Caring for the Retarded in America

A HISTORY

Peter L. Tyor
and
Leland V. Bell

Contributions in Medical History,
Number 15

GREENWOOD PRESS
WESTPORT, CONNECTICUT · LONDON, ENGLAND

Library of Congress Cataloging in Publication Data

Tyor, Peter L.
    Caring for the retarded in America.
    (Contributions in medical history, ISSN 0147-1058 ;
no. 15)
    Bibliography: p.
    Includes index.
    1. Mentally handicapped—Care and treatment—United
States—History. 2. Mentally handicapped—Institutional
care—United States—History. I. Bell, Leland V.
II. Title. III. Series.
HV3006.A4T96   1984   362.3'8'0973   84-6575
ISBN 0-313-20977-4 (lib. bdg.)

Library of Congress Catalog Card Number: 84-6575
ISBN: 0-313-20977-4
ISSN: 0147-1058

First published in 1984

Greenwood Press
A division of Congressional Information Service, Inc.
88 Post Road West
Westport, Connecticut 06881

Printed in the United States of America

10 9 8 7 6 5 4 3 2 1

Caring for the Retarded in America

Recent Titles in Contributions in Medical History

American Midwives: 1860 to the Present
Judy Barrett Litoff

Speech and Speech Disorders in Western Thought Before 1600
Ynez Violé O'Neill

Sex, Diet, and Debility in Jacksonian America:
Sylvester Graham and Health Reform
Stephen Nissenbaum

Shock, Physiological Surgery, and George Washington Crile:
Medical Innovation in the Progressive Era
Peter C. English

Professionalizing Modern Medicine: Paris Surgeons and
Medical Science and Institutions in the 18th Century
Toby Gelfand

Medicine and Its Technology: An Introduction to
the History of Medical Instrumentation
Audrey B. Davis

In Her Own Words: Oral Histories of Women Physicians
*Regina Markell Morantz, Cynthia Stodola Pomerleau, and
Carol Hansen Fenichel, editors*

Technicians of the Finite: The Rise and Decline of the Schizophrenic
in American Thought, 1840–1960
S. P. Fullinwider

Psychiatry Between the Wars, 1918–1945: A Recollection
Walter Bromberg

Compulsory Health Insurance: The Continuing American Debate
Ronald L. Numbers, editor

Disease and Its Control: The Shaping of Modern Thought
Robert P. Hudson

Pain, Pleasure, and American Childbirth:
From the Twilight Sleep to the Read Method, 1914–1960
Margarete Sandelowski

Understanding the Liver: A History
Thomas S. Chen and Peter S. Chen

To HJT and EB

Contents

ILLUSTRATIONS   viii

INTRODUCTION   ix

1. Optimism and Improvement, from Europe
   to America   3

2. Institutional Growth and Development   21

3. Professionalization and Specialization   45

4. The Rising Tide of Degeneracy: Custodialism and
   Its Rationale   71

5. Segregation or Surgery   105

6. A Return to the Community   123

7. Conclusion   153

   NOTES   161

   BIBLIOGRAPHICAL ESSAY   205

   INDEX   209

Illustrations

1. A group of boys and their teacher on the campus
   of the Ohio Institution for Feeble-minded Youth
   in the late 1880's   64

2. A classroom in the 1880's   66

3. A sewing class for girls in the late nineteenth-century
   institution   75

4. An institutional shoe shop for boys in the 1880's   77

Introduction

The history of the mentally retarded in America is a story of a hidden community, a group of persons, mostly children, traditionally viewed with pity, scorn, and contempt, who have been organized and contained on the periphery of society. They have represented an underclass of forgotten people. Throughout American history, there has been no sustained reforming drive or passion to aid the retarded. Over the years, the mentally retarded and the mentally ill have been linked together and identified as society's most unwanted citizens, its ultimate rejects. Some of this disdain has been conveyed in the labels popularly assigned to each disability: the mentally disturbed person has been tagged batty, nuts, cracked, looney; the mentally retarded individual has been called a dimwit, a simpleton, a fool, a dummy. The mentally ill, however, have had dramatic and colorful champions: Dorothea Dix, the nineteenth-century reformer, and Clifford Beers, the founder of the twentieth-century mental hygiene movement. There have been only a few crusaders for the mentally retarded; most of the heroes and heroines, if not all of them, remained local figures; not one really gained a national reputation for advocating the cause of the mentally deficient. A notable exception may be Samuel Gridley Howe, the pre–Civil War philanthropist, reformer, and physician who became an important educator of the "feeble-minded"; this work, however, represented only one of his many humanitarian concerns.

An overpowering stigma discouraged reform interest and intervention. Mental deficiency remains the most profound disability, a crippling handicap which can be ameliorated but never cured. Historically, it has carried a mark of shame, identifying the afflicted as a subhuman creature, a vegetable, or a blob of flesh. Tortured and dismayed by this reality, parents and relatives of the retarded have been overwhelmed with feelings of guilt, failure, and futility, and they, too, suffer social stigmatization. The traditional way out of this dilemma has been to isolate the retarded individual in an institution, where, out of sight and shunned as an outcast, the child—and later adult—can be forgotten.

A historical overview of American mental retardation social care may focus on three historical settings: in the 1850's experimental schools for mentally deficient children were established; around the turn of the century the large custodial facility was accepted as the most practical and beneficial way of caring for the retarded; and in the 1960's community residential care gained popularity. In effect, over the generations three different worlds were created for the retarded.

The school of the mid-nineteenth century represented a fresh, noble experiment inspired by the hopes, optimism, and enthusiasm of its founders who promoted an educational and rehabilitative ideal that the retarded could learn, improve, and eventually find a proper and meaningful place in society. Some unique features of the early school facilitated its goals. The small number of students generated a familial atmosphere in which the superintendent became a kind father figure who remained sensitive to the needs and problems of his children, the pupils. A selective admission and retention policy accepted the youngest, most promising students, screening out the incorrigibles and the severely retarded cases. Pupils kept in contact with their families and society through frequent visitations from parents, legislators, and other observers, and most students returned home for summer vacation. The school itself was not isolated in a remote area but usually located in the state's capital city, making it accessible to all interested groups. School administrators maintained strong ties in the community and aimed at educating the public about mental deficiency. For example, their annual reports were designed to create favorable opinion about the schools and argue the potential for ameliorating the condition of the mentally retarded person. In short, a few select students, a dedicated and vigorous staff committed to educating pupils, parents, and the public, along with a receptive and supportive community, created a setting, a unique educational milieu, which established a high quality of care and concern for retarded children.

By 1900, a second and far different world had been created for the retarded. Superimposed on the school was a large custodial facility where only minimal interest and effort went into training residents for life in the community. Its basic mission was the segregation of the deficient from the wider society, and superintendents extolled its custodial mission. In contrast to the school authorities of the 1850's, who confidently looked out on society anticipating that most of their pupils would participate in the life of the community, the custodial administrators of 1900 focused inward, assuming that the majority of their residents would never return to society. Self-sufficiency was a striking feature of the custodial institution. In the process of becoming a self-contained unit, the institution evolved into a unique community, physically and psychologically divorced from society. Ideally, superintendents characterized it as a "village of the simple" where around twelve hundred residents enjoyed hundreds of acres of land and utilized school, administrative, and maintenance buildings as well as a nursery, a chapel, an auditorium, a gymnasium, and several dormitories. It had a power station, railroad sidings, and fresh water, and the farm and gardens supplied food. It was accessible to the public but, in contrast to the experimental school, was usually located in a rural area of a state.

Psychologically, the institution offered a private, secluded haven where each resident functioned at his or her capacity in a noncompetitive atmosphere. There were no failures, no disappointments, no frustrations over someone's inability to attain the expectations of normal children. Residents were grouped with persons of the same potential and ability. While they were still trained and educated with the aim of attaining maximum self-sufficiency, the goal was independence at a specific task within the institution rather than employment in the outside world. They were assigned to tasks essential to maintaining the facility. The more capable inmates, for example, acted as attendants to care for less able residents. Superintendents emphasized that the retarded needed this world by themselves, a community made for them, a secure place suited to their needs and capacities. At the same time, the custodial institution satisfied societal demands that the retarded be permanently segregated, controlled, and prevented from propagating defectives.

Another world had been created for the retarded by the late 1960's. The custodial institution remained, but it was diminished in size and professional stature; it was accepted as a necessity for housing the most profound cases of retardation. The major trend was moving the retarded into a normal living and educational environment in the community. They found a place in sheltered workshops, public and private homes, and various supervised living arrangements. Professional attention focused on securing their human and civil rights, the pros and cons of labeling the handicapped, and the problems involved in integrating the retarded with normal children in the schools.

In the mid-nineteenth century, attitudes of the public and of the superintendents affected care. Then, and into the twentieth century, American ideas were often derivative and represented practicality rather than innovation. Most of the retarded were viewed as harmless individuals posing no danger to society. While the public held the common assumptions that the retarded were insensitive to the physical environment and had no capacity for growth, the mentally deficient remained a visible, integrated part of any community. Some school founders insisted that the presence of the retarded in daily life educated and sensitized people, making them aware of a social responsibility to aid the less fortunate members of society. For the superintendent of the 1850's, the uplifting of the retarded contributed to the broader reform goal of improving the nation.

By the turn of the century, this benign view had been replaced by a fear that the mentally deficient constituted a menace which had to be quarantined from society. Basic to this change was the acceptance of a deterministic hereditarian etiology, a notion that crystalized into a professional ideology late in the nineteenth century. It was assumed that degenerate families formed a major part of the lower strata mainstream of American life, where they spawned disease, disability, and dependency, costing taxpayers millions of dollars. Born of inferior stock, this group contained a large proportion of criminals and social misfits and constituted a major source of America's social problems. To professionals and to the public alike, a threat to the community existed, and proper measures were necessary to check the reproduction of hereditary defectives. Segregation and sterilization became the options for controlling what was called "the menace of the feebleminded." This perspective on retardation reached a crest around 1900 and represents the nadir in the history of the social treatment of the mentally deficient in America. Never again would the retarded be viewed in such negative terms, nor would such an extreme measure as surgical intervention be demanded as a solution to their control and care.

Beginning in the 1920's and continuing to the present day, the positive results of research and institutional change encouraged another view of the mentally retarded. The success of parole programs, research on the relationship between environment and IQ development, the growth and influence of organizations of parents of retarded children, and the medical impact of psychiatry and pediatrics represent some of the new factors that created the view that the majority of retarded citizens formed a positive community resource. Professional workers argued that the typical retarded person could live outside an institution, hold a job, and remain a harmonious member of the community. Clearly, by the 1960's, the retarded were no longer viewed as a menace to society.

The history of mental retardation care parallels developments in mental health care. The enthusiasm and optimism associated with the experimental schools accompanied the establishment of antebellum insane asylums. Here administrators practiced moral treatment, a therapy which involved removal of the patient to an institution in a peaceful environment, individualized care by a sympathetic physician, recreation, occupational diversions, and general avoidance of physical restraints. While school officials expected that most of their pupils would return to the community, asylum administrators anticipated that the majority of their patients would be restored to health fully capable of living productively in society. In the postbellum era, these hopes were dashed. By the 1880's, administrators ran overcrowded facilities; an aura of pessimism enveloped their work; societal fear and hostility were directed at both the retarded and the mentally ill. The long and slow ascent from this low point in institutional care began in the Progressive Era and culminated in the post–World War II years when workers displayed a renewed optimism and dedication toward their wards. New federal and state programs brought change and professional concerns dealt with reintegrating clients into the community, guaranteeing their basic legal rights, upgrading institutions, and initiating therapeutic innovations. In a sense, three historic settings have determined the fate of both the retarded and the mentally ill.

A conceptual continuity runs through the history of American mental retardation care. The labels identifying the problem have changed: feeble-mindedness, a term popular in the mid-nineteenth century, was replaced by "mental deficiency" late in the century. "Mental retardation" gained acceptance in the twentieth century and in recent years a retarded individual has been labeled a developmentally disabled or an exceptional person. While the terms changed, the basic concepts behind them remained the same—the educational model has dominated the care of the retarded. With this model, mental retardation was conceptualized as a condition of incomplete development, an impairment restricting a person's capacity to meet everyday living needs. It demands special attention and services if the retarded person is to realize his or her full potential. Retardation became analogous to a physical handicap, such as blindness or deafness, and the skills and the adaptability of the afflicted could be improved with training and instruction.

The educational model justified the institution, the school, or training facility, which provided pupils with a sheltered and controlled learning environment. It established the basic mode of care—a teacher-pupil relationship—placing the retarded individual in the role of a child. The emphasis on education also frustrated medical intervention. The professional concern for teaching, testing, and training inadvertently downgraded the biomedical approach to retardation.

A basic reality determined the care of the retarded. There was no cure, a fact proclaimed by the founders of the experimental schools, the superintendents of custodial institutions, and present-day workers in the field. Consequently, mental retardation care was dominated by a realistic perspective, devoid of overoptimism and extravagant claims and promises. The aim of such care has always been the improvement of the retarded person's condition. Mental health care, in contrast, has remained in a state of flux, supporting an array of therapeutics that have followed a roller–coaster pattern of fashionability. The search for a cure, or the promise of a cure, a major breakthrough which would alleviate suffering and restore health, was always a major element in the history of the care of the mentally ill. In the 1830's and 1840's, for example, the asylum itself became the therapeutic agent, and superintendents claimed fantastic recovery rates. Exaggerated claims of success accompanied the introduction of other therapies, and a familiar pattern emerged. The initial excitement and enthusiasm faded when additional research and follow-up studies challenged the original reports, suggesting that the therapy had only limited applications. Throughout the history of mental health care, expectations have been aroused and then dashed; there have been repeated cycles of hope and disillusionment. Mental retardation care, on the other hand, was locked to ameliorative aims and kept a low profile. It was characterized by timid demands, limited goals, and safe, modest accomplishments.

Few professional historians have ventured into the field of mental retardation. American social historians have made occasional references to the mentally deficient and the area of eugenics has received significant historical scrutiny. An important body of historical literature has been produced by psychologists, educators, administrators, and other workers involved with the developmentally disabled.[1] This study, while utilizing the work of these researchers, returns to the primary sources and focuses on institutional and professional development as well as the factors contributing to change and continuity in the treatment and care of the mentally retarded in the United States.

Caring for the Retarded in America

1
Optimism and Improvement, from Europe to America

Early in the morning of January 8, 1800, a boy about eleven or twelve years old was caught digging for vegetables in the garden of a tanner in the village of Saint-Sernin in the province of Aveyron in southern France. He wore only the tatters of a shirt and his body was covered with scars. Aside from occasionally uttering guttural sounds, he appeared deaf and mute. He had been seen intermittently since 1797 roaming the forests and countryside. This abandoned child was the "wild boy" or "savage" of Aveyron who became the object of an intensive investigation to determine his mental status and capabilities, marking the first significant nineteenth-century study of mental retardation.[1] In the past, other such "wild children" had excited much temporary popular interest but little prolonged study.[2] This case was to be treated differently. Enlightenment philosophers and naturalists saw the young boy as an example of a human being living in the original state of nature, free of socialization. With him they sought to test contending theories of human nature and of how humans acquired knowledge. The emerging spirit of scientific inquiry was challenged by the opportunity to educate the boy. The response to that challenge marked the beginning of a new period of educational history.

Despite the high hopes and attention accorded to him, the

boy proved to be a very difficult pupil. His personal habits remained bestial, and he made no progress in learning to talk.
One of his first observers, Pierre-Joseph Bonnaterre, a priest and
naturalist living in Rodez, capital of the Aveyron district, remarked that "a phenomenon like this would furnish to philosophy and natural history important notions on the original
constitution of man, and on the development of his primitive
faculties, *provided that the state of imbecility we have noticed in this
child does not offer an obstacle to his instruction.*"[3] Bonnaterre's last
point was given more significance when the youth was sent to
Paris and examined by Philippe Pinel, the country's foremost
expert on mental disorders. After studying the child and com-
paring him with others of limited mentality, Pinel asserted that
the boy was only a "pretend" savage, that he really was an idiot, and according to traditional belief, incapable of any improvement.

This diagnosis of idiocy was disputed by Jean-Marc-Gaspard
Itard, a former student of Pinel, who was the resident physician of the Institute for Deaf Mutes where the child was lodged.
Itard contended that the boy's wild conduct and lack of speech
were the results of isolation and of being entirely untaught
during his formative years. Since the boy lacked the stimulation and companionship of a normal childhood, his senses and
mental faculties had become focused narrowly on matters of
survival. Itard believed the proper course of instruction could
remedy these conditions. He named the boy Victor and for six
years attempted to restore him to society. In effect, he became
the boy's foster father.

Itard drew upon many sources in developing his pedagogy.[4]
In his overall approach he was guided by the analytic method
and sensualist philosophy of Etienne Bonnet de Condillac. To
Itard this meant: strict observation and concentration on his subject's progress and abilities; the division of learning tasks into
their most elementary components; steady progression from
simple to complex, known to unknown; training the senses
proceeding from touch to speech, ending with the achievement
of abstract thought and extended relationships.[5] Itard also availed
himself of contemporary advances in two important fields, the
education of the deaf, and the treatment of the insane. He

modified the devices and methods of the teachers of the deaf; first using the visually taught sign-based approach of Charles-Michel Epée and Roche-Ambroise Sicard, and later employing the tactile-oralist techniques of Jacob Pereire.[6] Finally, Itard adopted some of Pinel's principles of "moral treatment" of the insane, notably a concern for classification, the establishment of a therapeutic environment, and the necessity of personalized attention.[7] Combining all of these diverse contributions with his own intelligence, teaching skills, innovative abilities, and powers of observation, Itard pioneered in the use of behavior modification, instructional devices, and individualized learning.

Late in the year 1800, Itard began Victor's mental and moral education with an ambitious five-step program. His first aim was to make Victor's life more pleasant and "above all more like the life which he had just left." Second, he wanted to awaken the boy's "nervous sensibility by the most energetic stimulation, and occasionally by intense emotion." The third aim was "to extend the range of his ideas by giving him new needs and by increasing his social contacts." Teaching Victor to speak "by inducing the exercise of imitation through the imperious law of necessity" was the fourth aim. Itard's fifth aim was "to make him exercise the simplest mental operations upon the objects of his physical needs over a period of time afterwards inducing the application of these mental processes to the objects of instruction." In short, he aimed at training the boy to respond to others, to develop his senses, to extend his physical and social needs, to speak, and to think.[8]

After a year of vigorous effort, Itard was more successful in achieving his first three aims than in accomplishing the last two. According to his student, Édouard Seguin, Itard may have "suspected that there were other impediments besides savageness in his pupil," because "he framed, about 1802, an entirely new programme, more fitted for an idiot than for a savage."[9]

During the next four years, Itard concentrated on developing Victor's senses, intellectual faculties, and affective functions.[10] Although Victor made substantial progress in sensory discrimination, attention, memory, habits, and manners, Itard never fully achieved his most important goal. He could not teach Vic-

tor to talk. Itard believed that without language Victor had no
access to abstract concepts and no means of engaging in the high
mental processes; his social relationships would be forever limited. Regretfully, believing no more could be accomplished, Itard
returned to his work with the deaf, abandoning Victor to custodial care until his death in 1828.

Itard had originally undertaken Victor's education because he
had disagreed with Pinel's diagnosis of idiocy, and not because
he questioned the supposition that idiocy was an unchangeable
condition. If his limited success appeared to vindicate Pinel, the
fact that there had been any improvement at all was seen by
his colleagues as a stunning achievement in medical-educa-
tional therapeutics. The French Academy officially reported in
1806 "that if he [Itard] has not obtained a greater success, it must
be attributed, not to any lack of zeal or talent but to the imper-
fections of the organs of the subject upon which he worked.
The Academy, moreover, cannot see without astonishment how
he could succeed as far as he did."[11] Although it may never be
known whether Victor was truly retarded, Itard was celebrated
as "the first to educate an idiot with a philosophical object and
by physiological means."[12] His work profoundly influenced the
future of special education in Europe and America.

Before the nineteenth century, physicians and educators paid
relatively little attention to mental retardation. It was not strictly
differentiated from mental illness and was generally considered
a hopeless affliction. The most frequent and best treatment given
to the retarded was benign neglect in private homes or almshouses; otherwise they often suffered imprisonment with the insane. The lack of interest of the medical profession was indicated by a lack of precision in terminology. Two of the most
commonly used descriptors for the retarded were "idiot" and
"imbecile." The word idiot was derived from the Greek, meaning a peculiar or private person, one who is cut off from relationships with others and is alone. It was used generically to
refer to all varieties of mental defect. After 1800, however, the
generic denotation was gradually acquired by the term "feeble-
minded," and idiot was increasingly restricted to the profoundly or severely retarded, the lowest and most helpless
grades. Imbecile also had a generic connotation but it was more

frequently used to indicate retardates with a higher level of capability than idiots, who nevertheless still required guidance and control. Its derivation may be from the Latin, meaning weak or tottering. In the absence of any accepted standards, these terms as well as the plethora of others—such as dunce, fool, and simpleton—were used indiscriminately by physicians and laymen without reference to etiology, symptoms, or prognosis.

The eminent psychiatrist Jean-Etienne-Dominique Esquirol is credited with formulating the first medical definition of idiocy and differentiating it from insanity.

Idiocy is not a disease, but a condition in which the intellectual faculties are never manifested; or have never been developed sufficiently to enable the idiot to acquire such an amount of knowledge as persons his own age, and placed in similar circumstances with himself, are capable of receiving. Idiocy commences with life, or at that age which precedes the development of the intellectual and affective faculties, which are from the first what they are doomed to be during the whole period of existence . . . . A man in a state of dementia is deprived of advantages which he formerly enjoyed. He was a rich man who has become poor. The idiot, on the contrary, has always been in a state of want and misery.[13]

While this colorful depiction represents an important statement, the problem of distinguishing between mental deficiency and some types of mental illness persisted. Even late in the twentieth century, for example, competent clinicians continued to confuse catatonia with retardation.

Esquirol limited the application of the term idiocy to cases of congenital mental defect. Idiocy was to be inferred on the basis of a comparison of the subject's "knowledge" with that of like-situated contemporaries. Hence, this definition, like most others that followed it, was a comparative or social definition that relied upon an evaluation of the subject's abilities in relation to others. Esquirol's use of the word "doomed" was an indication of the prevalent belief in the immutability of idiocy.

Esquirol's pessimism was not shared by his pupil Édouard Seguin who had studied medicine and surgery with Itard. Seguin joined the methodological innovations of Itard with the theoretical advances of Esquirol to become the first professional to specialize in the treatment of mental defectives. He began his career in France, establishing an important reputation as an educator of the feeble–minded. After the Revolution of 1848, he emigrated to the United States where he aided in the operation of a number of the first institutions for the retarded while maintaining a private practice. He was one of the founders of the Association of Medical Officers of American Institutions for Idiotic and Feeble-minded Persons and served as its first president in 1876.

Seguin was born in 1812 in Clamecy and received an excellent education at the Collège d'Auxerre and the Lycée St. Louis in Paris.[14] Despite the forebodings of Esquirol, he established his own school in 1837 and, with Itard's guidance, he began the education of an idiotic boy. After a year and a half of arduous and continual work, the boy showed improvement: he could speak, write, and count. Esquirol conceded Seguin's success and the private institution gained recognition and increased enrollment. Three separate commissions, in 1842, 1843, and 1844, investigated Seguin's results and reported that he had conquered the problem of idiot education.[15]

Throughout his career, Seguin searched for better theoretical foundations to his work.[16] Like Itard, he was influenced by many sources as he created a system of special education that he called physiological instruction.[17] While he was critical of some of the concepts of Pereire, Epée, and Sicard, he selectively employed the instructional techniques of the teachers of the deaf. The medical treatment of insanity, as practiced by Pinel and Esquirol, impressed Seguin with the importance of individualized treatment based on thorough diagnosis and carried out in a well-planned therapeutic environment. Seguin also benefitted from the results of Itard's experience with Victor. But Itard's approach was only a starting point. Seguin carefully observed the mental development of normal children and he studied contemporary physiological research, aiming at perfecting a theory of learning that could be used in educating the retarded. As a result of these studies, he maintained that learning involved the reciprocal effects of sensory impressions and their corresponding neurological faculties whose actions reinforced each other; when properly considered together, they formed the basis for teaching conscious mental activity.[18] Finally, as he sought ways to implement his theoretical constructs, Seguin used many of the motivational curriculum innovations and physical training methods which were advocated respectively by the nineteenth-century educators Charles Rollin and Francisco Amoros.[19]

Seguin began the process of education by first examining the child's physical and mental condition as thoroughly as possible. He believed that every retarded individual, no matter how severely affected, exhibited some activity that could be discovered and cultivated by an observant educator. Once a case history was compiled, and a diagnosis was made, Seguin concentrated on strengthening the body and muscular systems and correcting any physical abnormalities. This was accomplished through the use of correctional gymnastic exercises, special training apparatus, stimulating baths and massages, proper diet, and pure air along with a wholesome environment.[20] Diet was considered especially important as improper nutrition was believed to have a negative effect on all the physical and mental functions. Next, the various senses were engaged as the pupil was led to make increasingly finer sensory discriminations.[21] Seguin believed that each sense organ had a passive as well as an active role: it received and sent out impressions and the mind responded with appropriate action. Accordingly, he worked at establishing relationships, encouraging students to make choices, judgments, and comparisons.[22] Finally, a series of sensorimotor drills carried the student from the elementary habits of muscular control to the complex mastery of academic and vocational skills. Seguin varied the setting, pace, and content of this training according to individual ability. Group activity provided the opportunity for learning through imitation and comparison while it created a wide range of mutual relationships for the class.[23]

Moral treatment worked in conjunction with physiological education.[24] In contrast to the physical methods, it emphasized the curative potential of a strong, positive relationship between master and pupil. For Seguin this approach was vital because "that which most especially constitutes idiocy, is the absence of *moral volition*, superseded by a *negative will*; that in which the treatment of an idiot essentially consists is, in changing his *neg-*

ative will into an affirmative one, his *will* of loneliness into a will
of sociability and usefulness; such is the object of the *moral
training.*[25] The force of the instructor's personality aroused in
the pupil a desire to overcome any handicap. Mere automatic
response or repetition was not sufficient, an action had to be
accompanied by conscious effort.[26] Only then, Seguin believed,
could all facets of a human being—activity, intelligence, will—
be brought into harmony.

Seguin's system of physiological education was successfully
employed in virtually every American and European institution
for the mentally defective. His books became the standard works
in the field. The combination of physical therapy and mental
discipline was so satisfactory that Seguin's methods underwent
remarkably little change or alteration during the period of institutional development. One consequence of this widespread
popularity was the curtailing of medical and scientific research
in remedial education. His work appeared to be so definitive
that his contemporaries devoted the bulk of their studies to other
areas such as etiology or institutional planning. Thus Seguin had
the distinction of being considered both a pioneering innovator
and an established authority.

The success of physiological education in the 1840's inspired
Americans to establish facilities solely for the care and treatment of mental defectives. There had been a number of earlier
attempts to ameliorate the condition of the retarded, who previously had been kept at home, or lodged in the county almshouse. Beginning in 1818, the American Asylum for the Deaf
and Dumb of Hartford, Connecticut, had accepted a limited
number of retardates who showed considerable improvement
when they were given some instruction.[27] Retardates were also
among the clientele of the Commercial Hospital and Lunatic
Asylum in Cincinnati, established in 1821, and the Ohio Deaf
and Dumb Asylum, created in 1827. In 1839 a blind youth, who
was also paralyzed and retarded, was admitted to the Perkins
Institution for the Blind in Boston. Samuel Gridley Howe, the
institution's director, helped the child by employing the new
methods he developed to educate the blind and the deaf. Howe
was so encouraged by the results that he accepted two similar
cases.[28] While these efforts demonstrated the feasibility of "id-

iot education" to a small group of interested physicians and reformers, there was no attempt at this time to enlist public support for the creation of specialized institutions.

In the United States, as in France, psychiatrists were among
the first professionals to be interested in the plight of the mentally retarded. William Awl, Superintendent of the Ohio Lunatic Asylum, set aside rooms for the mentally deficient, noting that facilities in mental institutions would never be adequate
for housing the "imbecile classes." At the 1844 founding convention of the Association of Medical Superintendents of
American Institutions for the Insane, he called for the establishment of institutions specifically designed for the care and
training of the "feeble-minded." Following the New York State
Census of 1845, Amariah Brigham, Superintendent of the New
York State Lunatic Asylum at Utica, used his *Annual Report* to
publicize the European educational methods that he believed
could be employed to instruct some of the 1,600 retardates
enumerated by the Census. The report enthusiastically described the progress made by such concerned Europeans as Seguin in France, Carl M. Saegent in Germany, and Johann J.
Guggenbuhl in Switzerland.[29] Brigham called upon New York
residents to undertake an experiment to aid the retarded: "We
are of the opinion that much may be done for their improvement and comfort; that many, instead of being a burden and
expense to the community, may be so improved to engage in
useful employments and to support themselves."[30] In his pleas
for state assistance, Brigham asserted that proper care would
not only improve the retarded but also financially benefit the
community. This argument, combining humanitarianism with
economy, would be invoked continually by those who sought
to institutionalize the defective.

The first legislative action concerning provision for the men-
tally retarded was initiated in the New York State Senate by
Frederick F. Backus of Rochester. Backus was influenced by
Samuel B. Woodward, Superintendent of the Worcester State
Lunatic Hospital of Massachusetts, whose *Annual Report* of 1844
contained a sketch of retardation developments in France with
the suggestion of adopting European techniques in America.
After corresponding with Woodward and preparing other ma-

terials, Backus, on January 13, 1846, "moved a reference of that
portion of the census relating to idiots to the Committee on
Medical Societies, of which he was chairman."[31] Two days later,
he presented the committee's report which narrated the successes of European institutions and urged New York to imitate
them. Finally, on March 25, Backus introduced a bill for the acquisition of a state and the construction of suitable buildings
for an "Asylum for Idiots." The bill was passed in the senate,
and initially was assured house approval, but it was defeated
for budgetary reasons. The same frustrating pattern was repeated in the following year.

Meanwhile, similar events were taking place in Massachusetts. On January 22, 1846, Horatio Boyington moved an order
in the House of Representatives to appoint a committee to
"consider the expediency of appointing commissioners to inquire into the condition of idiots in the Commonwealth, to as-
certain their number, and whether anything can be done for their
relief."[32] The order was passed and a committee of Boyington,
Gilman Kimball, and Samuel G. Howe, as chairman, was
formed. The committee's report recalled the success of treatment for the deaf, the blind, and the insane, noting that "all of
this change has been made by the substitution of knowledge
and kindness . . . for ignorance, neglect, and brutality."[33] The
committee urged the appointment of commissioners and Boyington, Kimball, and Howe were chosen. Although their preliminary report of March 31, 1847, disclosed little information
about the situation in Massachusetts, it did contain a most per-
suasive letter from George S. Sumner in Paris, who described
the methods and results of Seguin. Sumner forcefully ended his
letter with the telling comment:

For other nations, the education of the deaf, the blind, the infirm in
intellect, may be regarded as philanthropic provision, or as a comple-
ment to civilization,—for republics, it is an imperative duty—the necessary result of the principle on which they are founded, and by which
they are sustained,—*the principle of justice*, that accords to everyone—
not as a privilege, but as a right—the full development of all his faculties.[34]

In 1848, after learning that sending circular letters to town clerks yielded meager results, Howe personally visited 63 towns and examined 574 individuals. The outcome of this survey, the first by anyone with even a pretense to professional competence, was the famous *Report Made to the Legislature of Massachusetts Upon Idiocy*.[35] Howe found the level of care in almshouses and homes appallingly low. He characterized the treatment in almshouses as kindly but ignorant. There was no separation of the sexes; the food was poor; there was almost no bathing and little exercise or employment. Home care was worse, but as Howe explained: "This is not to be wondered at, when we consider that idiots are generally born of very poor stock."[36] The *Report* detailed numerous examples of deliberate cruelty. These apparent transgressions reflected the prevailing beliefs that the retarded could not experience pain, would willingly digest almost anything, and were unable to benefit from any type of human contact. Once it was known that the retarded could be educated and uplifted, such poor treatment would be severely criticized and condemned.[37]

Howe argued that the entire community had a social responsibility to aid the retarded because he considered "idiocy as a disease of society; an outward sign of an inward malady."[38] Believing that it was the result of violating natural and physical laws, he expected that idiots would be born to parents who "ignore the conditions upon which alone health and reason are given to men, and consequently they sin in various ways." Eventually the parents would become so degenerate that they could transmit this deterioration "and thus bring down the awful consequences of their own ignorance and sin upon the heads of their unoffending children."[39] Like others of his time, Howe was not aware of the precise mechanism of biological inheritance. He declared:

The transmission of any inferiority is not always direct. It is not always in the same form. It may be modified by the influence of one sound parent; it may skip a generation; it may affect one child more, and another less; it may affect one in one form and another in another . . . . Variety is the great law of nature, and it holds too in the transmission of diseased tendencies, as well as in anything else.[40]

Continued decay was not inevitable if the natural laws of health were obeyed, for Howe believed that healthful living "if strictly observed for two or three generations, would totally remove from any family, however strongly predisposed to insanity or idiocy, all possibility of its reoccurrence."[41] Idiocy was not a permanent affliction of society. Rather, it was like the first seven plagues of Egypt, a warning from God that society had to purify and redeem itself.

As a result of the survey, the number of retarded citizens in Massachusetts was estimated to be from twelve hundred to fifteen hundred. After some criticism of existing definitions of idiocy, Howe defined it as "that condition of a human being in which, from some morbid cause in the bodily organization, the faculties or sentiments remain dormant or undeveloped, so that the person is incapable of self-guidance, and of approaching that degree of knowledge usual with others of his age."[42] Modifying Esquirol's pessimistic view, Howe showed that idiocy existed in many forms and gradations, ascending from "drooling idiots" to fools and simpletons, "and that the difference between their intelligence and that of other men, is a difference in *degree*, and not in *kind*."[43] Almost all of the mentally defective were generally harmless to others, but Howe was aware of another variety of retardation often encountered in prisons. This was moral idiocy, which he defined as "that condition in which the sentiments, the conscience, the religious feeling, the love of neighbor, the sense of beauty, are so far dormant or undeveloped, as to incapacitate the person from being a law unto himself, in anything like the degree which is usual with others of his age."[44]

Howe clearly accepted the phrenological belief that the moral sentiments were finite entities, which, like intelligence or will, were capable of being impaired or invigorated depending on treatment and circumstances.[45] Postulating that moral idiocy was most likely to develop in classes that were exposed to brutalizing labor systems, such as domestic service in Boston or factory work in England, Howe dismissed the idea that all crime was the result of innate depravity. Some criminals, acting in a state of moral idiocy, were created by forces that were beyond the individual's control. Proper treatment and education, not

prison, were the only methods that could salvage these unfortunates, created, Howe concluded, "by the very operation of
our social system."[46]

He went on to enumerate the many benefits that would ac-
crue to Massachusetts if educational facilities were provided.
There would be a considerable financial savings, he said. Some
of the retarded could become self-sufficient, and many who
previously had cared for them could be freed for useful labor.
A moral evil would be removed from the community; as Howe
stated: "an ignorant vicious, or suffering class is a disturbing
force in society, it has no business there, it must be removed
or there never can be order."[47] There would be the satisfaction
of fulfilling a Christian duty to help a fellow human being, especially since it had been demonstrated that education was effective, and without it, the retarded would further decline. Howe
emphasized that in a democracy all have the right of access to
the means of self-improvement, not just in the common schools,
but through special educational facilities for those who require
them. The insane, the deaf, the blind were all receiving state
aid, why not the most helpless and brutalized class—the mentally retarded? Finally, Howe remarked on an especially ap-
pealing consequence if Massachusetts acted first: once again the
Commonwealth would be a model and a guide for all the other
states to follow.[48]

It is difficult to determine which tactics were most influential
with the legislature: the horrifying tales of retarded servants in-
structing their young charges in self-abuse, the democratic appeal to respect the rights of all citizens to an education, or the
thinly veiled warning that "were it not for the action of certain
principles which give the race recuperative powers, there would
be the danger of its utter destruction as a whole, by the sins of
so many of its individual members."[49] Nor can the originality
of Howe's research, his status as a humanitarian in the Greek
Revolution, or his international reputation as the teacher of Laura
Bridgeman, the blind deaf-mute, be ignored.[50] Underlying all
these points was the perfectionist faith of many reformers that
there was no limit to the improvement of humanity, and no
barrier that could not be overcome with the proper application
of faith, hard work, and knowledge.[51]

Most probably it was not any single argument but a combination of factors that motivated the Massachusetts lawmakers to resolve on May 8, 1848, to appropriate $2,500 annually to an experimental school for a three-year test period. Howe was appointed director of the Experimental School for Teaching and Training Idiotic Children, and it was located in the Perkins Institution. Ten indigent idiots, one from each judicial district, were selected as pupils. A teacher, James B. Richards, was hired and sent to Paris to learn firsthand the methods of physiological education.[52]

Before the experimental school accepted its first students in October 1848, another institution for the retarded, which was the first in America, had been in operation for three months. This private school in Barre, Massachusetts, was in the home of Dr. Hervey B. Wilbur[53] who had been so impressed by published reports of Seguin's achievements that he "sent abroad an order for any books treating upon the subject of the training and education of idiots."[54] In reply, he received Seguin's *Traitement moral, hygiène et éducation des idiots et des autres enfants arrières*. Having mastered the book, Wilbur began applying his knowledge immediately. He described his work as extending educational opportunity to all, noting that "this institution is designed for the education and management of all children, who by reason of mental infirmity are not fit subjects for ordinary school instruction."[55] The private school was organized on the family plan with students and staff eating at the same table and sharing the same facilities. With its limited enrollment and specialized services, it long remained an attractive alternative for wealthy parents who did not wish their children placed in a public institution.

In New York in the winter of 1851, Samuel G. Howe and some of his students were invited to appear before a special session of the legislature. This practical demonstration of the results of Howe's teaching and training proved decisive for the passage of the Backus bill. The legislature, in July 1851, appropriated $6,000 annually for a two-year period to an experimental school. Five trustees were appointed; they leased a house near Albany for the school, and "after some negotiation" made Hervey B. Wilbur its first superintendent.[56] The school opened in October

1851 with twenty pupils, one from each of the state's judicial districts. At the end of two years, the experiment was deemed a success, and the legislature approved plans to build a permanent institution. A site at Syracuse was selected where, in 1854, construction began on the first building for use as a school for the mentally retarded in America; two years later, the State Asylum for Idiots moved from Albany to Syracuse.[57]

The state of Pennsylvania acted in partnership with private interests to support a school. In 1852, James B. Richards left Howe in Boston to establish his own institution in Germantown, Pennsylvania. Although he had only four students, Richards interested prominent citizens of Philadelphia in his work.[58] With the assistance of Bishop Alonzo, Franklin Taylor, Dr. Alfred Elwyn, and others, a corporation was formed in February 1853 to operate the school. The Board of Directors retained Richards as teacher and arranged for a demonstration of him and his students before the state legislature in 1854. This event in Harrisburg was completely successful. A special act incorporated the Pennsylvania Training School for Idiotic and Feeble-minded Children as a private institution receiving an appropriation that provided for a fixed number of state-sponsored pupils.[59] The same system of finance had been adopted previously by Massachusetts in 1851, when the state incorporated the Massachusetts School for Idiotic and Feeble-minded Youth.[60] This mixture of private enterprise and public support was not new; it had been used in the past for other ventures, notably turnpikes and canals which were often privately originated but operated in the public interest.[61]

The Pennsylvania school prospered, grew, and was twice relocated. The second time the site was chosen by a committee that included Dorothea L. Dix, the mental health reformer, who took a continuing interest in the school. Seguin joined the staff in 1856, but as was the case in Boston and Syracuse, he remained for only a short time. Seguin was still having trouble learning English, and he proved to be a difficult man to work with when he was not in complete authority. As a result of the ensuing friction, both Seguin and Richards left the facility and Joseph Parrish, a graduate of the University of Pennsylvania Medical School, was appointed superintendent. Under his stewardship, the cornerstone of the new institution was laid in 1857 at Media, later named Elwyn in Dr. Elwyn's honor, and the entire school moved to the new site in two Conestoga wagons in 1859. Neighboring states which lacked their own facilities began sending retarded children to Pennsylvania in the following year; these states paid the same costs per pupil as Pennsylvania.[62] The practice of accepting out-of-state, paying students was adopted at virtually every American school. It was both a useful source of income and a good way to publicize special education.

In addition to those founded in Massachusetts, New York, and Pennsylvania, schools for the retarded were established in Ohio (1857), in Connecticut (1858), and in Kentucky (1860) before the Civil War.[63] In each case there was an initial struggle against public indifference and incredulity. The campaigns for state aid usually began with a public demonstration by teachers and students of existing schools, or with a survey of the treatment and number of retarded. There was some resistance to these efforts; for example, the Connecticut Commission on Idiocy found that it was the "settled opinion of a large majority of the citizens of the commonwealth, that idiots were as a class so utterly hopeless, that it was a waste of time even to collect any statistics concerning them."[64] It was doubly hard to collect accurate statistics because of the difficulties of diagnosis and the reluctance of relatives to volunteer information they probably considered embarrassing. But enumerations and statistics were influential with state legislatures to buttress support for educational facilities. Once public officials were made aware of the scope of the problem and the successes of existing institutions, they usually funded an experimental school for a trial period. Temporary quarters, frequently in a large private home or unused state building near the capital, were prepared, and a staff, often from the older schools, was hired. These arrangements were normally made by the Board of Trustees, the members of which generally included some of the individuals who led the efforts to establish the schools.

All of these institutions were intended to perform a variety of educational functions for individuals, parents, and society. The primary task of the school was therefore the cultivation and discipline of pupils' physical, mental, and moral faculties which also accorded with European theory. The major means employed were physiological instruction and moral treatment. The hope was that some of the retarded would become self-supporting while all would be less burdensome to their families and friends. Because mental defect was considered "one of the ways in which a righteous lawgiver punishes transgression," its occurrence had a didactic value.[65] "Humiliating as the thought may be," said Linus P. Brockett, a prominent advocate of the feeble-minded, summing up much opinion, "we are driven to the conclusion that the vast amount of idiocy, in our world, is the direct result of violation of the physical and moral laws that govern our being."[66] The schools for the retarded provided a model for an ordered, well-regulated way of life that complied with all the known natural laws. By reaffirming and practicing the proper standards of health—wholesome diet, sanitary housing, moderation in physical and mental exertion—the institution could operate as an example to the community and prevent the continued degeneration of its members.

While reasons of public health and individual improvement were important, Howe, Wilbur, Brockett, and others were motivated by a strong sense of Christian obligation and fellowship. Education of the retarded was undertaken "to show our reverence for God's plain will, and to acknowledge the common brotherhood of man, by taking these the most unfortunate of His children, and attempting to lift them up to a place, humble though it may be, upon the common platform of humanity."[67] The early superintendents believed that the increased attention given to the treatment of all types of defect was commensurate with the progress of civilization. America was becoming a finer and better society because it no longer abandoned the handicapped to lives of emptiness and misery. The provision of educational institutions for the mentally retarded was among the final steps in this process of communal self-improvement, or as Howe said, "it is a link in the chain of common schools—the last indeed, but a necessary link in order to embrace all the children in the State."[68]

2

Institutional Growth and Development

The early years of the American institutions for the mentally retarded were periods of learning and discovery, not just for the students but also for the trustees, superintendents, teachers, and staff. Working with few precedents or models, school officials had to define their mission, establish operating policies, and create the methods to implement them. The antebellum institutions were all established and operated with the intention that they were to function strictly as schools, not as custodial asylums. On this important point the statements of trustees and superintendents were clear and firm: the schools would not provide lifetime custodial care for the educable and trainable retarded. Instead, the primary mission was to give to the students' "dormant faculties the greatest practicable development," allowing the pupils to develop their full potential and return them to their homes and families.[1] Although the schools' founders had little practical experience to draw upon, they were guided by their generation's humanitarian and reformist faith in the perfectibility of man. They optimistically believed "that in almost all cases, and with very few, if any exceptions, those usually called idiots, under the age of twelve or fifteen, may be so trained and instructed . . . to learn some of the ordinary trades or to engage in agriculture."[2] To avoid custodialism and

to insure the educational character of their institutions, the school
authorities established a highly selective admission and retention policy. They tried to admit and retain only those children
who could continue to benefit from instruction. They reserved
the right to deny admission to unsuitable cases, and they fixed
a maximum age limit, usually sixteen, after which a pupil had
to be discharged.[3] These measures were adopted because the
experimental schools wanted to present the best possible records of progress, and because administrators sincerely shared
Samuel G. Howe's belief that a school "should not be converted into an asylum for incurables."[4] For the next two decades the founding goals and policies of the schools remained
officially intact but unanticipated needs and problems would
subtly alter institutional methods and procedures.

Based on the surviving institutional records of New York and
Massachusetts, it appears that the schools successfully avoided
becoming "a mere asylum for custodial purposes" during their
first twenty years.[5] Pupils were admitted while they were young,
retained for comparatively short periods of time, and discharged. Each of these factors—admission age, retention period, final disposition—is important in evaluating institutional
policy and performance. Low admission ages and relatively short
retention periods (those comparable to the common schools)
indicate that the institutions were adhering to their founding
purposes by accepting children who stayed only for the time
period necessary to teach and train them. Under these conditions the final disposition (meaning the way in which a person
is separated from the institution) of most of the students would
be either institutionally initiated discharge or removal by parents. Barring disease and accidents, relatively few individuals,
the superintendents held, would be retained long enough so
that they died in the school's care. This pattern of early admission, short retention, and live disposition was dominant in the
first two decades.

School authorities were firmly committed to an educational,
rehabilitative ideal. For this reason they requested the earliest
possible admission, which was "the most teachable age, the
proper school attending age of ordinary childhood," when "their
whole organization is more flexible, more susceptible of devel-

opment."[6] While the youngest children were considered the most desirable because their malleable natures were free from "confirmed habits," their youth made it difficult to diagnose insanity, epilepsy, or other unteachable conditions. To deal with this problem the schools instituted a trial admission period during which an individual's suitability was to be determined. In time, a bond was required to guarantee removal at no cost to the school. Even after the probationary period, the school officials retained the authority to discharge pupils who showed little promise of continued improvement. In admission and retention policy, the schools were concerned with the effective utilization of scarce resources. The rapid turnover of the institutional population assured that the schools' educational benefits would be distributed as widely as possible.

Other aspects of institutional organization discouraged the development of custodialism. Superintendents required all the students to return to their homes for periods of up to two months in the summer. Besides providing the staff with a needed rest from the seventeen-hour, six-day workweek, the vacations served two other important purposes. By annually leaving the schools, the students were reacquainted with their families and exposed to the conditions of everyday life: home ties were thus maintained. At the same time, the schools were divested of the character of permanent residential institutions; in Howe's words, they were "boarding schools for idiots."[7] Although there was some apprehension over the lack of suitable supervision, the summer vacations continued through the 1870's as the superintendents believed the benefits outweighed the risks. There were other sources of contact with society: Most of the schools were originally located near the state capital so the legislators could observe school operations. There were frequent visiting days for parents, inspectors from the governing authority, and the curious general public. This constant visitation continued the interaction of staff and students with the community. In later years these visits were curtailed by relocations to rural areas and the administrator's desire to limit disruptions in the daily routine. However, holiday celebrations, summer outings, religious services, and the like insured that the pupils were never totally isolated.

The schools quickly established well-planned, regular sched-
ules of activities that comprised the daily routine of institutional life.[8] Regimentation was avoided to a certain extent because the superintendents wholeheartedly adopted the
educational methodology of Seguin who emphasized the importance of personalized treatment. The primary task of the
physician-educator was to diagnose and ameliorate each student's special handicap. In actual instruction "each individual
case will be a study, and must be treated as its peculiarities demand. Mere routinism should be avoided in every exercise, and
at all times."[9] School authorities worried that pupils would not
receive the necessary attention, and they "expressed the opinion that more than 150 pupils can not be properly attended to
by one superintendent . . . . From the peculiarity of each case,
the pupils cannot be arranged in classes embracing large numbers; and when in classes, the training and education of each
must be guided by an experience, and steady hand; assistants
require constant oversight, and too many of them divert the attention of the superintendent from his appropriate duties."[10]
As Howe noted there was a further danger in rigidly categoriz-
ing the students, for "nature produces individual men and not
classes. Putting men into a class, is too apt to put them into a
caste; sometimes even it puts them out of the pale of humanity."[11] Thus, when the schools were small and Seguin's principles were dominant, the superintendents were educators, not
administrators, and they had the time necessary to know and
treat their students as individuals.

The early schools for the retarded lacked other characteristics
that were often associated with custodial asylums. There was
no prescribed manner of dress or uniform for the students or
the staff. Each child was supplied with clothing by parents, or
if indigent, by the county responsible for care. Funding came
from a variety of sources—the state treasury, county officials,
neighboring states, parents, and benevolent donors—producing a financial situation that was hardly amenable to central-
ized institutional control. A vital feature of any custodial organization, the involuntary internment and retention of the
residents, was also absent. Admission to the institution was
made on the basis of parental application supported by medical

testimony, and discharge could be demanded by the pupil's guardians at any time. The schools could neither initiate entrance nor deny withdrawal; they could only exercise the power of selection.

Although school officials wished to avoid the excesses of custodialism and regimentation, they were also keenly aware of the need for discipline, order, and authority in the educational process. The success of Seguin's program of moral training first depended upon the teacher's firmly establishing authority over the pupil, generally by force of personality but by physical means if necessary.[12] Once an orderly learning environment was created, it was "disturbed only by the noise and unruliness of some newcomers not yet broken in."[13] In most schools there was no corporal punishment; instead, the students were "governed and controlled with parental kindness" as they were taught "to comprehend the idea of obedience, of a God, and moral obligation."[14] In this respect the schools were modeled in the image of the nineteenth-century family, with character development and the inculcation of morality their most important goals.[15] The superintendents often referred to the entire institutional population as "the family" and they exercised their authority in a paternalistic manner. This type of familial governance was seen as being best suited to the students and most attractive to the general public.

A favorable popular opinion was vital to the continued existence of the schools. The Board of Directors in Pennsylvania, for example, realized that "to teach any given knowledge to those whom it was supposed were without minds had, . . . the appearance of a wild and visionary undertaking. It is this feeling which forms the chief obstacle to an entirely successful establishment of our Institution in public estimation."[16]

It was widely believed that an idiot had no mind and could not profit from an education. To negate this serious overgeneralization, the schools' *Annual Reports* repeatedly stressed that idiocy was a condition that existed in many forms ranging from profound to mild. While idiocy was not a disease that could be cured, all afflicted persons could be improved. School officials strove to make it clear that "we do not propose to create or supply faculties absolutely wanting,"[17] but they fervently believed "that there is nothing so low in the scale of human intelligence" that will not "reward an earnest effort for its elevation." [18]

In arguing their case for special education, school authorities continued to be hampered by the imprecise terminology of mental defect. When they referred to idiots they often used the term generically as a synonym for all the retarded. In the popular mind, idiots were the most severely retarded. During the 1850's, the potential for confusion was somewhat lessened by the adoption of a new classification format. Idiots were the lowest grade, who with constant training could improve their personal habits and possibly learn to care for themselves. Imbeciles were considered to have more ability; they could assist the less able or perhaps be self-sufficient under the proper supervision. The third and highest grade were the feeble-minded, who were thought to have suffered the least mental disability. Unfortunately for the sake of clarity, feeble-mindedness soon acquired the same generic connotation as idiocy, embracing all varieties of mental defect.

Since there was no way of authoritatively determining the extent, or even the presence, of retardation, almost all of the nineteenth-century diagnoses and classifications were questionable. Excepting those cases of obvious physical lesions, classification was mainly a product of deductive reasoning. For example, if individuals could not feed or dress themselves, they were idiots, or if they could perform these tasks but could not learn in school as well as their classmates, then they were feeble-minded. The majority of classifications, especially those of borderline cases, were really social and economic judgments.

From their descriptions of various cases, it is evident that superintendents used the tripartite classification (idiots, imbeciles, feeble-minded) to indicate differing levels of social competency, not unchangeable divisions of mental ability. They frequently mentioned that education and training not only improved the student's social functioning but also prevented degeneration from one grade to another. This was an additional reason why they had to disprove the public's belief that idiocy was a static, unchanging condition. To overcome public opinion, they called for a scientific test of their results "by the same

rigid rule which they would apply to any new theory in phys-
ics."[19] The test would compare the progress of the pupils after
training with their condition before entering the school. As
documented by case histories, in every instance there was some
degree of improvement. Thankful letters from parents were included with the case histories in the *Annual Reports* and provided ample testimony that the appearance of any improvement, whether it was in cleanliness, table manners, or speech,
was convincing proof of the school's ability to educate and uplift
the retarded.

Superintendents were aware that any dramatic change could
mislead some observers to expect complete recoveries, and so
they continually cautioned the public that there was no cure for
feeble-mindedness, only the potential for amelioration. Here the
school authorities had the difficult task of deflating unrealistic
hopes while still maintaining their claims of positive accomplishments. They tried to strike a careful balance. "Indeed, it
cannot be reasonably expected to educate *any* of them to such
degree as that they can become professional men, or procure a
livelihood by literary pursuits," said the commissioners of the
Kentucky institution. "Yet," they contended, "there are many
of them who can be taught, with comparative ease, some of the
simpler mechanical arts, and thus made useful to themselves
as well as society."[20]

While the nominal objective of the schools was the self-sufficiency of the pupils, superintendents warned that they could
not "convert them into intelligent and self-guiding individuals."[21] This was not seen, however, as a critical barrier to economic self-support in society. Most of the school officials would
have agreed with James B. Richards, first superintendent of the
Pennsylvania school, when he said, "The multitude of laborers
on our streets and farms, work by habit and routine; they are
not independent in their modes of thought, or life."[22] Richards
believed that only a few people were actually capable of truly
original thought, and those few were geniuses. Although the
feeble-minded were the most dependent, nearly all of humanity relied upon the initiative and intelligence of others. In making their way into the world, the retarded were merely like the
blind or the deaf, who would always require some degree of

helpful assistance or supervision after their periods of special education.

The retarded not only had to be taught how to work effectively, they also had to be trained in how to live harmoniously with others.[23] "The exhibition of greater self-control, and an increased perception of social and moral obligation" on the part of the pupils allowed the superintendents to continue to report "an increasing resemblance to ordinary persons of their own age." School authorities knew that this was the standard by which their work would be judged.[24]

As the effectiveness of educating the mentally retarded became more widely known and accepted, the schools experienced a moderate growth in enrollment that even the Civil War failed to halt. Starting in the 1850's, the institutional population increased on the average of nine new pupils a year. Even this modest addition quickly overtaxed the hastily converted accommodations that had been pressed originally into use. By the end of the decade, all of the schools had made some provision for expansion. In New York, Pennsylvania, and Massachusetts, the schools were relocated; the first two chose predominantly rural areas, Syracuse and Elwyn, with good transportation to urban centers, while the third moved to a healthful, but more constrained, seaside location in South Boston. Before the new facilities were completed, however, waiting lists of prospective students had grown. As soon as the new buildings were finished, they were filled to capacity. A cyclical pattern was established whereby institutions expanded to relieve waiting list pressures but the expansions were rarely sufficient to meet the demands of the state's increasing population. Construction always lagged behind applications for admission. As each new building was completed, the cycle began again.

There are a number of explanations for this situation. Obviously one factor was the states' fiscal priorities and the related question of demonstrated need. The states had limited financial resources that were generally spent in response to public pressure. In practical terms this meant that far more was spent on asylums for the insane than on schools for the retarded because the public believed that insanity constituted a greater and more immediate threat to society than did retardation. Even if sufficient funds were made available, there was the problem of accurately determining the number of the mentally retarded in society. In this regard the federal and state censuses were well known to underenumerate the retarded. Here there was the twofold difficulty of making a correct diagnosis and the reluctance of family members to admit to it.

There is one additional factor that must be considered, at least in the period prior to 1870. Since the schools were never intended to be custodial facilities, no provision was made for a permanent residential population. It was originally thought that as a short-term educational facility with constant turnover in the institutional population, the schools could effectively accommodate all the suitable cases in the state. The optimum size of the institution would be reached when the number of those returned to the community equalled the number of cases applying for admission. School officials expected a leveling off and a decrease in new admissions as society gained new knowledge about the causes of retardation and took the necessary steps to negate their effects. Authorities therefore thought that each new expansion would eliminate the waiting list and bring the school to its ideal size.[25]

The Civil War had relatively little effect on the activities and the personnel of the schools. Pupils continued to be admitted as the states maintained the prewar levels of their appropriations. There was even some expansion. Connecticut chartered the Connecticut School for Imbeciles at Lakeville in 1861 with Henry M. Knight as superintendent, and in the same year Kentucky completed the construction of the Institution for the Education and Training of Feeble-minded Children at Frankfort under James Rodman.[26] Naturally, there were some dislocations caused by the war. Elwyn in Pennsylvania found itself with ten pupils from the South that the school had to maintain at its expense. Hervey B. Wilbur of New York noted that rising prices increased the yearly costs of caring for a pupil from the prewar average of $160 to $210, but state funding did not increase proportionately. As with other schools, Syracuse went into debt, and Wilbur carefully watched its expenses. He also commented favorably on the fact that a number of students had enlisted and served in the Union Army.[27] Joseph Parrish, the superinten-

dent of the Pennsylvania Training School, left Elwyn to join the
United States Sanitary Commission. He was replaced by Isaac
N. Kerlin, his former student and assistant superintendent.[28]
Aside from these personnel changes, rising prices, and some
manpower shortages, there are few references to the war in the
annual reports and boards of trustees minutes.

Near the end of the Civil War, on February 18, 1865, the Illinois General Assembly approved "An Act to Organize an Experimental School for the Instruction and Training of Idiots and
Feeble-minded Children in the State of Illinois." Charles T.
Wilbur, the brother of Hervey, was chosen as superintendent.
Although he was only thirty, Wilbur had been previously associated with three other schools: he was a teacher in New York,
the assistant superintendent in Ohio, and the founder of the
school at Lakeville, Connecticut. After his graduation from the
Berkshire Medical School in 1860, he served in the Union Army
as a surgeon before coming to Illinois. Wilbur also was instrumental in the establishment of schools for the retarded in Iowa,
Indiana, Kansas, Nebraska, and Minnesota. In 1882, he began
publishing the monthly *Philanthropic Index and Review*, the first
periodical devoted to mental retardation. The following year he
left Illinois to open a private institution in Kalamazoo, Michigan.[29]

Wilbur guided the Illinois school through the slow process of
maturation that was to be repeated, in essence, in every succeeding institution. It took ten years of lobbying by the medical
profession and interested laymen before the General Assembly
authorized the expenditure of $5,000 per year for a two-year test
period. The Board of Directors of the Illinois Institution for the
Education of the Deaf and Dumb had been charged with orga-
nizing the school. They leased the home and grounds of ex-
Governor Joseph Duncan of Jacksonville and hired Wilbur and
engaged his wife as matron. This was not an uncommon arrangement. Nor was it unusual that the first teachers had held
similar positions in the older schools. As was often the case,
space was severely limited and the number of applications far
exceeded the school's capacity. Wilbur was able to get an additional $3,000 for another building in 1867, and he added a third
in 1870 so that the school could accommodate eighty children.

This was some improvement, but, as Wilbur pointed out, there were at least 1,750 retardates in the state, and the school had had 306 applications for admission since it opened. School authorities constantly emphasized the fact that as a group the retarded were as numerous as the insane but received far less institutional care.[30]

Like other superintendents in newly established and experimental schools, Wilbur in his *Annual Reports* discussed the relatively low costs and great benefits of his institution. Having a one-to-five ratio of staff to students, he argued that for every five pupils in school, four people who had previously attended the retarded could now be freed for more productive labor. It would not cost society any more to care properly for the retarded. The costs are simply shifted "from local authorities or poor families, who do not attempt to instruct them, and, usually at a lower cost per capita, places [retardates] under that discipline and training which often fits them to become producers, instead of allowing them to always remain an expense and burden to society."[31] There was a constant emphasis on the usefulness and practicality of the training. Wilbur reiterated that "all our exercises are made subordinate to, and terminate in, a capacity and disposition for some form of industry."[32] By means of such successful arguments Wilbur was able to have the Illinois institution incorporated as one of the permanent charitable institutions of the state in 1871.

Wilbur and the other school officials used the *Annual Reports* to influence and inform the state legislatures, which were the primary source of funds. They justified their requests for renewed or enlarged appropriations by calling attention to the large numbers of the retarded as yet uncared for, and by means of letters, testimonials, and surveys, they demonstrated the beneficial results they had already achieved.[33] Every year the same key facts and phrases were stressed and repeated. The superintendents apologized for the repetition, but given the turnover in nineteenth-century legislatures, they believed it was important that new lawmakers be informed of their situation.[34]

Starting in 1865, many school authorities began reporting to a newly created agency, a state board of charities. This happened first in Massachusetts, which was followed by Ohio and

New York in 1867; Illinois and Pennsylvania were next in 1869, and Connecticut acted in 1873. The boards had various titles, such as the Massachusetts Board of State Charities, the Pennsylvania Board of Public Charities, or most simply, the New York State Board of Charities. While they differed in scope, membership, and authority, the state boards had general supervisory, but not executive, power over prisons, jails, reformatories, insane asylums, hospitals, orphanages, and schools for the deaf, the blind, and the retarded. The *Reports* of these boards to the state legislatures varied considerably; in some states they only duplicated the *Annual Reports* of the various institutions, while in others, notably Massachusetts, they provided comprehensive examinations of the needs of the state.[35]

The general public was another important group that school administrators sought to impress. Hervey Wilbur correctly noted that the *Annual Reports* provided "our almost only opportunity of communication with the public."[36] The most common appeal was to the well-being of the family. The effort of caring for one retarded child, so this argument went, could completely exhaust any mother, deprive the other children of their share of attention, and drive a father to drink or some other excess. Remaining at home without ever getting the proper training that could prevent him or her from becoming a permanent public charge, a retarded child could destroy the viability of family life and pauperize a whole family. "The most intelligent parents are conscious of and confess their inability to discipline or properly instruct their unfortunate children. The result is that they grow up ungoverned, with passionate and perverse dispositions— making homes unhappy—a terrible burden and source of anxiety to friends as well as frequently an annoyance to neighbors."[37]

The *Circular* of the Illinois institution made it clear that the facility was committed to an educational mission: "The design and object of the Institution are not of a custodial character, but to furnish the means of education to that portion of the youth of the State not provided for in any of its other educational institutions, who are of proper school-attending age, and who shall remain such periods of time as shall, in the estimation of the Superintendent and the Board of Trustees, suffice to impart all the education practicable in each particular case . . . . Children between the ages of ten and eighteen who are idiotic, or so deficient in intelligence as to be incapable of being educated at any ordinary school, and who are not epileptic, insane or greatly deformed, may be admitted by the Superintendent."[38] As in the older institutions, the superintendent still determined which pupils were acceptable and for how long they would remain. School officials tried to admit an equal number of pupils from the different parts of the state, and they maintained the practice of a probationary period and a bond to insure the removal of a pupil with no cost to the state. Wilbur also retained the annual vacation in July and August, but students could remain at the institution with the superintendent's approval. Clothing was to be supplied by parents, or paid for by the county responsible for the child. Illinois would be the first state to provide free tuition, board, and laundry to all state residents, not only paupers.[39] This assumption of financial responsibility would be adopted in latter years by virtually every other state. Despite some changes, Illinois and succeeding institutions basically adhered to the operational patterns already established by the existing schools.

Wilbur's theories and methods of education were very similar to those of the other superintendents and were derived from the ideas of Seguin.[40] In the manner of Seguin's physiological approach, superintendents like Wilbur concentrated their efforts on strengthening the physical organs of sensation and then restoring the faculties of the brain. Historian Norman Dain has observed that nineteenth-century psychiatrists "shared the conventional belief in the existence of a non-material soul, which was equated with the mind and was thought to be separate from its physical agent, the brain."[41] School superintendents, such as R. J. Patterson of the Columbus, Ohio, institution accepted this tenet; he noted that "there can be no disease of the mind. . . . In idiocy, as in insanity, it is the mind's treatment that is at fault."[42] Patterson's successor, Gustavus A. Doren, emphasized the necessity of a physical approach to treatment: "Our efforts are always first directed towards securing the healthy action of every sense, limb, and muscle . . . . For imbecility is always the result of some physical cause, disturbing the bal-

ance or destroying the relations of the functions."[43] Superintendents believed that physical and mental functions were so
closely interrelated that "an unhealthy impression made upon
the digestive system will produce a similar effect upon the brain
and the moral nature."[44] Since retardates were considered to
be morally, mentally, and physically diseased, the task of the
school was to restore the vital balance that was originally disturbed by their affliction.

So long as school officials considered their mission to be primarily restorative and educational, they were gratified with their
achievements in individual cases. However, as the waiting lists
for entrance into the schools grew longer, superintendents expressed frustration that the basic causes of retardation, while
not beyond the control of human effort, were out of their hands,
a sentiment expressed more frequently after the Civil War. Howe
had voiced the widely shared opinion noted above "that it begins to be known that in almost every case, the imbecility of
the children is congenital, and that the causes of it are to be
found in the physical condition of the parents."[45] The retarded
were not responsible for their condition; the fault lay with their
parents, whose irresponsible behavior was increasingly in-
dicted by school authorities.

Most superintendents agreed with Doren when he found that
not all cases of retardation "but the majority of them must be
attributed to the violation of physiological laws, and the children of men must inherit their ills if they persist in fastening
these violations from a normal condition upon themselves."[46]
The types of violation were many and varied. The commonly
cited ones were excessive dissipation and amusements, especially alcohol and sexual relations, arduous physical or mental
labor, and consanguineous marriages. Any of these could ov-
erstrain and shatter the nervous system. Superintendents believed in moderate and prudent standards, and they condemned any type of excessive behavior in strong and vivid
terms. Kerlin, for example, denounced inebriation, saying "thirty
per centum of idiots have been referred to the transmitted poi-
son of alcohol, coupled with the attendant poverty and
wretchedness into which its children are so often born." Kerlin
righteously declared that "unlawful and excessive use of the

organs and functions of procreation, probably stands at the head
of all enervating and demoralizing influences."[47]

Unfortunately, the penalties for parental transgressions were
often paid by their offspring. Superintendents believed that nature was a strict accountant and "repeated abuse and indulg-
ence establish a condition at variance from that which is normal. The enfeebled or congested brain becomes habitual, the
diseased condition of the body becomes chronic, and the law
of hereditary transmission explains like begetting like."[48] In
common with other American thinkers of that era, superintendents were uncertain of the exact processes of the law. They
saw the influence of both immediate and remote causes as they
felt "that not only the peculiarities which are ours by inheritance, but the influence of acquired habits, is transmitted."[49]
Howe had pointed out that "the transmission of any inferiority
is not always direct. It is not always the same form."[50] However, regardless of its method of transmission or ultimate man-
ifestation, school authorities were convinced that hereditary
weakness was responsible for nearly all congenital retardation.
In this way of thinking, environmental factors ultimately cor-
rupted heredity.

Americans seemed to be caught up in an "age of extreme"—
an age when "the head and the heart, the intellect and affec-
tions, run away from each other, in the giddy race for life."[51]
Retardation was one result of the "terrible strain that is kept
up, both physically and mentally, upon our people in the
'scramble'—for it is nothing else—for money and position."[52]

Administrators of insane asylums presented a similar analysis in accounting for the increase of madness in mid-nine-
teenth-century America. They attributed the high rate of insanity to the stresses and strains caused by the loss of stability and
order in American life. In every field of human activity, America produced the driving, compulsive person eager for power
and wealth. This individual lived at a fervid pace, blinded by
unrealistic goals and inflated ambition. An individual caught in
such a life-style ignored the basic rules of good health and invariably developed behavioral patterns which led to insanity.
In making this critique, mental hospital administrators were, like
those concerned with the retarded, offering a guide around the

pitfalls leading to mental illness. Both were interested in preventing insanity and urged Americans to pursue a life of moderation and self-restraint; good mental health was maintained
by accepting modest ambitions and by striking a balance between mental and physical activities.[53]

Along with sharing common etiological concerns, administrators of insane asylums and superintendents of schools for the
retarded became increasingly involved in the problems associated with custodialism. In the case of the mentally deficient, the
primary influence in this alteration of institutional function was
the growing awareness that the early estimates of the number
of retarded who could be returned as self-supporting to the
community were far too high.

It had always been known that a certain percentage of the
mentally defective were so severely retarded that little if any
improvement could be achieved from even the most persistent
efforts. Members of this class were considered to be unimprovable, and they were generally excluded from the schools so that
the superintendents could concentrate on what they believed
to be the far larger numbers of retarded who could be educated. As early as 1856, Howe raised the question of what to
do with those "past the hope of improvement." He recognized
that the school had no proper facilities for them, but he felt that
the correctional value of retardation would be most strongly
impressed on the public by "leaving adult idiots who are harmless scattered in the community."[54] These sentiments were
shared by other school officials who were preoccupied with the
difficulties of establishing the educational programs of their institutions. Even if there had been significant interest in creating
homes for the unimprovables, it would have been difficult to gen-
erate legislative support for expensive custodial facilities once
the lawmakers had been already convinced that the schools were
most effective as economical short-term educational institutions. Later, the superintendents would have to struggle to
modify these beliefs as they changed their own opinions concerning the proper mission of the schools.

After the Civil War, when many pupils who had been admitted as young children in the 1850's were ready to leave, superintendents more accurately evaluated the results of their

work. In most cases, they had overestimated the potential for improvement. They had been misled by the high rate of initial development when the students first entered the schools, and they assumed the pupils would continue to improve at this rate until their discharge. Now, as they approached that critical time, superintendents realized that few of their charges were able to support themselves even with the kindly assistance of family and friends. The actual experience of working with the retarded on a daily basis over a period of years made it clear that the rapid initial gains were primarily due to the combined influence of the childrens' natural process of growth and their entry into the therapeutic-educational environment of the school. The effects of these factors diminished with time, and the rate of development of most pupils slowed at the age of puberty and then declined. Thus, by the late 1860's, school authorities were becoming aware that only a small proportion of their students would ever be able to support themselves in society.

It was true that a number of the retarded, generally of the highest grade, were able under capable and constant supervision to earn enough to offset the cost of their maintenance at home. But often the parents did not want to remove their children from the schools where they could receive continuing professional care. In other cases, parents had died or moved away, and the students were left friendless and alone. In this situation there was no other place to go but the almshouse, where atrophy and deterioration were almost certain. Even if the schools could have found proper accommodations for all who were capable of supervised self-support, there was still the problem of providing for those retardates who could contribute only some fraction toward their maintenance, and then only in an institutional environment. Finally, school authorities were confronted by the claims of the even more helpless, who had originally been denied admission to the schools but who had a valid right to some form of institutional care. Faced with these conditions, school administrators began to consider alternatives to their traditional methods of operation.

In 1867 Kerlin in Pennsylvania mentioned publicly the need for a separate facility for "such children as are unsuited to our schools, but who are a heavy burden to their afflicted fami-

lies."[55] Devoting his 1869 and 1871 *Annual Reports* to a detailed
analysis of the dispositions of all those admitted to the school
since its founding in 1853, he reported that out of a total of 500,
only 81 (16.2 percent) were able to support themselves fully,
while 140 (28 percent) could provide for some portion of their
expenses, 118 (23.6 percent) were capable of performing small
services and chores, and 161 (32.2 percent) were hopelessly dependent. More than half of those admitted were unable to make
any significant financial contribution towards their care. Kerlin
next estimated the family resources of his pupils from their admission blanks. Using this data he extrapolated the financial
condition of the estimated 3,500 retarded individuals in the
Commonwealth. If the Elwyn population was a representative
sample, Pennsylvania had 717 retardates who came from families fully able to support them, 664 could call upon half support, and 1,619 had families who were poor but not willing to
resort to the almshouses, where 569 did reside.[56] Kerlin concluded that many retardates were unable to provide for themselves and came from families too poor to support them. Given
these findings, the Board of Trustees decided that an "asylum
is the natural outgrowth of the school, and as there are several
in the present family who are either adults or approaching adult
life, the time has come to make such provision . . . for many
candidates awaiting such a home."[57]

While Kerlin considered these measures, school authorities at
Syracuse discussed the possibility of creating a separate custodial institution. In 1865, the Syracuse *Annual Report* noted that
the age of discharge might have to be extended. Originally, the
age limitation had been established in reference to the ages of
development of normal children, but it was later learned that
the retarded developed more slowly over a longer period of
time.[58] Gradually, Syracuse, and the school at South Boston,
retained pupils beyond the mandated leaving age. There was
no official notification, but in this instance changes in actual
administrative practices preceded modifications in policy. The
same thing was true regarding the summer vacations; as a matter of official policy they continued, but in fact each year fewer
and fewer pupils returned home.[59] These practices of modifying the upper age limit and restricting the annual vacation could

be interpreted as attempts to strengthen the educational capabilities of the schools by giving them a greater period of time to work with their students. However, as the policies were implemented in the 1870's, they nurtured the emerging custodialism by creating a supply of trainable, adult, full-time residents who could serve as a necessary and inexpensive source of labor.

The type of custodial facility discussed by school officials in the 1860's was similar to the asylum for the insane poor at Ovid, New York. Such an institution for the retarded required a healthy environment and sufficient land for growth. It would accept two classes of inmates: one group would be the estimated 20 percent of the retarded who could not be educated but only improved in their habits, a class generally not admitted to the school. The second class would be "graduates" of the school who could not function successfully in society but had all the training the school provided. Superintendent Wilbur of Syracuse emphasized that the growing numbers of both classes provided the impetus for planning a separate custodial institution.[60]

The legislatures of New York and of other states did not immediately favor the creation of separate custodial institutions; instead, support went to enlarging and differentiating existing physical plants. In many cases this was acceptable to school authorities because of the long-standing practice of student segregation. Schools had divided pupils into groups, sometimes on the basis of sex, or the separation of the noisy from the quiet and timid, or keeping the sleeping quarters of the incontinent apart from the toilet-trained. Most often a combination of these factors produced a separation of students who possessed a greater capacity for education from those who did not. This division would provide the basis for the creation of custodial services within institutions.

Student segregation, or "proper classification" as it was called, was considered vital to any nineteenth-century asylum, and it was believed particularly important in facilities for the retarded because of the highly imitative nature of the pupils.[61] It was feared that the well-trained or advanced students would relapse into poor habits if they were kept in close contact with less able residents. In theory, the necessary separation could be achieved by careful scheduling, so that the different grades never used the school rooms, gymnasium, playgrounds, and dining room at the same time. Not only was this difficult to achieve in practice, it left unsolved the problem of keeping student dormitories separate while making the necessary fire precautions for a quick exit. The solution was to abandon the large, solitary structure that housed all classes and served all functions in favor of separate buildings and facilities for the exclusive use of the different grades of students. In this way pupils could interact with others equal in development to themselves, and when their condition warranted, they could change services.

The process of internal segregation proceeded at different rates in the various schools. Elwyn and Syracuse had more land than South Boston and found it easier to expand. The larger schools, such as Columbus, had a greater number and variety of students to form into classes and grades than did the smaller schools at Jacksonville, Frankfort, and Lakeville. Moreover, as the schools expanded facilities, new needs appeared. The necessity for a separate hospital became evident at one school during an attack of infectious disease, but its usefulness was apparent at an earlier date elsewhere simply because of the poor physical condition of the students.[62] As schools accepted and retained the more profoundly retarded, there were residents who required continuous hospital care since they were confined to beds, or in more helpless cases, to cribs.

When school officials realized that their institutions would have to make some provisions for the lifelong guardianship of the retarded, the existence of this pattern of internal segregation greatly facilitated the arrangement of custodial accommodations. In many ways it was easier, and, as has been noted, from the legislator's point of view, cheaper to enlarge the schools rather than build new custodial institutions.

Thus, by the 1870's, the institutionalized mentally retarded would be divided into three groups: the highest and most educable were known as the school grade; those trainable to some degree were called the custodial grade; and the most helpless and dependent became the hospital or asylum grade.[63] The superintendents had committed themselves to the care of a wide variety of the retarded, including those who had previously been considered unteachable. The tripartite division of school populations was one response to this new class of residents.

The admission and retention of an ever growing number of custodial and asylum grade cases created the two interrelated problems of proper care and increased costs. The solution to these difficulties was found in the increased utilization of resident labor. For years most schools had employed some of the pupils in small farms or gardens. This work was considered an adjunct to the formal training in the classroom and gymnasium. It provided a healthful means of exercise, instilled discipline, and developed coordination while only incidentally serving as a source of revenue.[64] Since the object of the school was to return the student to the community, some form of occupational training, especially in agriculture, seemed appropriate. For the winter months, when outdoor activities were impractical, Syracuse and South Boston introduced shoemaking to keep pupils occupied and to test their mechanical abilities. Gradually other forms of manufacturing were tried in an effort to suit the tasks to student abilities.[65]

When it was recognized that many of the trainable pupils would never live in society, superintendents employed them within the schools. Men assisted in various forms of institutional maintenance, in farming, and in the rudimentary industries of making brooms, mats, brushes, mattresses, and cane-bottomed chairs. Women worked in the kitchens and laundries, or were employed in the sewing of linens and clothing. The residents participated in all the chores necessary for maintaining a large Victorian household. In addition, many of the custodial grade residents were useful as nurses or attendants for the more helpless asylum cases. All of this resident labor reduced costs by allowing school personnel budgets to remain relatively constant while the institutional populations increased.

By the mid–1870's, schools for the retarded were not fully developed custodial institutions, but neither were they the educationally oriented schools of the past. As Hervey Wilbur noted, "the school exercises" remained a "prominent feature" of the facility, "but now in subordination to the more practical objec-

tive of the institution."[66] The realization that many of the retarded could not be brought to self-sufficiency had caused superintendents to shift the emphasis of the curricula away from
academic lessons towards a reliance upon industrial or agricultural training. Kerlin felt it was "obvious that a large percentage of children admitted to institutions of this character become their permanent wards."[67] He estimated that 10 to 15
percent could be fully educated, 20 to 30 percent would be returned home somewhat useful, and 55 to 70 percent would have
a lifetime home in the institution. Clearly, for residents remaining in the asylums, learning occupational skills, rather than abstract concepts, would be the best suited and most economical
preparation.

Almost all of the officials accepted these trends; the most
prominent exception was Samuel G. Howe. He recognized that
some of the retarded might never be able to support themselves, but he believed that close congregation and lifelong association of large numbers of the retarded was medically and
socially wrong. It was medically wrong because the retarded
needed exposure to people of normal mentality, and it was socially wrong because it implied "social and moral isolation and
ostracism."[68] Howe felt that institutions represented a social evil
that was justified only by preventing a greater evil. His hope
was that many of the retarded could be educated in the common schools while "residing in the neighborhood." For some
children this would not be possible, and in these cases the institution was justified. But all pupils should be returned home
at the end of their term of years. When this was not feasible,
custodial cases should be boarded with families, and the state
should appoint guardians of the feeble-minded. Kerlin strongly
disagreed, pointing out that boarding could never be properly
supervised, and that a central institution with all of its specialized facilities was a vital necessity. He concluded noting that
"it is not invidious to declare that the most economical and the
most humane provision that can be made for the idiot and imbecile classes is that of the General Asylum or Institution."[69]
Kerlin's reply to Howe temporarily satisfied the superintendents, but ultimately Howe's ideas of "diffusion among the
normal population" would prevail.

The schools were changing both their methods and their goals, yet officials were not sure that they could control or guide the change. The transformations came about partly because of the failure to accomplish the original educational mission. This fact, along with the interest in hereditary debilitation and extramural guidelines for healthy living, demanded a redefinition of institutional goals and priorities. Also many retardates were deemed unsuitable for life in the community and only a small percentage actually lived in proper institutions. Previously there had been little mention of the consequences of having the retarded at large; there merely had been some discussion on the disruption they caused in the family.

In 1870, while referring to the usefulness of the schools, the Board of Trustees of the Columbus school pointed the way to future institutional importance:

As a protection to society, we believe such institutions have a value far transcending their cost . . . . The facilities afforded in such institutions to learn the causes which produce such a sad deterioration of humanity, and so suggest the appropriate means for prevention will, we presume, be generally recognized as a still more important benefit.[70]

As the institutions grew, their administrators placed increasing importance on the protection of society and the prevention of mental retardation.

3

Professionalization and Specialization

By the mid–1880's, school authorities agreed that greater custodial provision was necessary for the mentally retarded. This
was considered important for the mutual benefit and protection of both retardates and society. The schools never totally
abandoned educational goals, but the role of formal education
declined as it was supplanted by the industrial or manual training necessary for an economical custodial operation. The retarded were less often thought of as helpless children needing
the ministrations and uplift of Christian charity. Instead, apparent scientific investigations combined with a new sense of
administrative professionalism and mission increasingly identified the retarded as potential sources of social disruption who
required isolation and control in specially equipped facilities.

Although some of these thoughts were evident in 1875, they
were by no means fully developed. As was frequently the case
in American history, interested foreign visitors provided some
of the most informative observations of American activities. In
the summer of 1876, two Englishmen, George E. Shuttleworth,
Medical Superintendent of the Royal Albert Asylum, and Fletcher
Beach, Superintendent of the Metropolitan District Asylum for
Imbecile Children, traveled to all nine of the American institutions and reported their findings in a short pamphlet.[1] Begin-

ning the account with a brief history of the founding of the
schools, Shuttleworth divided the facilities into two types: first,
the private, incorporated institution which relied primarily upon
public funds for the care of state beneficiaries who were nomi-
nated by local officials. These schools, notably South Boston,
Lakeville, and Elwyn, also accepted private pupils whose parents paid up to $500 annual tuition. The state institution was
the second type of school and included Columbus, Frankfort,
Jacksonville, Randalls Island, and Syracuse. Established by the
legislature, this facility was primarily for state beneficiaries but
accepted some paying students, generally from out of the state.
Shuttleworth found little difference in the care or accommodations given to the various classes of pupils. He mentioned that
the profits derived from the higher payment cases at Elwyn established a fund to provide for a custodial branch of the institution. In this way, the wealthier subsidized the less fortunate.[2]

The two Englishmen were impressed by the educational aspects of the schools. Shuttleworth noted that "the excellent
school arrangements are perhaps the most noteworthy feature
in American institutions."[3] Established as part of the public educational system, the schools were intended primarily for the
reception of educable cases and he quoted from the Syracuse
bylaws as an example of the probationary periods employed to
ensure the educational character of the institutions. He felt "the
effect of careful selection, and the weeding out of bad cases, is
that in the State Institutions generally the physical and mental
condition of the inmates presents a higher average than that seen
in British institutions, and, consequently the death-rate is lower,
and standards of scholastic education higher."[4] However, some
schools, notably Lakeville, Frankfort, and Elwyn, did not ex-
clude epileptics, especially those suffering from a mild form. In
fact at Elwyn epileptics made up approximately 10 percent of
the student body. Overall, Shuttleworth found that "the class
of 'Feeble-minded Children' would indeed appear to prepon-
derate over that of pure Idiot in the American institutions."[5]

Much favorable comment went to the "large and intelligent
staff of Teachers, and admirably appointed Schoolrooms and
Gymnasia." The student-teacher ratio was one to twenty or

twenty-five, and female teachers were employed almost exclu-
sively. At this time the sexes were not rigidly segregated into
separate classes; each group of boys and girls had its own room
and teacher. The classes were often subdivided into smaller
groups in an effort to individualize instruction. These sections
were devoted to writing, manual operations, or simple imitation exercises. Classroom equipment, such as desks, horseshoe
tables, and blackboards, was the same as in the public elementary schools, but what Shuttleworth found of "special interest
were various ingenious devices . . . for quickening the perceptions, and educating the senses of the Feeble-minded."[6] He
noted the peg-board, and the use of the word method of teaching reading. In this system pupils were first shown that a picture denoted a definite object and they were taught to associate
the word printed under the picture with the object. For many
students, speaking and articulation lessons were necessary before they could correctly pronounce the words.

Shuttleworth observed that "the Gymnasium is everywhere
regarded as an important preliminary and adjunct to the school
exercises proper."[7] This was due to the emphasis placed on the
functional relationship between a healthy body and an active,
inquiring mind. The gymnasia were large, close to the school
rooms, and fully equipped with gymnastic ladders, wands,
dumbbells, rings, and Indian clubs. The simplest exercise began with the teacher throwing soft objects at the pupil in an
effort to fix attention and arouse some form of voluntary movement. By imitating the teacher, the student attempted simple
extension movements of the arms and legs. More advanced use
of the gymnastic ladder, by climbing or walking, would fix attention, develop the will, and strengthen the muscular system.
Ultimately, pupils would perform rhythmic drills with wands
or Indian clubs to music. The use of musical instruments, weekly
dances, and marching corps were highly successful at all the
schools. These amusements, and others such as plays and as-
semblies, were good diversions for students and excellent ad-
vertisements for the schools on visiting days or national holidays.

The administrative organization of American institutions was
described in detail. The management was vested in a Board of

Trustees that was either appointed by state officials or jointly chosen by them and the members of the corporation. The Board elected a president, secretary, and treasurer and supervised the affairs of the school. The entire responsibility for internal administration rested with the superintendent, a qualified physician appointed by the Board. The matron, "looked upon as the Mother of the Family," advised attendants—mainly women, controlled nurses, and administered out-of-school care. The housekeeper was in charge of domestic duties, while the steward kept the stores and occasionally directed the male attendants and other workers. Teachers and their assistants were ranked and paid by seniority. In general, the ratio of staff to students was one to four or five, and the ratio of attendants to pupils was one to ten. Shuttleworth found the food, clothing, and housing more than adequate. He also remarked that the annual cost of maintenance, averaging $200 per pupil, declined as the size of the institution increased.[8]

Besides their interest in the educational and organizational features of the American schools, the Englishmen commented on other important developments. The diversity of industrial and agricultural occupations met with approval. They found that the making of mats, brushes, chair seats, and rope had been introduced with "good results," but that there was less success in tailoring and shoe-making. Most of the men were engaged in some phase of farming because the majority came from agricultural districts so "the most appropriate industrial training is such as will fit them for working on the land."[9] Every school, except South Boston, had a farm or garden, the largest being four hundred acres at Columbus. Women were employed in several branches of domestic industry or in sewing and fancy knitting work. Training for specific skills appeared as important as acquiring a general education.

Shuttleworth had previously noted the preponderance of "Feeble-minded children" over "pure Idiots." He reported that "great stress is very properly laid upon the importance of keeping the two classes entirely distinct. This is effected in several instances by providing accommodation for the low-grade cases in a building detached from the main-block, with separate exercising ground."[10] He mentioned the use of a detached infirmary in Ohio and the segregation of the different grades in New York as examples of this differential treatment. In these schools, the admission, retention, and segregation of different classes of the retarded was already in practice and was obviously accepted. Shuttleworth found that "the question how best to provide for teachable and adult idiots—whether in connection with existing Schools, or in entirely separate custodial institutions— is the subject of considerable diversity of opinion."[11] Here it is important to note that the question under consideration was not whether or not any provision at all should be made but what kind of accommodations should be established.

The report ended with a summary evaluation of institutional successes. After noting that the schools only cared for approximately fifteen hundred of the country's estimated forty thousand retardates, Shuttleworth observed that these institutions were viewed as useful facilities producing beneficial results. The statistics, however, quoted to support this contention revealed that only a small percentage of the pupils were successfully returned to the community: 26 percent in Lakeville, 25 percent in Columbus, and 10 percent in Elwyn. Shuttleworth felt that "facts like these are of course the most striking results of training."[12] However, the return of 10 to 25 percent of the retarded to the community was not the original objective of the schools; the founders optimistically believed that almost all their pupils would rejoin their communities. What clearly had occurred was a change in the criteria in judging success. In nearly three decades of school operation, the superintendents accepted the fact that only a minority of their students would eventually be discharged. In the mid–1870's, their new source of pride was in the size of that minority.

Although the original intentions of the administrators of the retarded were not fully realized, there was a significant increase in the number of state institutions.[13] The newly established schools continued, remarkably enough, to replicate the patterns of growth and development similar to those of the older institutions. Many were first located in temporary sites and were given small legislative appropriations that were commensurate with an experimental status. During this period, they generally stressed educational and rehabilitative work, and carefully monitored admissions and retentions in order to maximize records of achievement. School officials emphasized the economic benefits of the institutions, noting how they relieved the family, reduced pauperism, crime, and dependence, and at the same time secured the rights of the retarded to educational amelioration. As the schools became better known, they attracted larger numbers of students which necessitated the construction of larger, permanent facilities. The schools received increased financial support from the state which funded a variety of specialized buildings, including classrooms, gymnasiums, industrial shops, hospitals, laundries, dormitories, and custodial residences. The new superintendents frequently had teaching or administrative experience in the older schools and a few had previously worked with the insane.[14]

Naturally, the superintendents derived their beliefs about the treatment of the mentally retarded from their own experience and backgrounds as well as from contacts with one another. After 1876, communication between them was greatly enhanced by the creation of two professional societies: the National Conference of Charities and Corrections (NCCC) and the Association of Medical Officers of American Institutions for Idiots and Feeble-Minded Persons (AMO). The formation of both organizations facilitated the exchange, collection, and amplification of professional opinion concerning the mentally defective in the United States.

Although modest about his role in founding the AMO, Isaac N. Kerlin played a most significant part in its establishment.[15] He recognized that the time was right for acting on Seguin's long-standing proposal that "every year the Superintendent of the various schools for idiots should meet, to impart to one another the difficulties they have encountered, the results of their experience, and mostly to compare the books containing their orders and regulations."[16] Kerlin used the celebration of the American Revolution Centennial at Philadelphia as his opportunity to suggest a meeting of superintendents at the Pennsylvania Training School for discussions on topics of mutual interest. Accordingly, on June 6 and 7, 1876, E. Seguin, G. A. Doren, Henry M. Knight, Hervey B. Wilbur, Charles T. Wilbur, and George Brown joined Kerlin at Elwyn and adopted a constitution forming the AMO, a permanent professional organization. Its objective was the discussion of questions relating to the causes, condition, and statistics of idiocy, including the management, training, and education of retarded persons. Annual meetings would occur at the different schools, and membership was limited to the medical heads of institutions and such persons who distinguished themselves in working with the retarded. Seguin was elected the first president, Hervey Wilbur vice-president, and Kerlin secretary and treasurer.[17]

While the AMO was the primary professional organization of the superintendents, association with the NCCC introduced them to professionals in the field of social welfare, acquainting them with a wider variety of community problems. The NCCC was founded on May 20, 1874, when the Boards of Public Charities of Massachusetts, Connecticut, New York, and Wisconsin gathered together in New York to organize the Conference of Boards of Public Charities.[18] In 1875, it became the Conference of Charities and met in conjunction with the American Social Science Association until 1879, after which it assembled independent of its parent organization and adopted the more descriptive name, Conference of Charities and Corrections. In 1882, it became the National Conference of Charities and Corrections.[19]

Almost all the original members were active on their respective state boards of public charities, and it was their belief that the Conference "is simply an exchange for the comparison of views and experiences, not a convention for the adoption of any creed or platform, nor a body organized to accomplish any scheme or undertaking."[20] The NCCC's orientation was toward the practical problems encountered in the daily administration of the varied institutions supervised by the state boards. Its meetings were devoted to such diverse concerns as provisions for the insane and the retarded, plans for penal reform, and the difficulties of administering relief to the poor. Because of the catholicity of its interests, the NCCC overlapped the work of other organizations, notably the American Health Association (founded in 1872), the National Prison Association (organized in 1870), various charity societies (started after 1877), and, of course, the AMO.[21]

The creation of the AMO and the NCCC were critical in developing a sense of professional identity among the superintendents. The chief executive officers of institutions for the retarded had been previously just a group of physicians bound together by ties of common interest, informal correspondence, and exchange of *Annual Reports*. However, when they created the AMO and established the standards of membership for it, they were implicitly announcing the criteria for, if not the very creation of, their profession. Their organization was modeled after the Association of Medical Superintendents of American Institutions for the Insane which was founded in 1844. With some success, this older association had worked for three important goals: establishing the standards of entry and practice of the profession; creating autonomy in the operation of institutions; and becoming the spokesman to government and the public on matters of concern to the membership. The AMO would try to achieve similar results for itself in these same areas.[22]

From the time of its founding, the AMO was a service organization and a public relations platform for the profession. At the second annual meeting, provisions were made to record and publish the transactions of the association for distribution in states that were considering the establishment of institutions for the retarded.[23] Each year as the membership list and published *Proceedings* increased in length, the section devoted to "Status of the Work Before the People and Legislatures" reported small but steady advances in all areas of the country except the South.[24] The value of the AMO to its members was best summarized at the tenth annual meeting in the Presidential Address of F. M. Powell of Iowa: "Here interchange of ideas and experience take place; our own methods are confirmed or corrected, as well as new plans and impressions received. The benefit of acquaintance with co-workers establishes confidence and prepares the way for concerted action."[25] Powell made the nature of this "concerted action" perfectly clear, saying that because "other classes of defectives have largely monopolized philanthropic movements, public and private," it was the duty of the AMO to press the claims of the retarded for proper care.[26]

To support these claims, one of the first steps taken by the

AMO was to collect accurate and reliable data concerning retardation. The third annual meeting (1878) created a committee to
prepare a system of descriptive admission blanks and institutional records for the "uniform and exhaustive inquiry into, and
record of, the phenomena and causes of idiocy."[27] Two years
later, Kerlin presented a report from the Committee on Statistical Records with examples of the descriptive, etiological, and
physical examination blanks used at Elwyn.[28] Although the
schools never adopted a uniform data recording format, the superintendents were justified in their concern to document the
facts of retardation. School officials believed:

Public opinion is shaping a decision that most of the diseases, suffer-
ings, and ills of life are not to be attributed to accidental and fatalistic,
but to avertible and removable causes; if this doctrine can be sustained
by the honest testimony of our Institutions for Charity, Reformatories,
and Prisons—a testimony that gives its figures and that cannot be
gainsaid—they will furnish a valuable aid to the arguments for such
legislation and education as will correct or abate all tendencies, habits,
and practices that can be reached by those means.[29]

For this reason, many superintendents provided information
about their pupils and the retarded population of their states,
just as their predecessors had in the first decades when schools
were established. It was assumed that by gathering and publishing facts and charts, the superintendents would dramatize
the inadequacies of existing facilities, demonstrate the harmful
consequences of retardation, and discover some means of reducing the social and economic costs of mental deficiency.

Finding the causes of retardation and the ways to prevent or
minimize it were matters of increasing concern to school authorities in the 1870's. Although dedicated to improving the
condition of the retarded, they now accepted the fact that educational techniques of the previous twenty-five years had not
produced the results that were originally anticipated. Consequently, two courses of inquiry and action were pursued: first,
to devise and implement new instructional methods and institutional facilities for retardates who were considered incapable
of self-support and self-control. These innovations took the form

of specialized industrial or manual training and the creation of separate custodial departments within the schools. The second approach was to identify the causes of retardation and if possible negate their effects. This encouraged more emphasis to be placed on the role of hereditary factors in the creation and perpetuation of mental defects. Both approaches were responses to the realization that the traditional educational methods were not achieving the desired results. If the schools could not rely upon education alone to restore a significant number of the retarded to productive lives, there would be attempts to care for those already afflicted while trying to prevent any further increase in their numbers.

The significance of the relationship between heredity and mental retardation was known from the beginnings of institutional care in America. By the 1870's, it was widely believed, as one superintendent noted, that "no fact in science is better established than that there is a most intimate mental as well as physical relation between the parent and the child—between each generation and the succeeding one."[30] Most superintendents agreed with Kerlin's summary concerning heredity as a contributory agent in retardation: "Idiocy and imbecility are dependent *generally* on hereditary and prenatal causes, *occasionally* on the diseases or accidents of infancy, *rarely* also, upon certain debilitating influences of childhood."[31] Despite the generality of these beliefs, there had been almost no detailed investigation of the actual long-term effects of heredity by a qualified observer.

It was partly because there had been so little work done on the social effects of heredity that Robert L. Dugdale's book, *"The Jukes:" A Study in Crime, Pauperism, Disease, and Hereditiy*, had such a dramatic impact.[32] Dugdale was not a professional penologist or social worker; rather, he was a merchant whose avocation was reform and the investigation of social problems.[33] This combination of interests was not unusual in the nineteenth century when many businessmen and professionals regularly served state and private institutions. Dugdale became involved with the Juke family in 1874 when he was on an inspection trip for the New York Prison Association. In a rural Ulster County jail he found "six persons, under four family names, who turned out to be blood relatives to some degree."[34] This appeared to be more than just a coincidence, and as he was concerned with penal reform, it aroused his curiosity and became the origin of what would be, as Haller notes, "the most influential American work on heredity during the nineteenth century."[35]

Dugdale tried to learn as much as possible about the family of the six jail inmates. He was assisted by two lifetime residents of the county who were physicians, one of whom was eighty-four years old. Other sources included the "testimony" of neighbors, relatives, employers, and officials as well as the records of local doctors, town postmasters, county clerks, and sheriffs. Dugdale described his research method as "one of historico-biographical synthesis united to socio-static analysis."[36] That is, he studied the life histories of family members of each generation, and subjected the data to statistical analysis. From this work he hoped to determine the responsibility of both hereditary inheritance and environmental influences in producing criminals, paupers, alcoholics, prostitutes, and mental incompetents.

The progenitor of the Juke family was identified as Max, a colonial backwoodsman of early Dutch ancestry born between 1720 and 1740. Max was described as a "hunter and fisher, a hard drinker, jolly and companionable, averse to steady toil" who became blind in his later years.[37] Two of Max's sons married into a family of six sisters, and it was their progeny that Dugdale traced for five generations. He found information on 540 who were related by blood and 168 by marriage or cohabitation, a total of 708 persons. He admitted that there were probably 1,200 family members but because of out-migrations they could not be located.[38] Neither he nor any contemporary reader expressed reservations that this missing data might invalidate or at least qualify his conclusions.

What Dugdale did discover about the 708 known Jukes aroused considerable attention. In the family, 128 were prostitutes, 18 kept brothels, 76 were convicted criminals, 45 were intemperate, 85 were diseased or defective, and 208 received poor relief. In addition, 23 percent of all Juke children were illegitimate.[39] Instead of finding a random distribution of criminals, paupers, or whatever in each branch of the family, Dugdale found "groups which may be considered distinctively industrious, distinctively uncriminal, distinctively pauper, and specifically diseased." The attached genealogical charts showed that "these features run along lines of descent so that you can follow them from generation to generation."[40] One of the original six sisters was known as "Margret, the mother of criminals" because of the propensity of her descendants for crime. The majority of the book was devoted to discussions of representative cases from each branch of the family, illustrating the concentration of specific traits or tendencies in that line of descent.

In accounting for the antisocial careers or vocations[41] of the Jukes, Dugdale portrayed heredity and environment as complementary and interrelated forces. In some cases where the body was structurally modified or organically weak, then "heredity is the preponderating factor in determining the career, but it is, even then, capable of marked modification for better or worse by the character of the environment. In other words, capacity, physical and mental, is limited and determined mainly by heredity." But in other cases where conduct depended on training, knowledge, and education, then "the environment has more influence than the heredity." Dugdale believed that some acquired traits could become hereditary, and that "the tendency of heredity is to produce an environment which perpetuates that heredity." After he assessed the influence of both factors, he concluded that "environment is the ultimate controlling factor in determining careers, placing heredity itself as an organized result of environment."[42] Despite this important conclusion, Dugdale's readers concentrated more on his findings about the possibilities of hereditary inheritance of disease, dependency, and disability, and gave less attention to his suggestions for the relief of these serious social problems.

In a number of instances, Dugdale indicated that changes in the environment could and did curtail prostitution, crime, and pauperism, although success or failure in reform was largely dependent on the individual's mental and physical condition. Dugdale accepted the contemporary belief that "the whole question of crime, vice, and pauperism rests strictly and fundamentally upon a physiological basis, and not upon a sentimental or metaphysical one."[43] He believed there was an underlying physical defect responsible for antisocial activities which had to be rectified before the offending behavior could be altered. While the causes of some defects were hereditary, notably disease in parents producing idiocy in their children, in most cases the etiology lay in such environmental factors as nutritional deficiency, unsanitary living, and educational neglect. Any of these conditions could cause an "arrest of cerebral development at some point, so that the individual fails to meet the expectations of the civilization in which he finds himself placed." The only effective "cure for unbalanced lives is a training which will affect the cerebral tissue, producing a corresponding change of career."[44]

Dugdale's suggestions for reform were principally environmental. Remove the Jukes from their "ancestral breeding spot" where they occupied overcrowded shanties of one or two rooms which encouraged sleeping or "bunking" together with no provision for modesty or privacy. Put them into decent housing, or if they were young board them with good families who would encourage them to learn a trade. This productive labor would divert their "vital force" or energies into constructive channels rather than into deviant sexual behavior or criminal activities.[45] In addition, state institutions, especially prisons and reformatories, would have to modify their operations in accordance with new educational goals. "Every reformatory should take for its model of school training, either the kindergarten education or the method of object lessons . . . for the youth of this class, if not moral imbeciles, are moral infants. The advantage of the kindergarten instruction rests in this, that it coherently trains the senses and awakens the spirit of accountability, building up cerebral tissues."[46] Dugdale believed that within fifteen years there would be a significant decrease in crime if children of the "criminal population" were given this proper form of training.

As a summary and conclusion, Dugdale provided a type of "human cost accounting" that purported to calculate the expense caused by the Jukes to the people of New York. Much quoted by his readers, the grand total was $1,308,000 created by 1,200 people over a seventy-five-year period. Some of the data were undoubtedly accurate, such as the costs of poor re-

lief and of trials and imprisonments. Other figures were merely
rough estimates, notably wages lost due to illness and death.
In a few cases, the entries appear to be ludicrous, especially in
those that calculate the cost per year of debauchery by prostitutes. But no one criticized Dugdale's estimate that syphilis was
responsible for $600,000 in lost wages or questioned why the
sum was charged as a cost to New York. Indeed, Dugdale and
most of his readers believed that he was being conservative; if
better records existed and the study continued, the total costs
would have been much higher.[47]

The Jukes became the model for future studies of "defective
families." Despite Dugdale's disclaimers that "the study here
presented is largely tentative, and care should be taken that the
preliminary generalizations announced be not applied indiscriminately to the general questions of crime and pauperism,"[48] his methods and selective parts of his conclusions were
widely copied and accepted. All successive studies would have
long pedigree charts of genealogies, complete with full sets of
abbreviations to record the failures and shortcomings of individual family members. There was something at once alarming
and fascinating about the thought of whole families, even entire communities, living off in the hinterlands free of law and
morality that were the breeding grounds of crime, vice, pauperism, and degeneracy. To many readers, the situation demanded prompt action to stop any further increase in the numbers of defectives and degenerates.

Dugdale's study quickly became the subject of widespread
professional interest. Besides being one of the first works to claim
scientific exactness, *The Jukes* informed readers what they had
traditionally believed about the sins of the fathers being visited
upon their sons. As the Massachusetts State Board of Charities
concluded, "The hereditary relation has, we believe, a far greater
agency in producing social evils than has generally been con-
ceived," and "the more evident it becomes that in order to check
the increase of pauperism, crime, and insanity, the remedy must
be applied to their primary sources."[49] In short, some effective
method had to be devised and implemented to halt the cease-
less reproduction of lunatics, paupers, and criminals.

Although Dugdale established that only one Juke was idiotic,[50] it was a common assumption that retardation was merely another variant, such as laziness, licentiousness, or tuberculosis, resulting from a hereditarily defective constitution. The same preventive measures which were proposed to lessen the burden that families like the Jukes imposed on the state appeared to be equally serviceable when applied to the mentally defective. In 1878, Josephine Shaw Lowell, the first female member of the New York State Board of Charities and the spokeswoman for its Committee on the Condition of Poor Houses, called for the establishment of a separate custodial institution for feeble-minded women of childbearing age.[51] Her recommendation was prompted by investigations of county poorhouses, where she encountered weak-minded women who repeatedly bore illegitimate children fathered by male inmates or other men willing to take advantage of such women. The children of these unions seemed destined to inherit the weaknesses and propensities of their parents and become additional liabilities of the state. At the prompting of Mrs. Lowell's committee, the Board of Trustees of the Syracuse institution agreed to open an experimental home at Newark, New York. The legislature responded very quickly and in 1878 appropriated $18,000 for the New York State Custodial Asylum for Feeble-minded Women. It remained under the control of the officials at Syracuse until 1885 when it became fully independent.[52]

The goals of the Newark asylum were the custody and maintenance of feeble-minded women, the improvement of their physical, mental, and moral condition, and the prevention of the continual "misassociation of the sexes." During the first years of its existence, Hervey Wilbur complained that well–meaning but over zealous county officials persisted in sending wanton, but not feeble-minded, women to the institution. He maintained that the proper "home" for such profligate women was in the reformatory, and not in an asylum for feeble-minded women.[53] The difficulty of selecting the proper inmates, taking those who were feeble-minded and not just licentious, was compounded by the belief that promiscuous behavior indicated retardation. If a woman's sexual behavior was the only criterion, it was difficult to determine if promiscuity was the result of retardation or moral perversity. Custodial officials thought

that they could correctly make this crucial distinction in determining the cause of immoral conduct. They believed that the
retarded women suitable for inmates at Newark were "ungoverned and easily yielding to lust"; because of limited mentality,
they were truly "denied the power to choose the good, or the
aid of the Golden Rule."[54] In this period before the use of intelligence tests, custodial officials frequently had only personal
experience to guide them in diagnosing retardation.

The creation of the Newark asylum occurred when the schools
were already modifying admission and retention policies. In
some cases, especially regarding women, custodial practices
preceded the formulation of announced custodial policies. This
can be substantiated by an examination of the institutional records of Syracuse and South Boston, the only material available
for the entire period. Compared to the 1850's and 1860's, the
mean age at admission increased 11 percent, while the mean
period of retention grew by 43 percent in the 1870's (Table 3.1).
These statistics are more revealing when the differential treatment of men and women is examined. For men admitted in the
1870's there is a modest rise in admission age and a more significant change in period of retention. However, for women institutionalized in the 1870's compared with the previous two
decades, there are dramatic increases to both mean age at admission (23 percent) and mean retention period (80.7 percent).
Women were being admitted at older than traditional school attending ages and were being retained for longer periods of time
because "an imbecile woman is the steady prey of vile imposi-
tion, and unless she be well guarded by her kindred, should
promptly be acknowledged by the State as prominent among
its wards."[55]

The rapid creation and acceptance of Newark as a custodial
institution was one indication that the timely prevention of retardation, through the segregation of potential hereditary
sources, was considered important. Certainly part of Newark's
appeal was the insistence that the chastity of helpless, defense-
less women had to be protected. This was a powerful argument in Victorian America when the "cult of true womanhood" mandated sexual innocence until marriage and only
sanctioned those sexual acts necessary for the fulfillment of

Table 3.1
Admission Age, Retention Period and Disposition by Decade of
Admission and Gender

Decade		Age at Admission in Years	SD	Period of Retention in Years	SD	Percent Discharged	Percent Died	N
1851-59	Male	11.5	4.0	6.0	9.9	79	21	24
	Female	10.1	2.8	5.8	7.7	93	7	41
1860-69	Male	10.6	2.9	5.6	7.8	86	14	14
	Female	10.0	3.7	4.7	3.5	95	5	21
1870-79	Male	11.6	4.3	7.0	8.6	82	18	39
	Female	11.8	3.7	12.6	18.3	74	26	19
1880-89	Male	12.1	6.3	14.1	13.2	57	43	115
	Female	13.4	6.0	14.7	12.9	50	50	80
1890-99	Male	15.6	10.8	11.9	14.3	51	49	278
	Female	15.4	9.7	14.1	15.2	46	54	242
1900-09	Male	14.5	8.2	10.9	13.7	55	45	510
	Female	16.4	10.4	12.8	14.7	57	43	408
1910-19	Male	14.4	8.7	8.9	11.1	67	33	747
	Female	17.7	9.8	12.0	14.0	64	36	658

wifely responsibilities in bearing children. Equally compelling in Newark's favor was the perception that a long-standing abuse of poorhouse management would finally be corrected: retarded women would be removed from the unsavory influences of un-principled men, and would be placed in an orderly environment where both they and society would be protected.[56]

Once Newark was established, nearly all of the school officials used its existence as part of their own campaigns for the creation of comparable facilities in their states. Generally they did not agitate for special institutions for women; instead, they attempted to gain acceptance for the concept that the state had an obligation to care for all the mentally defective, including those incapable of benefiting from educational activities and constituting a potential threat, hereditary or otherwise, to the well-being of the community.[57] Superintendents had numerous motives in seeking this more comprehensive commitment to a larger number of the retarded. The construction of proper accommodations would permit better classification and care for all the school's population. The operation of Newark demonstrated that custodial facilities were less expensive than the existing schools. In a supervised custodial environment, the higher grade inmates could provide valuable services for the less able, or they could work in the fields and shops, further reducing costs. In this manner, the more capable, but not safely dischargeable, residents could be provided with lifetime employment at minimum expense to the state.

The attempt of school authorities to establish custodial care on a large scale was expressed in the ways officials modified institutional policies and operations. In most cases these efforts began with remarks in the *Annual Reports* questioning the value of summer vacations, or commenting on the difficulty of placing some students in the community, especially women and low-grade cases, or calling for extensions of the school-leaving age, or requesting funds for the creation of facilities to train older pupils for institutional employment. One of the best examples of this process occurred at the South Boston facility. Until the time of Howe's death in 1876, this school had been molded by his belief that it should remain a short-term, educational institution. But Howe's successors, Henry Tuck, George G. Tarbell, and Asbury G. Smith, saw the need for changes.

Tuck believed the school had to make some provision for retardates, possibly a third of the pupils, who either could not or should not return home. The almshouse was not a proper place for them, but they "could not go out into the world and earn a livelihood in competition with intelligent laborers."[58] Tarbell acted on these suggestions by introducing sewing as a source of employment for older girls, which he found quite successful. He traveled to other schools and was impressed by their farms, believing them to be both educational and economical. In 1881, a custodial wing for unimprovables was opened, and a small farm, ironically named for Howe, was purchased to serve as a custodial facility for the more capable older boys. The state legislature formally recognized the thrust of these new programs in 1883 when it reorganized the institution. Renamed the Massachusetts School for the Feeble-minded, it was divided into separate school and asylum departments. Its state appropriations were reduced as funds were to be sought from individuals or towns of settlement; its inmates were to be admitted by probate judges; and it was to be placed under the financial scrutiny of the Board of Health, Lunacy, and Charity.[59]

According to Tarbell, the institution should receive only those who could benefit from instruction or who could not be guarded properly at home, while "the much larger number of harmless and unimprovable imbeciles can be better and more economically cared for by their natural guardians in their own families."[60] However, the new superintendent, Asbury G. Smith, realized that "it is impossible to prevent the accumulation of some unimprovable cases," and the situation would shortly have to expand its custodial facilities to care for them.[61]

In other states, the movement toward the provision of custodial care made steady but less dramatic gains. After the Illinois asylum was relocated to Lincoln in 1877, and its population nearly doubled, Charles T. Wilbur renewed requests to acquire a farm for the training and employment of school "graduates" who could not function in society and "must always be under guardianship."[62] At the same time, his brother, Hervey B. Wilbur, made a similar appeal in New York. As with other schools which were mandated to accept only the teachable, improvable retarded, in Syracuse "this original purpose [had] been somewhat departed from, and for causes quite beyond the reach of the officers."[63] Since some pupils were homeless and others very troublesome, it was "not easy, always, to rigidly enforce the restrictions contemplated in the by-laws as to admissions, or as to dismissals of improper cases once admitted."[64] He advised the purchase of a farm for the employment of older custodial boys, estimated at 20 percent of the school's population, and the appropriation was granted in 1882. In the same year, Kerlin obtained $60,000 from the Pennsylvania legislature for land to be used for an agricultural department of his facility.[65]

The schools best known for industrial and agricultural vocational training, Frankfort and Columbus respectively, continued to strengthen these programs. This was particularly true in Ohio, where after a disastrous fire in 1881, Doren recommended increasing the school's property from four hundred to

A group of boys and their teacher on the campus of the Ohio Institution for Feeble-Minded Youth in the late 1880's (*From the Gustavus Adolphus Doren Photograph Collection, courtesy of the Ohio Historical Society.*)

one thousand acres, which he felt would fully support all the residents.[66] Even the officials of the recently established schools in Iowa, Indiana, Minnesota, Kansas, and Nebraska called for the provision of some custodial facilities and institutional employment on the grounds of better classification, relief of families, reduction of expenses, and public safety.

The increasing emphasis on custodialism had corresponding effects on educational methods and goals. As the schools placed less emphasis on educating the retarded for their return to society, they began to alter the nature of the training. "So predominating is the practical training in our institution," said the Syracuse Trustees, "that if the term 'school' were applied at all, it should be industrial school for idiots."[67] They still worked for the physical, mental, and moral improvement of their charges, but now the objective was to educate a growing percentage of them to self-sufficiency within an institutional setting. As Kerlin forcefully wrote:

It is hard to convince parents that old forms of letters and numbers do *not* constitute an education for an imbecile child, even when they may be acquired. The best end attained in his training is in reality to introduce in him the simplest conformity to the habits and actions of normal people—that he speak seldom; that he repress his emotion; that he move willingly and easily; so that he shall become an unobserved member of the common population, if thrown into it, or if retained under institutional regulation, that his cost and care shall be as moderate as possible.[68]

School administrators agreed that it was "useless to attempt to arouse these dormant facilities by forcing upon them the abstract truths of ready-made knowledge. Our teaching must be direct, simple and practical."[69] They had traditionally urged the early admission of retardates primarily for educational purposes; the earlier and longer instruction was undertaken, the more beneficial it proved. Without setting aside these pedagogical motives, officials in the 1870's and 1880's stressed that since the feeble-minded seemed destined to become public charges of one kind or another, it was true statesmanship and economy to begin their training and control before they acquired vicious habits or had the opportunity to reproduce.

A classroom in the 1880's (*From the Gustavus Adolphus Doren Photograph Collection, courtesy of the Ohio Historical Society.*)

Justification for this concern with expansion and with custodial care was ably provided by Kerlin in his report to the NCCC
in 1884. This was the first report by his committee, the Standing Committee on Provisions for Idiotic and Feeble-minded
Children, and he sadly remarked: "It is not strange that the
claims of idiotic and feeble-minded children should have waited
a hearing until your twelfth conference; for this clientage is almost a voiceless one, hidden away often from its nearest
neighborhood, shunned of companionship, and until the last
census, but half reported."[70] Indeed, it was the Census of 1880—
inaccurate as Kerlin and others believed it to be—that deeply
disturbed the school officials. In contrast to the 1870 figure which
set the number of retarded at approximately 30,155, the 1880
census reported the total number of feeble-minded to be 76,985,
showing a gain of about 155 percent, with only some 2,429 in
institutions. Over the same ten years, the general population
increased about 30 percent. Despite the expansion of facilities,
institutions provided for only a little more than 3 percent of the
known mentally defective, and conservative estimates assumed
there was an underenumeration of 20 to 30 percent.[71] Kerlin
devoted the bulk of his report to the dangers of this situation,
and some suggestions for its improvement.

After a brief discussion of the "degrees and grades of idiocy," and the "susceptibility to improvement" which drew upon
the work of his colleagues in the AMO,[72] Kerlin proceeded to
examine "the obligations of society to its defective members."[73] This was done from two perspectives:

1. That of the preservation of society itself from a baneful, hinder-
ing, or disturbing element generated within itself and too often from
avoidable causes.
2. The right inherently existing in a defective and irresponsible
member of society to protection from the body in exact ratio to his necessities.[74]

Kerlin saw the need for a government that would assume the
relation of parent to child, "abridging personal liberty where its
exercise is attended with a crusade against the rights of the
peaceable . . . . "[75] For an apt example, he turned to Max and

Ada Juke, who "rarely fail of an introduction in these Conferences," and expressed the hope that their grandchildren "might
have been recognized as unfit members, and very consistently
with the public welfare and their own best interests, have been
detained for the better part of their lives in jails or sequestered
in asylums."[76]

Concerning the Jukes, Kerlin had a ready explanation to account for the low incidence of retardation found by Dugdale.
He believed the Jukes, like blacks, were so mentally enfeebled
as a class that only the most profound cases of idiocy were recognized for what they were. Kerlin also felt that other groups
of deviants—criminals, tramps, prostitutes, alcoholics—were
defective in much the same manner. However, Kerlin believed
that there was a scientific way of identifying these heretofore
undetected disabilities by means of pathological examinations.
He noted the similarity between the findings of Moriz Benedikt
in his examination of criminal brains and the results of Alfred
W. Wilmarth, the pathologist at Elwyn, who studied the brains
of feeble-minded children.[77] The existence of similar convolu-
tions on the brain surfaces of criminals and the feeble-minded
led Kerlin to the conclusion that there was a definite relationship between crime and mental retardation.[78]

Kerlin did not require the results of any pathological examinations to answer his own question of "How many of your
criminals, inebriates and prostitutes are congenital idiots?"
Simple observation was enough to reveal that the tramp ("the
stamp of his intellectual weakness is clear in his features") and
the prostitute ("a class so feeble in will power, so ignorant, and
of so uncontrolled emotion that . . . very many are unsound
and irresponsible") were truly mental defectives. Kerlin called
for the early recognition and permanent sequestration, with little probability of release, of these "special, upper, and more
dangerous forms," of retardation. This would prevent "their
assuming social relations under marriage, or becoming sowers
of moral and physical disease under the garb of professional
tramps or degraded prostitutes."[79]

When Kerlin stated that "there is no field in political economy which can be worked to better advantage for the diminu-
tion of crime, pauperism, and insanity than that of idiocy,"[80]

he was making a significant shift in the perspective from which the value of treatment had been viewed. Previously it had been accepted that mental deficiency in itself was deserving of care. With the failure of the schools to return a sizable number of pupils to society, the authorities could no longer urge institutionalization for educational and rehabilitative reasons alone. They had to persuade legislatures and the public that their institutions were truly contributing to the general welfare. Naturally they continued to expound the benefits bestowed upon the retarded, their families, and their communities. At the same time they alluded to the civic and Christian obligations of the state to provide for its most helpless and needy citizens. But now with the linkage of heredity and retardation to numerous social problems, they had the opportunity to promote their institutions as solutions to crime, pauperism, disease, prostitution, alcoholism, and vagrancy. To many people, this new, additional function would be the sole, or at least the most important, mission of the institutions.

Kerlin devoted the last portion of his report to a description of the ideal institution which would suit the more broadly defined goals of the superintendents. Much of his plan was based on facilities already existing at Elwyn. The future institution would be able to accommodate 1,200 inmates who were divided into seven grades. Hundreds of acres would be provided for the central buildings of the school and industrial departments, the nursery department, the asylum department, and colonizing of adults as they passed the school age. An abundance of pure water, strong light and fresh air, combined with a homelike setting, would be necessary for the buildings. There would be a chapel, gymnasium, and an auditorium. The best fire escapes, sewers, construction techniques, storage and sanitary facilities would be incorporated. The site would allow for seclusion and privacy of the various grades, and would have sufficient arable land for the cultivation of the institution's food supply. The goal of such an institution, or more accurately of such a community, would be to provide comprehensive, self-contained, and lifelong care for all the mentally defective.[81]

Kerlin recognized the high initial expense of such an establishment, but he believed that the state would ultimately save money. "Only the education of the people and perhaps some prohibitory legislation" was necessary "to diminish the number of the wards of any Commonwealth by choking the sources whence they spring."[82] By gathering statistics and investigating the causes of retardation, the institutions might urge citizens to convert "to better forms of living."[83] The increased utility of institutions for the retarded held such a promise, and in his 1885 report to the NCCC Kerlin rhapsodized about the future. Speaking for his professional colleagues, he said:

The future of this work contemplates far more than the gathering into training schools of a few hundred imperfect children . . . . The correlation of idiocy, insanity, pauperism, and crime will be understood as it is not now . . . . Here and there, scattered over the country may be "villages of the simple," made up of the warped, twisted, and incorrigible, happily contributing to their own and the support of those more lowly . . . in truth; havens in which all shall live contentedly, because no longer misunderstood nor taxed with expectations beyond their mental or moral capacity. They "shall go out no more" and "they shall neither marry nor be given in marriage," in those havens dedicated to incompetency.[84]

4

The Rising Tide of Degeneracy: Custodialism and Its Rationale

With growing accord by the mid–1880's, institutional officials were defining their most important function as actively preventing rather than passively responding to the host of social problems attributed to mental retardation. Changes in the ranks of executive officers and greater knowledge about the variety and extent of mental defects were partly responsible for this activist posture. Three distinct types of retardates requiring institutionalization were identified: the profoundly retarded who generally had been denied admission to the schools, the "feeble-minded women of child-bearing age," and finally, a new class known as moral imbeciles who represented a threat or undue burden to society. In addition, the budding eugenics movement, the Federal Census, and the creation of special educational programs in the public schools all underscored the necessity of institutional intervention in preventing any further growth in the "defective" population.

Responding to a situation they now perceived as "the menace of the feeble-minded," officials further modified institutional policies and operations. Their *Annual Reports* and other publications constantly repeated that permanent custodial segregation was the most humane and effective measure that could protect society from the proliferation of Juke-like families. All of these pressures in the 1880's and 1890's created new demands for admission and increased retention that greatly stimulated institutional expansion. Case records reveal that custodial operations and ideology were already in place before the rediscovery of Mendel's laws and the development of intelligence testing would give custodialism an even greater importance after the turn of the century. However, despite the increasingly inward focus of institutional life and the prominence of custodialism in official rhetoric, the links to the past were never entirely severed because the schools continued educational services, vocational training, and short-term care for their pupils. Thus custodial care is most accurately described as a supplement to, rather than a replacement of, the traditional institutional services.

The deaths of many of the original leaders and founders of the movement to educate the mentally retarded broke one of the ties to the schools' past. Samuel G. Howe died in 1876, followed by Édouard Seguin and Henry M. Knight in 1880, and Hervey B. Wilbur in 1883. The next decades brought the deaths of Joseph Parrish in 1891, George Brown and Isaac N. Kerlin in 1893, leaving only Gustavus A. Doren as the last active founder of the AMO. He served as the Superintendent of the Ohio Institution for Feeble-minded Youth for the impressive total of forty-six years until his death in 1905. These men were often replaced by their assistants, or by others trained in the mental health field. In two instances there was literally a second generation of leadership as George H. Knight succeeded his father at the Connecticut School for Imbeciles (Lakeville) and George A. Brown followed his father at the Private Institution for the Education of Feeble-minded Youth (Barre).

The second generation of superintendents began work in a somewhat different atmosphere than the first. The institutions were not the small, tentative, experimental schools that sought to educate a few carefully selected pupils; they had matured into large, multipurpose facilities which were committed to custodialism as well as to education. As inmate populations swelled, the superintendents had neither the time nor the ability to know their charges on a personal basis. Instead, the authorities were concerned with the proper classification of "cases" into the appropriate grades, divisions, or classes, where the orderly administration of routine procedures would provide the necessary care and treatment under the management of well-regulated subordinates. To some extent, the new men could not have shared the optimism, excitement, and personal involvement of the first generation of physician-educators. As a second generation, they inherited established policies and operations. They could, and they did, innovate and make changes, but given the size and complexity of the institutions they had to manage and administer, bureaucratic skills, as well as the ability to deal effectively with state boards, legislatures, professional societies, and other interest groups, made for a successful new superintendent.[1]

The younger men did possess a degree of historical detachment from the earlier pioneering days. They were capable of objectively surveying the profession's past and were astutely critical of some aspects of it. James C. Carson, Wilbur's successor at Syracuse, found that "when the training and education of the feeble-minded were first attempted the benefits attained were so obvious that certain enthusiasts were led to hope and even to believe and predict that many could be raised to a mental status which would enable them to pass unnoticed in the outside world."[2] Carson and his contemporaries rejected such grandiose aspirations. They believed that only a small percentage of their residents made enough social and educational progress to safely warrant their discharge into the community.

Carson's use of the term "the outside world," from which many retardates would be excluded, suggested the existence of an alternative "inside world" where they could live happily protected and productive lives. From the 1870's, superintendents devoted much effort to the construction and to the inhabitants of this other world within the asylum. It is not possible to fully reconstruct what life was like under these conditions. Every individual had his or her own abilities, limitations, sources of joy and sorrow; each had a unique experience as an inmate. In addition, generalizations have to be made with caution since the institutions and their records changed as much over time as they differed with each other. However, using examples, models, and statistical methods, some common patterns of institutional development and inmate populations can be discerned.

As the institutions grew larger in both size and numbers, they assumed the appearance and provided many of the services of small towns. After the 1870's there were constant appeals to the legislatures concerning special appropriations for such capital improvements as land, buildings, railroad sidings, reservoirs, water systems, electrical generators, boilers, heating systems, even telephones and other communication devices. This was in addition to the regular requests for larger budgets for routine items including farm implements, laundry machinery, food–processing equipment, and industrial shop supplies. Although periods of economic depression accompanied by fiscal re-trenchment delayed the granting of some demands, in most cases the necessary funds were supplied. The capital improvements were clearly necessary to replace or update equipment and buildings that had seen twenty or thirty years of hard service and were woefully inadequate to meet the demands placed upon them. It made equally good economic sense to approve suffi-cient annual appropriations so the institutions could perform maintenance and repairs (carpentry, brick-making, masonry, painting), produce food (cereals, vegetables, meat, dairy prod-ucts, baked goods, preserves), and provide household and per-sonal needs (furniture, printing, mattresses, brushes, shoes, clothing, linens), all with a minimum of hired outside labor.

Although these activities were not pursued in any single in-stitution, each did provide vocational training and employment in domestic, agricultural, and industrial occupations. This in it-self was not new. But there was a most significant change in the benefits the authorities associated with inmate labor. The change can be illustrated by examining the comments of two successive superintendents of the Pennsylvania Training School for Feeble-minded Children (Elwyn). The first is from Joseph Parrish's *Tenth Annual Report* of 1863: "The pupils in this Insti-tution are employed at manual labor, not to get work *out* of them, but to get it *into* them. It is a secondary consideration whether the work is profitable to us; it is a *primary* object that it prove profitable to them."[3] Compare Parrish's sentiments to Kerlin's comments in the *Fortieth Annual Report* (1892): "The Sewing

A sewing class for girls in the late nineteenth-century institution (*From the Gustavus Adolphus Doren Photograph Collection, courtesy of the Ohio Historical Society.*)

Room—This has become thoroughly organized as a profitable auxiliary, not only to the young women who are employed in it, but to the institution itself, having turned out a large amount of work, the assessed value of which labor is $1,200"; Kerlin then made note of the shoe shop boys "the combined work of whom, with their instructor, pays the entire expenses of wages and material, with a not inconsiderable profit to the clothing account"; and finally he mentioned "The Laundry School" in which "we gather so many boys and girls, who without the labor it furnishes would necessarily be turned into the world incapable and unhappy." The "Laundry School" had done so well that "the paid labor of this entire department has been reduced to three employees, while the net weekly wash for over one thousand people amounts to thirty thousand pieces."[4] In short, profits for the institution, reductions in paid staff, and increases in production were being celebrated in the 1890's, while thirty years earlier the primary goal of the vocational programs was individual improvement.

The value of inmate labor combined with the economics of scale of large institutions did lower the net per capita costs. A typical example of these savings was furnished by Superintendent Ambrose M. Miller of the Illinois Asylum for Feeble-minded Children (Lincoln). Over a twenty-year period he reported a net per capita cost of $280 in 1875 with an average of 81 inmates, $184 in 1885 with 312, and $135 in 1894 with 546.[5] One of the most significant contributions of the inmates in reducing expenses was the services they provided as attendants. In Massachusetts the superintendent observed: "The older girls and women are of great assistance in the care of the feeble and helpless children. The instinctive feminine love for children is relatively quite as marked with them as with normal women. . . . This responsibility wonderfully helps in keeping this uneasy class happy and contented." But the key point was that "without this cheerfully given service we could not well care for the large number of helpless and feeble children in our asylum department without a largely increased number of paid attendants."[6]

In addition to the monetary value of inmate labor, these last statements touch upon several other important issues. For the

An institutional shoe shop for boys in the 1880's, a way of utilizing inmate labor to pay for institutional expenses (*From the Gustavus Adolphus Doren Photograph Collection, courtesy of the Ohio Historical Society.*)

most part, contemporary gender roles determined vocational training and employment in the institutions as much as it did outside of them. Officials assigned women to work in the dormitories, sewing rooms, kitchens, dining rooms, and laundries, while men were employed in the fields, shops, and around the grounds. It was assumed that this sexual division of labor best suited the innate capacities of the inmates, and it allowed institutional life to more closely resemble working conditions in society. In this regard, at least one institution, the Iowa Institution for Feeble-minded Children (Glenwood), paid its inmate workers nominal sums "as a means of teaching them to think and act for themselves; in other words, to develop a spirit of self-reliance—self-help—as a means to prevent, as far as possible, institutionalizing the individual."[7]

Although these measures may have had some success with the more capable, custodial grade retardates, officials felt that far less could be accomplished with those in the hospital or asylum department. These "helpless and feeble children" were given only the most elementary habit training, and the simplest, if any, work assignments. Their need for almost constant care and attention would have severely strained institutional resources without the labor of the higher grade inmates. Whether this reality was "cheerfully given service" is hard to determine accurately without more data, but considering the positive emphasis that society placed upon self-support and the virtues of labor, it is not surprising that administrators reported that 20 to 40 percent of the inmates did some useful work, which "wonderfully helps in keeping this uneasy class happy and contented."[8]

To provide this employment and to accommodate the increased number of custodial and asylum inmates, the institutions had to enlarge facilities. Naturally, this expansion took different forms and proceeded at different rates in each institution, but it is possible to formulate a three-stage model of growth based upon common features of institutional development that have already been touched upon. In the initial phase, when the schools were first established, either private homes or older institutions were converted for use. These buildings provided basic shelter for students and staff with some accommodations for classrooms and other instructional necessities. But such facilities soon proved inadequate for more than a limited number of pupils, and when the schools were no longer considered temporary or experimental, they were relocated to permanent sites. In this second stage, impressive multistory buildings were constructed on spacious grounds. The typical arrangement was a central section for administration, staff quarters, and food service, with connecting wings housing the dormitories, classrooms, gymnasiums, and auditoriums. Several outbuildings enclosed boilers, pumps, and cold storage. When more space was required, the tendency was to either add another story or build an additional wing; thus, literally keeping the school under one roof.[9]

The hospital was usually the first building to be constructed away from the central structure, and in many institutions it was utilized as a resource for the asylum or lowest grade retardates. As admissions increased, and custodial grade retardates were retained, the outbuildings became shops and workrooms, marking the beginning of the third stage of growth. In many cases the central building could not be economically enlarged, and officials now wanted separate, secure living quarters for certain worrisome groups such as epileptics, moral imbeciles, and older custodial retardates, especially women. A series of "cottages" or dormitories, often with food services as well as vocational and recreational facilities, were built to accommodate from fifty to two hundred inmates each. Frequently, land was acquired for construction and for farming. The original school buildings, now surrounded by special purpose structures, became central storage, administration, and staff quarters, and sometimes served the school departments or sheltered the most feeble of the asylum cases.

The basic purpose of institutional expansion was to provide comprehensive care for all the mentally retarded. The institutions grew larger as they broadened goals and services. Starting with special programs for the educable retardates, they added hospital or nursery care for the profoundly retarded, vocational education for the trainable cases, and finally custodial facilities for persons who could not or should not be returned to society. Moral imbeciles were prominently included in this last group.

Over thirty years earlier, Samuel Gridley Howe had discussed moral imbecility, describing it as a "condition in which
the sentiments, the conscience . . . are so far dormant or
underdeveloped, as to incapacitate the person from being a law
unto himself, in anything like the degree which is usual with
others of his age."[10] Howe believed the moral faculties were
finite realities, separate from intelligence or willpower, but like
them capable of being impaired or invigorated. His intriguing
comments elicited little response. It was not until the late 1880's
that the subject aroused significant professional concern. Isaac
N. Kerlin of Elwyn developed moral imbecility into the most
serious interest of the last years of his life.[11] While his writings
and activities alerted the profession to the apparent threat of
the moral imbecile to society, Kerlin's perspective on this question clearly abandoned the optimistic, hopeful view of the antebellum period and pointed toward the more deterministic,
pessimistic outlook of the early twentieth century.

Kerlin discussed moral imbecility in several of his *Annual Reports* (1886, 1887, 1889), as well as in papers presented to the
AMO (1887) and the NCCC (1890). The last work, entitled "The
Moral Imbecile," was his most complete analysis. Kerlin found
that "the fundamental disorder is manifested in the derange-
ment of the moral perceptions or emotional nature rather than
in the intellectual life, which not frequently is precocious."[12]
Examples of inappropriate behavior defined and identified the
condition: "Unaccountable and unreasonable frenzies . . . mo-
tiveless and persistent lying: thieving, generally without ac-
quisitiveness . . . a blind and headlong impulse toward arson;
delight in cruelty . . . habitual wilfulness and defiance, even
in the face of certain punishment . . . these are some of the
forms in which the congenital deficiency of the moral sense
evidences itself."[13] Moral imbecility was analogous to other forms
of retardation; the moral imbecile suffered from an irreparable
defect of the moral faculties that was comparable to the affliction of the intellectual faculties of the retarded. The same sense
of irreversibility concerning other types of mental defectives was
extended to moral imbeciles. Although the extent of the disability varied, producing different grades of moral idiocy, the
defect itself was considered permanent and incurable.[14]

Kerlin was aware of the contemporary debate that raged over the very similar concept of moral insanity, but he was confident enough of his position to state: "During the thirty years' contemplation of the subject, a marked change in professional opinion has been noted, so that it is no longer hazardous to reputation to believe in the existence of a condition termed 'moral insanity' nor to refer to it as of commonly congenital origin, and hence better denominated 'moral imbecility.' "[15] The moral imbecile was diagnosed entirely on the basis of action, behavior, and attitudes; there was no other symptomatology. Kerlin recognized that it is "hard to answer 'What is there in all this to distinguish it from simple wickedness or badness?' " He could only reply, "The answer is contained in the persistency of the trait and the utter destitution of any reason for it, as is indicated in the confessed helplessness of the child to do differently."[16] There was an element of tautology in this reasoning; the moral imbecile was defined as someone who acted like one because he or she could not behave in any other way. With no other explanation to account for this behavior, the moral imbecile was officially defined "as 'a person who displays from an early age, and in spite of careful upbringing, strong vicious or criminal propensities, on which punishment has little or no deterrent effect.' "[17] Of course, at that time, many phenomena, especially in medicine, had no reductionistic explanation.

Kerlin supported the concept of moral imbecility with evidence from the field of criminal anthropology. He quoted extensively from "the recent Second International Congress of Criminal Anthropology in Paris, at which were assembled distinguished representatives of science, law, medicine, and the administrative world."[18] Although a factious group, the criminal anthropologists agreed that hereditary degeneration—a type of regressive evolution that produced declining mental, moral, and physical powers in each generation—was at the heart of much antisocial activity.[19] The degeneration may have originated with some mental or physical excess, but once introduced into a family unit, it was subject to inheritance. The presence of degeneration was revealed by various stigmata—mental or physical aberrations that skilled observers could detect and interpret—but there was no widespread agreement re-

garding what specific stigmata correlated with what instance of
degeneration. When describing the consequences of hereditary
degeneration, criminal anthropologists employed such terms as
atavism, arrested development, or reversion of type, all of which
referred to a return to a supposedly instinctual behavior of
primitive man, thus confusing degeneration proper with the
concept of hereditary throwback. In common usage, degeneration was a stripping away of qualities and abilities developed
over the ages by the process of human evolution. Since Kerlin
believed that "the moral sense [is] the latest and the highest
attribute of our rising humanity," it is thus "the first and the
most to suffer from the law of reversion to lower type."[20] Moral
imbecility was the result of the degeneration of man's moral
nature.

Kerlin identified four classes of moral imbeciles: alcoholics,
tramps, prostitutes, and habitual criminals; in each category one
character defect prevailed: "There is a radical lack of will power
to be other than they are, to do otherwise than they do."[21] The
incorrigible nature of moral imbecile received endless comment. "There is," wrote a superintendent in 1887, "a lack of
proper moral impulse, or a perversion of the sense of right and
wrong."[22] Another official commented: "With a moral imbecile
it is not a question of yielding to temptation, but rather a question of yielding to his natural instincts, which are almost, without exception, instincts for evil."[23] The most effective way to
deal with this class was lifelong custodial care which prevented
"those who are congenitally unfit" from mingling "their lives
and blood with the general community." Kerlin felt they should
not be taught to read and write; instead, "intellectual entertain-
ment for these people is provided in the exercise of the shop,
the field, the garden."[24] He concluded: "I trust that there are
some—yes, many—in this Conference, who may see in these
suggestions a line which followed will lead to the relief of many
of our institutions, to a better understanding of this worst form
of moral perversion, and to a partial arrest of the apparently
increasing degradation of our race."[25] The NCCC responded by
placing on record: "*Resolved*, That any person who is aware of
the moral inbecility of a child shall not place that child either at
board, or free of expense in the community."[26]

This concern for the correct treatment of moral imbeciles strengthened the appeals of superintendents for adding custodial facilities to their institutions. Kerlin incorporated an admonition for the professional care of moral imbeciles in a report to the Committee on the Care and Treatment of the Feeble-minded to the NCCC (1888). But he used the report mainly "to formulate a series of propositions which may represent to this body the status of this work in America, and to suggest the principles on which . . . its further development may wisely be directed."[27] He reasserted the value of special education for the improvement of feeble-minded children, and their right to this instruction as guaranteed in public law. The only suitable place for this training was in institutions established expressly for the purpose and not in jails, county infirmaries, almshouses, or hospitals for the insane. Based on his earlier research, Kerlin estimated that only one-fifth of all retardates had comfortable financial resources, one-fifth were paupers, and three-fifths came from the middle and poorer classes, where "the sadness and burden are found to be especially severe in the families of mechanics and artisans, who are bravely striving to keep themselves above pauperism."[28]

Kerlin proclaimed: "The experience of the past thirty years proves that . . . ten to twenty percent are so improved as to be able to enter life as bread-winners; that from thirty to forty percent are returned to their families so improved as to be self-helpful . . . and further, and of greater importance, that one half of the whole number *will need custodial care so long as they live*."[29] He divided the custodial class into two groups—the severely retarded and the moral imbeciles,[30] and recommended that this "large class of the permanently disabled" be sheltered in custodial departments located in buildings away from the educational and industrial facilities. Such a "broadly classified administration" would allow the employment of moral imbeciles "thereby diminishing greatly the burden to the charitable and the tax-payer."[31]

Although the severely retarded and the moral imbeciles were both classified as deserving custodial care, a different rationale existed for each group. It was evident that the profoundly retarded were incapable of self-support, and would be enormous

burdens to their families if they were retained at home. Starting with Pennsylvania, an increasing number of states made
provisions for the permanent care of this class in existing institutions and in specialized asylums devoted to their needs.[32]

In summary, moral imbeciles were viewed by Kerlin and other
administrators as a danger to the community, and they had to
be protected from the consequences of their irresponsible actions. This is why they were candidates for custodial treatment. Being congenitally deficient in judgment and willpower,
they were unable to exercise self-control; they were dominated
by emotional desires and unrestrained egos. While they were
able to move at will because their behavior and appearance were
less obvious than other retardates, their condition was frequently misunderstood and undiagnosed. Some were treated as
criminals or prostitutes, while others became mindless alcoholics, wandering tramps, or debauched paupers. Unless they were
recognized as moral imbeciles, and were retained in the appropriate institutions, they would be discharged from the jails, infirmaries, or almshouses to continue their deviant careers and
the endless reproduction of their own kind.

The serious consequences of uncontrolled degeneracy were
vividly illustrated in Oscar C. McCulloch's paper, "The Tribe of
Ishmael: A Study of Social Degradation," presented to the NCCC
in 1888. McCulloch, a Congregational pastor active in social
welfare programs,[33] drafted the law establishing the Indiana
Board of State Charities, founded the Charity Organization Society in 1878, and was president of the NCCC in 1891. His research was indebted to Dugdale's earlier work: "It extends,
however, over a larger field, comprising over two hundred and
fifty known families, thirty of which have been taken out as
typical cases, and diagramed here."[34] In all, McCulloch traced
1,692 individuals from the thirty families during a period of eight
years, but he estimated the total number to be over five thousand. As with the Jukes, there was the same baneful chronicle
of pauperism, illegitimacy, prostitution, and crime.[35]

McCulloch identified four main factors that influenced the
family's decline: physical depravity, physical weakness, heredity, and unscientific charity. The first manifested itself in the

form of prostitution and illegitimacy "due to a depravation of nature, to crowded conditions, to absence of decencies and cleanliness."[36] "The physical depravity," he continued, "is followed by physical weakness. Out of this come the frequent deaths, the still-born children, and the general incapacity to endure hard work or bad climate." The power of heredity was obvious as "each child tends to the same life, reverts when taken out." What really disturbed McCulloch was the contribution of unregulated public and private charity to the survival of the degraded family. Public relief was distributed by the township trustee, an elected official, and "about the time of nomination and election the amounts increased largely."[37]

McCulloch insisted that "charity—falsely so-called—covers a multitude of sins, and sends the pauper out with the benediction 'be fruitful and multiply.' Such charity has made this element, has brought children to birth, and insured them a life of misery, cold, hunger, sickness. So-called charity joins public relief in producing still-born children, raising prostitutes, and educating criminals."[38] Indiscriminate benevolence, without systematic method or permanent supervision, enabled the tribe of Ishmael to survive and reproduce. To correct this situation, McCulloch called for comprehensive care in specialized institutions staffed by trained professionals thoroughly familiar with social problems. The tribe of Ishmael, along with the Jukes, warned of the high costs exacted from the community and the state treasury when hereditary defectives went unregulated.

Other critics demanded governmental intervention to resolve the matter. "Hereditary taint, sensual excess, drunkenness, intermarriage of relatives, the disabilities of extreme poverty, are all factors in the propagation of idiocy, and all of them, to some extent are within the purview of intelligent legislation."[39] Institutional officials used *Annual Reports*, the NCCC, and the AMO to alert legislators and the public to the possibilities of positive state action. They emphasized repeatedly that "it is not enough that the state provide temporarily for this division of unfortunates; it must be a life school for its inmates, thereby preventing the transmission of infirmities to a still more degraded progeny." Superintendents agreed that "where it is possible for professional interference to obviate the conditions favoring a degenerated offspring, it should engage our earnest attention."[40]

While the state was being urged to "legislate in the interests of morality and hygiene," the members of the AMO had already started the process of "professional interference" by broadening the scope of their institutions. In 1883, for example, the Massachusetts School for Idiotic and Feeble-minded Youth (South Boston) became the Massachusetts School for the Feeble-minded.[41] This change reflected the more comprehensive care being offered to retardates of all ages and grades. Other states acted in a similar fashion, substituting "school" or "institution" for "asylum" and replacing "idiotic" with "imbecile" with "feeble-minded." For South Boston, the 1883 legislation established an asylum department "for idiots who are beyond school age, or are not capable of being benefitted by school instruction."[42] This feature was retained in an act of 1886 that reorganized the school into separate educational and custodial departments.[43]

South Boston still had two major shortcomings. Despite its healthy seaside location, it had no room to expand, and it had no permanent resident superintendent to plan for the future. Both difficulties were remedied in 1887 when the legislature provided $20,000 for land and $200,000 for buildings at the school's new location in the Boston suburb of Waltham. As the trustees commented, this expenditure finally put Massachusetts' total capital spending on a par with other leading states: Pennsylvania ($198,000), New York ($223,500), and Ohio ($650,000).[44] At the same time the expansion was approved, Walter E. Fernald was appointed the institution's first resident superintendent.[45] In many ways, he was a model of the second-generation executive official. A medical school graduate with experience in the mental health field, he quickly established an excellent working relationship with the board of trustees and within a short period of time became a leading spokesman for his profession.[46]

Under Fernald's direction, Waltham acquired a farm colony at Templeton, Massachusetts.[47] Its first inmates, transferred from the home institution in 1900, were housed in temporary accom-

modations while they worked on the construction of permanent dwellings. Located about sixty miles from Waltham, the
colony was provided with good water, drainage, timber, stone,
and other building materials.[48] In the winter the colonists stored
ice, hauled supplies, and cut wood, while the summer was devoted to land clearing and building activities. As capable adult
inmates accumulated, they were transferred to the farm colony
and the construction cycle was repeated. Waltham would provide "a market for the milk, beef, potatoes, and other vegetables, fruit, poultry, eggs, and other food products produced by
this farming community."[49] Fernald described Templeton in an
almost idyllic manner: "We have created a little community
suited to the need and capacity of these feeble-minded boys, or
men—a little world made for them, where they live the natural
life of a country boy."[50]

Superintendents agreed that a majority of the mentally retarded belonged in a special environment. Discussing reasons
for public support of their work, Arthur C. Rogers, Superintendent of the Minnesota School for the Feeble-minded, declared:
"If you ask why, the answer is found in the simple statement
that it reaches the homes, the primary units of society, upon
the perfection of which the highest type of civilization de-
pends. Whatever affects the homes whether for good or evil affects the community, the state, and the nation."[51] Rogers repeated the now familiar argument that attempting to provide
adequate care for a mentally defective child could exhaust a
mother, forcing her to slight her responsibilities to other family
members resulting in the disruption of the entire household. If
familial dislocation was severe enough, the family would be
demoralized and soon pauperized. Protecting the integrity of
the family, "the primary unit of society," was accepted as an
important responsibility of institutions for the feeble-minded.[52]

The superintendents also felt that it was equally important to
institutionalize those retarded who were a perennial source of
crime, pauperism, and moral indecency. The detection of moral
imbecility revealed that, according to Walter E. Fernald, "the
brighter class of the feeble-minded, with their weak will power
and deficient judgement, are easily influenced for evil, and are
prone to become vagrants, drunkards, and thieves."[53] Perma-

nent segregation would relieve society of this burden by removing an important cause of social problems at considerable
financial saving.

While protection of the home and society were valued objectives, superintendents did not ignore the benefits to the retarded themselves. Just as stated earlier, the refrain continued,
the retarded would no longer be subjected to disappointment
and repeated failures because of the impossible demands of
competing as equals in society. They would learn, live, and work
with others of the same potential and—depending on their capabilities—might derive pleasure from caring for themselves or
the less able. The feeble-minded would also be protected. Superintendents believed that "a feeble-minded girl is exposed as
no other girl in the world is exposed. She has not sense enough
to protect herself from the perils to which women are subjected."[54] Mentally defective men would no longer be the "town
fools," the guileless dupes of brighter criminals, or the perpetrators of senseless, brutal crimes.

By the 1890's then, there was an overwhelming professional
demand for permanent custodial care for the mentally retarded.[55] Superintendents emphasized constantly that "the state
should hasten to care for its feeble-minded as a measure of social self-preservation, for the greater health, physical and moral,
of the body social."[56] They drew on census figures to support
this position. The Eleventh Census (1890) recorded a total of
95,609 mental defectives of which only 5,254 were in special institutions. This followed the pattern of the previous census which
had pointed to the large number of retarded persons and the
small number kept in special facilities. Again, superintendents
used census figures with caution; many observers agreed that
significant underenumeration occurred because of the reluctance of family members and friends to identify the feeble-
minded. The Tenth Census (1880) had sought to negate this
difficulty by requesting physicians to report all known cases of
mental retardation to the census office; this procedure was directly responsible for the counting of 29 percent of the 76,895
feeble-minded reported in 1880. The Eleventh Census (1890) did
not, however, utilize these special physicians' reports. Its total
of the mentally retarded at large—disturbing as they were—may

therefore have been less accurate than those of 1880.[57] Generally, the superintendents employed the census data to indicate
the extent of the problem facing society and the necessity of reducing the percentage of feeble-minded who were under no form
of strict supervision.[58]

In response largely to the urgings of superintendents, a
number of states established their first institutions: Michigan
(1895), Wisconsin (1899), New Hampshire (1901), North Dakota
(1902), Rhode Island and Oregon (1907).[59] A few state legislatures created additional or specialized facilities. In 1895, New
York provided for the Rome State Custodial Asylum, reserved
for the unteachable adult retarded; Pennsylvania built the
Western Pennsylvania State Institution for the Feeble-minded
at Polk in 1896; and Massachusetts added the Wrentham State
School in 1906.[60] The new institutions provided the AMO with
additional members. At this time membership was still restricted primarily to the chief medical officers of the institutions
and prominent persons interested in the feeble-minded whom
the Association wished to honor.

Following the death of Isaac N. Kerlin in 1893, the AMO
underwent a transformation. Kerlin had been held in great es-
teem by the Association; he served as secretary, was its foremost spokesman, and was elected president in 1892. His death
and the attendant sense of being cut off from the past permitted the superintendents to appreciate the danger of the Associations becoming narrow and inwardly focused, giving too much
praise for departed greats and ignoring the challenges of the
present. They recognized that the Association should do more
to arouse interest in its work and publish more information about
its methods and progress.[61] Martin W. Barr, Kerlin's successor
at Elwyn, expressed these sentiments in his 1896 presidential
address, calling for a modernization of the organization. He
suggested three reforms: a change in name, accomplished in 1906
when the Association became the American Association for the
Study of the Feeble-minded (AASF); the formation of committees of specialists (e.g., pathologists, custodians) to hold meetings and issue reports concurrently with those of the Association; and the publication of a quarterly professional periodical,
the *Journal of Psycho-Asthenics*, begun in 1896 under the editor-

ship of A. C. Rogers. These changes made the organization better able to capture and hold the attention of the general public and fellow professionals.[62]

While the superintendents were improving efficiency and communications within their professional organization, contemporary developments in education were arousing considerable public interest in mental retardation. Within a ten-year period, beginning in 1896, a number of public school systems organized special classes for mentally defective children: Providence, Rhode Island (1896), Springfield, Massachusetts (1897); Chicago (1898), Boston (1899), New York (1900), Philadelphia (1901), Los Angeles (1902), Detroit (1903), Washington, Bridgeport, Connecticut, and Rochester, New York (1906).[63] In 1893, Providence had established special disciplinary schools for troublesome pupils. "The teachers in the regular grades experienced so much relief when their disorderly pupils were removed, that they soon urged the transference of those who were mentally deficient."[64] A reason for this development was the enforcement of compulsory school attendance laws which brought greater numbers of educationally handicapped children into the schools.[65] Over the years other school systems followed a similar pattern of development.[66]

Typically, teachers were requested to notify school authorities of students who appeared feeble-minded. The students would be examined by the school physician or in diagnostic clinics.[67] Any physical impediment—eyesight, hearing, tonsils—would be corrected. If retardation in schoolwork persisted, the student would be transferred to a special class. These classes relied primarily on manual training, and the teacher adjusted the substance and tempo of instruction to suit the individual student's potential.

The rapid expansion of these special classes,[68] presented retardation specialists, educators, and the public with a variety of issues. Educators accepted a "Department for the Education of the Deaf, Blind, and Feeble-minded" as a part of the National Education Association in 1897.[69] Although a few important papers were read before it, the Department of Special Education,[70] as it was renamed in 1902, was too diverse a group to achieve significant results.

Superintendents recognized the value of special classes[71] and the difficulties they presented to the average teacher. In 1902, the New Jersey Training School for Feeble-minded Children became the first institution to offer a summer school course to train teachers for the new classes.[72] Institutional officials approved of the ungraded system designed to restore the pedagogically backward child to his or her proper level, but they had more serious reservations about the future of feeble-minded children enrolled in special classes.[73] Yet, despite the slight difference in professional opinion, the public schools functioned as rudimentary detectors of retardation. The most conservative estimates in 1904 showed that 1 percent of the school population was, in some way, defective.[74] This observation coupled with the new school programs made the public more aware of the presence of the feeble-minded in the community.

Superintendents advanced an explanation to account for the apparent increase in the numbers of mentally retarded. A. E. Osborne, for example, Superintendent of the California School for the Feeble-minded, noted "that the demands of our age, the various requirements of the time, are largely responsible (aside from heredity) for the vast number of incompetents that exist."[75] Administrators contended that the new America, the emerging urban, industrial order, required an exacting style of mental life. Some individuals who previously could have coped with the slower-paced, agricultural community of the past were now incapable of either supporting or controlling themselves. The feeble-minded were characterized as persons who "interfere with the harmony of normal society,"[76] and are "less able to work harmoniously as cogs in the school machine."[77]

Superintendents argued that the retarded would suffer in a complex social order which required competitive as well as cooperative and conforming patterns of behavior. Those who did not "fit in" were likely to be exposed by the new forms of social discipline—compulsory school attendance, the industrial obedience of the factory, and the proximity of urban life. Thus, the "results of education and training," as James C. Carson of Syracuse pointed out, "marvelous as they are in many cases, fall short, as we have seen, of developing that indescribable something which removes the stigma of feeble-mindedness."[78]

There is irony in this complaint that educational methodology was unable to remove the mark of retardation; it had been emphasized that the moral imbecile's role in crime, pauperism, prostitution, vagrancy, and alcoholism was responsible for the stigmatization. Superintendents continued to warn society that "the great neuropathic family which springs from degeneracy and throws out degeneracy is undoubtedly increasing, and society must give permanent custody to the insane, epileptics, feeble-minded, the neurotic tramps, criminals, paupers, blind, deaf, and consumptives, so as to stop the stream at its source, or we must expect an increase."[79] There were few distinctions made among the different components of the "neuropathic family" or the defective class, but there was a sense of almost absolute separation between it and the remainder of humanity: "In dealing with the defective class, we are not dealing with average humanity . . . but with humanity of low grade, less able to grapple with the stress of honest self-support and less able to work harmoniously as cogs in the social machine."[80] The "dependent, defective, and delinquent" elements even became an accepted field for scholarly research.[81]

As noted earlier, superintendents were self-consciously aware of the changes that had occurred in both their institutional and their professional roles. Barr depicted this consciousness of change in 1898, noting that early in the nineteenth century philanthropy inspired work among the retarded; in his own day, however, government intervention was a necessity "to preserve the nation from the encroachments of imbecility."[82]

Fernald pointed to another factor—immigration—which also affected the changing functions of institutions. Previously men like Howe believed idiocy to be a didactic form of divine punishment. After a few years of instruction, the idiot would return to his or her home or parish and serve as an example to other members of the community. This was why Howe did not want the school to become custodial, although, in addition, he believed that residence in the New England village of the 1840's was itself a partial curative. The times, however, had changed. As Fernald stated, "the Doctor wrote before the tide of immigration had set so strongly to our shores . . . . What is to be done with the feeble-minded progeny of the foreign hordes that have settled and are settling among us?"[83] Increasing immigra-

Table 4.1
Nativity of White Parents of Massachusetts Inmates

	Total	Native Born	Foreign Born	Mixed Parentage	Percent of Native Born
1880	113	100	13		88 %
1890	267	126	28	112	47 %
1903	861[a]	347	172	154	51 %

Sources: For 1880, Department of Interior, *Defective, Dependent, and Delinquent Classes*, p. 216; for 1890, Department of Interior, *Insane and Feeble-minded*, p. 294; for 1903, Department of Commerce and Labor, *Insane and Feeble-minded*, p. 220. Nationwide, data exists only for the years 1880, 1890, when 94 percent and 66 percent, respectively, of the inmates were native born.

[a] includes the inmates of the private Elm Hill School, who were most likely to have had native-born parents. Excluding their total enrollment—seventy— the percentage of white inmates at Waltham with native-born parents in 1903 was 45 percent.

tion and a decline in native New Englanders (see Table 4.1) precluded the possibility of returning large numbers of mental defectives to a remedial environment. In addition, urbanization, industrialization, and immigration had transformed the environment itself.

By the turn of the century, Fernald and other professionals believed that the power of inheritance was the foremost agent in the perpetuation of mental defect. This factor also forestalled any mass return of the feeble-minded to their homes and communities. Interest in heredity, as typified by the superintendents' concern for the adverse influence of defective families on society, was even more in evidence than in the antebellum years. Barr rhetorically asked, "Shall we isolate those who, seemingly in a normal condition, may, nay *will*, through the stern laws of heredity, pour such a flood of imbecility upon the nation as is shown in the record of the Tribe of Ishmael . . . ?"[84] Fernald flatly declared, "Retain in our institutions the feeble-minded of both sexes, and there will be no more Juke families."[85]

Even before 1900, as biologists rediscovered Gregor Mendel's laws of heredity,[86] superintendents experienced a surge of interest in the relationship of heredity to retardation.[87] Rather than performing biological studies, they used compilations of statistics—taken from inmate admission blanks—to argue a causal relationship between heredity and mental defect. James C. Carson, who had been recording such information since 1884, found that of 2,000 applications to Syracuse only 673, or less than 33 percent, were wholly free of parental degeneracy or hereditary taint.[88] Barr, in *Mental Defectives: Their History, Treatment and Training* (1904),[89] the first comprehensive text since Seguin, *Idiocy and Its Treatment by the Physiological Method* (1866), found "heredity is herein proven law, as inexorable in its descending as it is beneficent in the ascending scale; heredity—whether it be direct from parent to child, collateral as from other relatives, or reversional reappearing ever and anon through generations—which none may escape."[90]

Around 1900, the *Journal of Psycho-Asthenics* rarely mentioned the leading figures of biological and genetic inquiry,[91] although superintendents were definitely exposed to August Weismann's ideas as early as 1895.[92] Administrators accepted some notions about the mechanics of heredity. In the mid–1890's, Rogers had formulated four laws that appeared to govern the transmission of defective heredities: (1) violation of the laws of health lead to degeneracy; (2) latent degenerative tendencies can be directly inherited or varied, depending on parental proclivities; (3) parents with the same traits intensify those qualities in their children; (4) only by intermarriage with individuals of sound constitutions and heredities can the malignant effects of a defective heredity be dissipated.[93]

While it was commonly accepted that "of all the neurotic conditions, no one is perhaps as easily transmissible to succeeding generations as feeble-mindedness,"[94] there was also a recognition that "it is not necessarily a specific neurosis that is transmitted, but may be such instability or disorder in arrangement of nerve tissues as may evidence itself by different types in various generations according to the degree of prepotency in the mingling of the parental elements."[95] Thus, a variety of conditions—insanity, alcoholism, blindness, tuberculosis—which appeared in the families of the mentally defective were interpreted as confirmations of some fundamental genetic defect, presumably in the nervous system, that was transmitted from generation to generation. At any rate, by the turn of the century, superintendents were aware that "heredity is not a freakish and occasional thing, showing itself only by peculiarities of nature or of conduct, but is a steady and constant element, that gives a trend to the whole of man's condition."[96]

A major concern of the nascent American eugenics movement and its foremost champion, Charles B. Davenport, was to develop a heightened appreciation of the importance of heredity. Eugenics—"the effort to improve the inborn characteristics of man by the study of human heredity and the application of those studies to human propagation"—had been given form and direction by the work of Francis Galton and his disciple, Karl Pearson.[97] Davenport, a Harvard Ph.D. in biology, was impressed by the attempts of the English eugenists to enumerate, through the use of statistics, the pedigree of human inheritance.[98] In 1902, while affiliated with the Zoological Laboratory of the University of Chicago, he applied to the Carnegie Institution of Washington for a position to direct an experimental study of evolution. The next year, he was established as Director of the Station for Experimental Evolution at Cold Spring Harbor, Long Island.[99]

Davenport began his research with studies of animals, insects, and plants. By 1907, however, he had become Secretary of the Committee on Eugenics of the American Breeders Association, an organization devoted to improving the biological stock of the race, and was more interested in investigating the application of Mendel's laws to human heredity.[100] He saw his main work as "discovery of general principles or laws"[101] and he became a rigid biological mechanist, believing that every aspect of human behavior had its origin in definite physiological and anatomical mechanisms subject to scientific classification and explanation through the use of simple Mendelian ratios.[102]

Many superintendents were receptive to the analytic techniques and the goals of Davenport's movement because eugenic research reinforced their own long-held convictions on the necessity of preventing the propagation of the manifestly defective. While advocating the adoption of custodial provisions, superintendents knew that a great many of the mentally defective were outside the proper institutions, hence beyond the reach of segregation. As a measure of eugenic control for this large, ever–increasing class, they recommended the passage of restrictive marriage laws that would forbid the legal union of the retarded.[103] Connecticut acted first (1896), followed by Kansas (1903), New Jersey and Ohio (1904), Michigan and Indiana (1905).[104] To overcome the difficulty of uneven enforcement, one commentator asked: "Should there not be a national marriage law, forbidding the marriage of all idiots, insane, and feeble-minded persons . . . ?"[105] A demand for stricter regulation of marriages became a regular part of the National Conference of Charities and Corrections appeals for limitations on defective procreation.[106]

Administrators realized that such measures as segregation and marriage restrictions were only partly effective. Since both methods required supervision of the retarded, success was a function of the degree of control provided. Segregation for eugenic purposes required custody until the individual was incapable of propagation, not merely until a certain level of education or skill was achieved. Even with the improvement of farm colonies, this was a lengthy and expensive undertaking.

As the superintendents understood more fully the genetic hazards presented by the feeble-minded, they began to question the desirability of releasing many ostensibly trained inmates, even to parents. Barr commented: "The sudden removal from a paternalism, which protects while it also supports the weak, is a drop from freedom into license. With a class in which the moral sense is stultified if not altogether absent, the emotional nature exalted, the sexual impulse exaggerated, what is more natural than just such a result?"[107] Superintendents complained that the public did not completely comprehend the disabilities of the retarded. Parents believed that mental defectives entered institutions and trained workers, able to assist the family finances, came out. Frequently, inmates were removed from institutions when their guardians mistook slight improvements for total cures. Although superintendents had maintained that mental retardation was a defect and a cure was impossible, they now asserted an inability to effect any but the most modest improvement.[108]

These changed attitudes were best exemplified in a paper read to the NCCC by Walter E. Fernald in 1904. Admission to the institutions, as he observed, was "based upon the relief needed for the mother, the family, or the neighborhood, with the prospective educational benefit to the child himself as a secondary consideration. A feeble-minded child is a foreign body in a family or a modern American community."[109]

A retarded child could worry a mother into a nervous breakdown or an early grave, drive a father to drink, a brother to the "gang," and a sister to the streets. When the child grew up, he or she became a community problem.

> The adult males become the town loafers and incapables, the irresponsible pests of the neighborhood, petty thieves, purposeless destroyers of property, incendiaries, and very frequently violators of women and little girls. It is well known that feeble-minded women and girls are very liable to become sources of unspeakable debauchery and licentiousness which pollutes the whole life of the young boys and youth of the community.[110]

Fernald's sense of indignation at the community's pollution through the unrestricted presence of the mentally defective indicates how much professional opinion had changed. Once this expression of outrage had been reserved for those who mistreated or ignored the retarded; the feeble-minded had been characterized as the most helpless, pitiful, and deserving of Humankind. After the detection of moral imbecility and its relationship to a host of social problems, superintendents were condemning the mentally handicapped—especially the moral imbecile—as primary sources of social disruption that the community dare not neglect.

The community could not disregard the feeble-minded, Fernald insisted, because "under any conditions these defectives must always be supported by the public . . . . The public always pays the bills."[111] As a "simple business proposition," it was a wise investment to prevent feeble-minded women from reproducing. He quoted examples of the Jukes to demonstrate that the savings realized in a few generations would repay the cost of maintenance. These were well-known considerations, but

Fernald pointed out that the superintendents "have only begun to apply our knowledge of obvious defectives to the study
and treatment of juvenile incorrigibles and adult criminals."[112]
This was a relatively new field of social investigation in which
superintendents could play a substantive role.

Observation of the inmates of prisons and reform schools
suggested that a considerable number were "defectives where
the intellectual defect is relatively slight and is overshadowed
by the moral deficiency."[113] Here again was the moral imbecile, the type of retardate identified and observed by Samuel G.
Howe, before the Civil War, and by Isaac N. Kerlin in the decade of the 1880's. While recognizing the danger the moral imbecile posed to society, Howe believed this person was re-
deemable; Kerlin labeled the moral imbecile an unworthy
individual requiring permanent incarceration.

Echoing Kerlin's observations, Fernald characterized the moral
imbecile as lazy, cruel, destructive, perverse, incorrigible, irresponsible, immoral, and, most important, beyond redemption.
Such individuals necessitated lifelong care and supervision in
special facilities which would combine the educational and correctional features of a school with the custodial and security arrangements of a prison.[114]

In discussing moral imbecility, as well as other varieties of
mental defect, Fernald emphasized the irreversible aspects, insisting that "all degrees of congenital mental defect" resulted
from permanent "brain abnormalities."[115] This meant that a
mentally handicapped person lived with an irremedial condition and Fernald argued that little could be done to improve it.
Believing that the work of the pre–Civil War teachers produced
only meager results, he stressed the inability of the retarded to
become "self-controlling." He curtly stated: "Under the best
conditions, feeble-minded persons do not become desirable
members of a modern American community."[116] This remark
reflected how adversely an outstanding and representative
member of the profession viewed the retarded.

While administrators agreed that society was best protected
by the lifelong care of the feeble-minded, especially those of
childbearing age, several problems militated against permanent
segregation. A. W. Wilmarth, a Wisconsin pathologist, dis-

cussed a particularly troublesome one—the premature removal
of inmates by parents—in a report (1902) to the NCCC. Some
parents abandoned retarded progeny until they became potential contributors to family income. When they reached the age
of employment, parents demanded that their children be returned home. Wilmarth also noted that many parents still viewed
institutions as schools and assumed that their children, the
pupils, would be released after a fixed period of instruction.[117]
Other administrators argued—for a combination of professional, educational, and eugenic reasons—that they alone should
determine when and if an inmate should be discharged. They
recognized that "institutions have changed their character,
largely, to furnish a permanent residence . . . . "[118] If institutions were to succeed, they must retain the power to retain inmates. Insisting that their professional experience and continued observation of inmates made them, not the courts or the
parents, the best arbiters of retention policy, superintendents
further argued that many mental defectives could be content and
self-supporting only within the sheltered environment of the
custodial facility, where they would also be prevented from reproducing more social problems for society.[119]

   While advocating such measures as marriage restriction and
involuntary retention, superintendents were conscious of potential conflicts regarding individual rights. Speaking of marriage restriction, George Knight of the Connecticut School for the
Feeble-minded said, "I am well aware that this suggestion carried out would strike a blow directly at the root of what is called
the law of individual right." He maintained, however, "that the
mentally unfit have no individual right to reproduce themselves."[120] Many state regulations barred the insane, the epileptic, and the idiotic from marriage because they could not le-
gally enter into contracts. Since these restrictions were made on
the basis of public policy, superintendents wanted the principle extended to hereditary defectives. Barr aptly summarized
his colleagues' position: "The spirit of our Constitution protects
every man in his inalienable right of the pursuit of happiness,
it is true, but only when that pursuit does not conflict with the
rights of his neighbor."[121] Administrators insisted that the
community had the primary right to safeguard itself: "Guiteau

and Czolgosz, terrible in their work, were only warning signals thrown up from the great volcano of irresponsibility, which, never extinct, is sure to have its periodic outburst, bringing destruction to life and property." The conflict between society's demands and the citizen's rights was judged to be largely illusory, since "it must be remembered that we are dealing not with men, but with an arrested development which constitutes a perpetual childhood, as incapable of the responsibilities of parenthood as it is of intelligent suffrage."[122]

One of the most formidable obstacles to achieving the large-scale permanent segregation of the mentally defective was the lack of proper institutional facilities. Despite the efforts of superintendents and the implementation of the colony plan, there still were accommodations for only approximately one defective in ten. Superintendents compared the situation of the feeble-minded to that of the insane, arguing that the numbers of each group were equal, yet there were far better provisions for the mentally ill. Alexander Johnson, Superintendent of the Indiana School for the Feeble-minded, explained that "the average citizen is afraid of the insane. A few among them are so dangerous that the whole class is feared . . . . The dangers of the idiotic are less obvious."[123] Johnson suggested that the public had to be made more aware of the claims of the feeble-minded; when this was accomplished, the institutions would receive the appropriate degree of public consideration.

Superintendents were determined to make the best use of the limited space available until funds for expansion were found. Due to the policy of custodial care, many institutions accumulated large numbers of less improvable older inmates yet, as in other fields of education, the young were believed the most susceptible to improvement. Fernald recognized the dimensions of the problem in 1893, observing that without more state aid sacrifices were necessary. He suggested that the older inmates be returned to the county workhouses to allow the younger mentally retarded to benefit from the educational programs of the training schools, still a part of institutional care.[124]

Returning the feeble-minded to workhouses or even to their homes would have created institutional vacancies, but it also would have allowed the retarded to escape competent supervision, increasing the possibility of sexual relations. There was a need for a means to prevent the defective from reproducing while they were not in custodial care.

Asexualization offered a way out of this dilemma. The perfection of sterilization techniques, as distinct from castration, was a relatively modern development. In America, the castration of criminals was suggested by Orpheus Everts, an insane asylum administrator, in 1887. Its use precipitated a lively debate between those who favored it for punitive, therapeutic, and eugenic reasons and those who considered the physical and emotional effects too severe and doubted its legality.[125] In 1892, Kerlin expressed the opinion that "life long salutary results to many of our boys and girls would be realized if before adolescence the procreative organs were removed."[126] He recommended castration primarily for its therapeutic benefits, notably the prevention of masturbation. Acting on this basis, F. Hoyt Pilcher, Superintendent of the Kansas State Home for the Feeble-minded, castrated ten inmates between 1894 and 1895. By 1899 he had castrated an additional forty-four males and removed the ovaries of fourteen females, supposedly for eugenic reasons. He proceeded, however, without any legal authority and was forced to halt by adverse public opinion.[127] Despite assurances that castration would provide a "double release" for the retarded—freeing them from the possibility of harming themselves and society as well as lessening the need for strict segregation—public sentiment demanded something less spartan.[128]

Two operations, salpingectomy and vasectomy, achieved the desired result—the prevention of procreation without severe physiological and psychological side effects.[129] Vasectomy was first used by Harry C. Sharp, physician at the Indiana Reformatory, to help cure an inmate of incessant masturbation. The operation was successful and Sharp noted: "It was then that it occurred to me that this would be a good method of preventing procreation in the defective and physically unfit."[130] The importance of the operation was clear. Sharp believed that the survival of the nation was at stake:

Idiots, imbeciles and degenerate criminals are prolific, and their defects are transmissible. Each person is a unit of the nation, and the nation is strong and pure and sane, or weak and corrupt and insane in proportion that the mentally and physically healthy exceed the diseased. Nor can any nation live if there is a reverse ratio. So we owe it not only to ourselves, but the future of our race and nation, to see that the defective and diseased do not multiply.[131]

Because sterilization was less drastic than castration, officials found that they could arouse more public support for it. Even before the popularization of vasectomy, however, there had been attempts in Michigan (1897) and Pennsylvania (1901) to pass laws for the asexualization of criminals and defectives.[132]

Martin W. Barr was the foremost administrative advocate of asexualization for eugenic and institutional reasons. In 1897, he addressed a questionnaire to the heads of sixty-one institutions for the retarded, twenty-five American and thirty-six foreign, asking their opinions on asexualization and prevention of defective reproduction. Despite a dishearteningly small response (twelve), Barr concluded that although "all agree that procreation is not advisable—that defect must breed defect—there is evident cautiousness in advocating asexualization in all grades, but a consensus as to the necessity being greatest for those of high grade."[133]

Barr recommended the passage of a "Bill for the Prevention of Idiocy" which would have empowered a committee of experts (a neurologist, a surgeon, and the chief physician) acting in accordance with the board of trustees "to perform [on inmates judged incurable] such operation [sic] for the prevention of procreation as shall be decided safest and most effective." After passing both Houses of the Pennsylvania legislature, the bill was returned by the governor for, as Barr put it, some "trifling technicality."[134]

Supporters of asexualization saw it as a means to restore the process of natural selection, which they believed had been hampered badly by the misguided philanthropic and charitable efforts of man.[135] In their rhetoric one can detect a sense of regret over how the defective was no longer allowed to die off. Asexualization appealed to them as a scientific means by which society could partly undo the damage that it had done. The large class of existing defectives could not be changed, but asexualization could prevent any further increase. The primary cause of the large number of degenerates was heredity and the surest way to eliminate defective heredity was to prevent reproduction. Nevertheless, when the Barr bill[136] was passed again by the Pennsylvania legislature in 1905, it was vetoed. The governor did not believe that available scientific evidence supported such drastic acts, which seemed cruel experiments beyond state authority and were performed without the consent of the imbecile children or their guardians.[137] This position represented a sizable body of public opinion.[138]

Indiana passed the nation's first asexualization law in 1907.[139] The act was more comprehensive than the Pennsylvania bill; it applied to "confirmed criminals, idiots, rapists, and imbeciles," who, when declared unimprovable by a committee of experts, would be rendered incapable of reproduction.[140]

Professional opinion was not unanimous in favoring asexualization. The division of thought was illustrated best by the majority and minority reports of the Committee on Colonies for Segregation of Defectives, read to the NCCC in 1903. Alexander Johnson, chair of the committee, presented the majority view, arguing for segregation and against sterilization.[141] He discussed neither the legality nor the appropriateness of sterilization, but removed the examination of the issue to the realm of sentiment and emotion. On this basis, Mary E. Perry, Vice President of the Missouri State Board of Charities and Corrections, justified the use of surgery. She took issue with Johnson:

I believe the remedy is largely in the hands of this conference . . . . It would not be well to prepare our several states to call to our assistance the surgeon's knife to prevent the entailing of this curse upon innocent members of yet unborn children . . . . It is time we looked this question squarely in the face and as it is humane, so it is righteous if resorted to for the sake of the child.[142]

Segregation and sterilization were both initially endorsed by administrators for reasons of institutional policy. Segregation evolved out of the failure of the schools to restore a significant number of their pupils to productive places in society. At the conclusion of a student's instruction, officials discovered, the

only useful role a pupil could assume was within the institution. Schools continued to replace the academically oriented
cirriculum with vocational instruction, and to train the feeble-
minded for a lifetime of custodial service. In Barr's words, classes
that "partake of the industrial and manual training given in the
ante-bellum days on the plantations, which were, in fact—as
the world is fast acknowledging—training schools for a backward race, many of whom were feeble-minded."[143] The image
of dealing with a troublesome, backward race, genetically inferior but capable of prodigious reproduction, was not far from
the minds of superintendents. An editorial in the *Journal of Psycho-Asthenics* proclaimed: "If the day ever comes—let us say
bravely when the day comes—that all or nearly all, the degenerates are gathered into industrial, celibate communities, how
rapidly the 'White Man's Burden' of distress, pauperism, and
disease, which he must be taxed to support, begins to diminish."[144]

Around 1900, sterilization appealed to some superintendents
as a means of insuring the celibacy of the feeble-minded, regardless of whether or not they were institutionalized. The need
for such controls seemed urgent: for over a decade the eugenics movement had emphasized the importance of preventing the
reproduction of defectives; the growth of special classes in public schools pointed to the existence of a large number of retarded children; and after the rediscovery of the moral imbecile, observers detected ever increasing threats to society. In his
presidential address to the NCCC, a presentation devoted solely
to the feeble-minded, Amos W. Butler quoted Indiana hereditary studies and declared: "This record is doubtless nothing more
than typical of what can be gathered, by care, in other states.
It shows one of the most potentially destructive factors in our
civilization; one of the most terrible forces acting against society; a fact we have to face, a condition to meet, a power that
must be kept under."[145]

5

Segregation or Surgery

The development of intelligence testing further hardened the attitudes of superintendents toward the retarded, stirring anxiety that the feeble-minded did indeed constitute a menace to society.[1] Although it was recognized that the mentally deficient could become social problems and that mental handicaps were subject to hereditary transmission, there was no clear understanding of the true incidence of retardation in the general population, nor of the role of heredity and mental defect in the causation of antisocial behavior. These questions had been noted as early as 1895, when Isabel Barrows, editor of the *Proceedings of the Association of Medical Officials of American Institutions for Idiotic and Feeble-minded Persons*, expressed the hope that "some way could be devised by which our public schools could be examined . . . . If prisoners and inmates of reformatories could in the same way be subjected to a careful analysis and the result presented to the public . . . it would enlighten the people. . . . If institutes of heredity could be induced to make imbecility a . . . branch of investigation, that too, might help . . . . "[2] Subsequent events proved Barrows to be remarkably accurate in foretelling both the early direction and the impact of intelligence testing.

From the 1890's onward, institutional officials became interested in psychological testing and measurement. In 1900, Barr established an "anthropometric" laboratory at Elwyn, premised on the belief that various measurements of human ability and anatomy, notably lung capacity, grip, muscular control, and head size, could be utilized as indices of an individual's mental and physical development.[3] It was along these lines that Henry H. Goddard proceeded when he became Director of the Research Department of the Vineland, New Jersey, Training School for Boys and Girls in 1906. The decision to create the department and appoint Goddard was made by Edward R. Johnstone, Vineland's superintendent. Johnstone's background was more academic than medical, but when he established the Vineland Summer School for special class teachers, he faced immediately questions he could not answer. He sought the advice of a group of colleagues informally organized as the "Paidological Staff" or the "Feeble-minded Club." They suggested the establishment of a research department, and G. Stanley Hall recommended Goddard, a former student with a Clark Ph.D. currently holding the Chair of Psychology and Pedagogy at the Pennsylvania Normal School in West Chester.[4]

Goddard began his research in an institutional atmosphere arranged "for proper study and investigation, with a view of finding the cause and prevention of defectiveness, and so aim[ing] to dry up the stream at its source."[5] He conducted a variety of experiments, many of them employing the learning of numbers, in an attempt to gauge the abilities and potentialities of the retarded.[6] Goddard became aware of the work of Alfred Binet and Thomas Simon during a trip to Europe in the spring of 1908.[7] Binet and Simon, at the request of the French Ministry of Public Instruction in 1904, had devised a series of tests to identify and classify feeble-minded children for placement in special classes. The tests were compiled from empirical studies which sought to determine exactly what tasks children of different ages could accomplish. When they found that a majority of children of the same age could successfully complete a given task, they incorporated that task into their schema for the measurement of intelligence. Binet and Simon offered revisions of their 1905 tests in 1908, and again in 1911. Each new scale was the product of additional research as they sought to perfect a testing procedure that could evaluate innate intelligence and not be influenced by education or environment.[8]

When Goddard learned of the improved 1908 scale, he felt that "it seemed impossible to grade intelligence in that way. It was too easy, too simple; . . . "[9] yet he realized "that we have great need for some sort of classification which will tell us at the outset very closely where the child is in mental development and what we may expect from him and what methods of treatment shall be applied."[10] After using the Binet scale with every inmate at Vineland, Goddard reported to the American Association for the Study of the Feeble-minded (AASF) that it was remarkably accurate. Because of his initial doubts, Goddard employed some additional controls such as duplicate testing with the older methods and a group conference of staff members where the development of each inmate was appraised according to the traditional criteria, all of which confirmed the results of the Binet tests.[11]

Goddard reached a number of important conclusions. He established an apparently objective set of criteria for the evaluation of varying degrees of mental defect. He determined that a mental age of twelve was the upper limit of retarded development; none of the examined Vineland inmates passed many of the tests designated for normal twelve-year-old children.[12] Thus, any adult who failed to score a mental age above twelve was highly suspect of being feeble-minded, as was any child who was two or more years mentally below his or her chronological age. Goddard found that the tests achieved a tripartite division of the Vineland inmates. Idiots with a mental age of less than two years were the lowest, followed by imbeciles ranging from two to seven, and a third group Goddard first called "proximates" (meaning they were nearly normal) and later named morons (from the Greek for slow, sluggish) who were mentally eight to twelve. This terminology received official approval and adoption by the Committee on the Classification of the Feeble-minded of the AASF in 1910.[13]

At the same time that Goddard and the AASF were determining the parameters of retardation, the prestigious British Royal Commission on the Care and Control of the Feeble-minded was defining the different grades in an entirely social context.

The highest type of defective was "one who is capable of earning a living under favorable circumstances, but is incapable, from mental defect existing from birth, (a) of competing on equal terms with his normal fellows; or (b) of managing himself and his affairs with ordinary prudence." The imbecile was "one who, by reason of mental defect existing from birth, or from early age, is incapable of earning his own living, but is capable of guarding himself against common physical dangers." Finally, an idiot was "a person so deeply defective in mind from birth, or an early age, that he is unable to guard himself against common physical dangers."[14] To many observers these definitions appeared to correspond with those established on the basis of mental age. For example, a two-year-old child could not guard himself against common physical dangers but a seven-year-old could. Although the Binet scale classifications were made on the basis of mental age, they were frequently conceptualized in terms of chronological age.

Superintendents accepted this type of oversimplification because they believed, as one noted in 1911, "the new classification based upon mental tests will give something definite and tangible and something readily understood by the nonprofessional mind." An observer summarized the results in terms that anyone could understand: "These defectives are always children regardless of years or stature. Their mental processes have been arrested, and though an adult in stature, they have the mind, judgement and impulses of a child."[15] This characterization represented child stereotyping, a perennial problem of popular and professional perception of the retarded. In line with all types of stereotyping, it contained an element of truth—the mentally deficient often exhibit socially immature forms of behavior. Later in the twentieth century, however, mental retardation workers would argue that the depiction of the deficient person as a child encourages a self-fulfilling prophecy, that is, it allows one to expect, reward, and favor childlike responses in a retarded individual, and, at the same time, the representation assumes a patronizing attitude which frustrates effective care and development.

Goddard and his research staff had established the utility of Binet intelligence testing for the categorization of the mentally retarded confined to special institutions; the Binet testers were eager to expand its application.[16] In 1911, after testing 2,000 normal children by the Binet method, Goddard concluded that the tests were highly accurate for use in schools and that they did not measure conscious learning but actually gauged basic mental processes. To maximize efficiency and educational benefits, he suggested that all students be tested upon entrance to insure placement in the proper grade.[17] Goddard investigated the New York City public school system and found that 2 percent (15,000) of the enrollment was feeble-minded and 15 percent dull.[18] This disclosure prompted him to institute training in the administration of intelligence tests to the public school teachers attending the Vineland Summer School.

The advent of intelligence testing provided public officials with a scientifically approved means of ascertaining what the superintendents had been asserting for generations: mental retardation was responsible for a great deal, if not the majority, of crime, prostitution, vagrancy, and other social problems. In numerous experiments the role of mental retardation in the causation of antisocial behavior was inferred from the results of Binet testing which revealed that a large percentage of inmates or known offenders failed to pass the twelve-year level and many scored even lower.[19] A well-publicized example of this technique was the Massachusetts *Report of the Commission for the Investigation of the White Slave Traffic, So-Called*, written apparently by Walter E. Fernald in 1914. The commission found in its examination of 300 prostitutes that 154 were mentally defective enough to warrant institutionalization. Their average mental age was nine and a half years, and of those rated as normal, "no more than six of the entire number seemed to have really good minds."[20] There was little uniformity in the figures presented by these researchers. Goddard noted: "It is the most discouraging to discover that the more expert is the examiner of these groups, the higher is the percentage of feeble-minded found."[21] Whether or not the discovery of mental deficiency was dependent upon the examiner's abilities remained an open question; early twentieth-century observers were more concerned that the studies revealed a widespread prevalence of retardation.

Criminals and juvenile delinquents were among the groups

of "social debtors" most often examined and found with alarm-
ingly high percentages of mental defectives.[22] The Massachusetts legislature passed a resolve in April 1910, empowering a
commission "to investigate the question of the increase of criminals, mental defectives, epileptics and degenerates."[23] It determined that the growing population in state institutions was
not the result of an increase in the absolute numbers of defectives, dependents, and delinquents; rather it was a product of
better public understanding, simplified identification, and a
general desire to provide more comprehensive facilities for the
unfortunate.[24] The possibly comforting effect of these conclusions was offset by the discussion of a newly identified menace
to society—the defective delinquent.

For a number of years Fernald had remarked that Waltham
was receiving an increasing number of inmates in whom mental and moral deficiency was more pronounced than mental defect. These individuals appeared prone to committing destructive and criminal acts and were a bad influence on their more
impressionable and mentally weaker inmates.[25] In 1910 Fernald
urged that the term "defective delinquent" be adopted to identify cases where "the mental defect is relatively slight, and the
immoral and criminal tendencies are strongly developed, but the
mental weakness is the cause of the moral delinquency, and is
a permanent condition."[26] Fernald drafted the bill, which became a Massachusetts law in 1911, providing for the establishment of custodial facilities to care specifically for defective delinquents. These institutions would combine the security features
of a penal institution with the educational programs of an industrial training school; inmates could be transferred from existing institutions or be committed directly from court. In either
instance, they were subject to an indeterminate sentence and
were given only liberty at the discretion of institutional officials.[27]

Previously, defective delinquents were tagged as moral imbeciles, high-grade defectives, psychopaths, criminal imbeciles,
or imbeciles with criminal instincts. Intelligence testing was responsible for their identification as true mental defectives.[28]
Fernald noted: "The field of mental defect has been so broadened and extended as to include large groups of persons who

would not have been included even a decade ago. Naturally this extension has been almost entirely in the higher grades of defect."[29] Defective delinquents were classified generally as morons or borderline cases, which meant that they scored higher on Binet tests than the obviously retarded but lower than the normal individual. Without intelligence testing they would rarely have been diagnosed as mental defectives. Since they were unable to learn from past mistakes, punishment had little or no deterrent effect. There was a "close analogy between the defective delinquent and the 'instinctive criminals' who formed a large proportion of the 'prison rounder type.' "[30]

Further studies revealed that defective delinquents were responsible for a wide range of crime, from petty theft to arson, murder, and rape.[31] These findings led many to concur with Goddard's judgment that "every feeble-minded person is a potential criminal . . . since the feeble-minded lacks one or the other factors essential to a moral life—an understanding of right and wrong, and the power of control."[32] The exact percentage of feeble-minded criminals was subject to debate—Goddard maintained that 25 to 50 percent was a conservative minimum—but few questioned that the retarded were responsible for a disproportionate share of criminal activities. One observer noted that "in the courts we find the defectives forming the very backbone of recidivism, appearing for disposition over and over again, apparently unable to profit by what is done for them."[33] Authorities agreed that education, not punishment, constituted proper treatment for defective delinquents. The Massachusetts program of control was viewed as an excellent short-term solution, but stronger measures were required. "In order to restrain and ultimately put an end to the production of defective delinquents," an expert concluded, "it is necessary to restrict the propagation of the feeble-minded variety of the human race."[34]

Although defective delinquents presented officials with some unique difficulties, the question of their disposition was considered a part of the larger, overall problem of the feeble-minded. The combined efforts of Goddard and leading American eugenicists brought this problem into sharper focus. In 1910, Goddard presented a paper to a meeting of the American Breeders

Association which dealt with the relationship of heredity to mental retardation. His research was the result of curiosity to know more of the family history of his Vineland patients. He devised a special "after admission blank" that was used by two field workers employed to work on the project. Utilizing this research, Goddard displayed striking charts that showed the appearance of mental handicaps in generation after generation. Many interpreted this as indicative of Mendelian transmission.[35]

Goddard's research was highly suggestive to Charles B. Davenport, who by 1909 had turned his primary interest to studies of human heredity.[36] Through the generous funding of Mrs. E. H. Harriman, Davenport had established the Eugenics Record Office in 1910 as a center and clearinghouse for American eugenic research. Each summer, he delivered a series of twenty-five lectures to train field workers in the principles of eugenics. Some of these students would be dispatched to cooperating institutions to conduct heredity and background studies of inmate families; others would remain associated directly with the Eugenics Record Office, working under Davenport and helping to organize the data that poured in from the field.[37]

Davenport was convinced that "social progress is largely, if not chiefly, due to socially desirable fecund matings . . . [and] permanent social improvement is got only by better breeding. The only way to secure innate capacity was by breeding it."[38] Society must heed eugenic warnings, he insisted, because the future of America lay in the nation's germ plasm. Socially beneficial traits (aristogenic) had to be multiplied through the breeding and rearing of large healthy families, while those with debilitative and degenerative traits (cacogenic) should be suppressed and destroyed. Many persons accepted "eugenics as a religion"; Harry M. Laughlin, a leading eugenicist, stated that if the eugenics movement was to succeed it must become "a part of the American civic religion."[39]

Davenport believed that eugenics provided scientists with "a clear insight into the hereditary basis of conduct," meaning that virtually all of human behavior was genetically determined.[40] In the case of retardation, he contended that low mentality resulted from "the absence of some factor, and if this factor that determines normal development is lacking in both parents, it will be lacking in all of their offspring. Two mentally defective parents will produce only mentally defective offspring."[41] His belief that feeble-mindedness was a simple recessive trait—a unit character—was given strong support by two of Goddard's books, *The Kallikak Family: A Study in the Heredity of Feeble-mindedness* and *Feeble-mindedness: Its Causes and Consequences.*

Working in the Dugdale tradition, Goddard became interested in the Kallikak family (a word meaning "good-bad family") after investigating the ancestry of Deborah Kallikak, one of his patients. He engaged Elizabeth S. Kite as a researcher and together they discovered a remarkable story. The founder of the family, Martin Kallikak, Sr., fathered two half-brothers, one by a promiscuous tavern maid, and the other by his wife, a product of a good family. Goddard traced 496 descendants of the legitimate union and found all to be normal, many in distinguished positions in their communities. But the 480 descendants of Deborah's great–grandfather, Martin Kallikak, Jr., known as "Old Horror," presented an almost unbroken line of degeneration: 143 feeble-minded, only 46 normal, 36 illegitimate, 33 immoral persons, 24 alcoholics, 8 pimps, and a total of 82 who died in infancy.[42] Goddard believed that the Kallikak family constituted "a natural experiment in heredity" since both branches of the family lived "out their lives in the same environment, except insofar as they themselves, because of their different characters, changed that environment."[43]

In *The Kallikak Family* Goddard suspended judgment on the utility of Mendel's laws: "Our own studies lead us to believe that it [Mendel's Law] also applies in the case of feeble-mindedness, but this will be taken up in a later work . . . ."[44] This more comprehensive treatment came in *Feeble-Mindedness: Its Causes and Consequences* in which he and his field workers investigated the families of Vineland residents. Based on the data of 300 families, he concluded that 164 cases were definitely hereditary, 34 probably hereditary, 37 had neuropathic ancestry, 51 were accidently caused, and in 8 no cause could be discovered. These figures indicated that 77 percent of feeble-mindedness was hereditary, and only 19 percent could be considered accidental.[45] After a recapitulation of Mendel's laws and their application to his data, Goddard concluded: "Since our figures agree so closely with Mendelian expectation and since there are few if any cases where the Mendelian formula does not fit the facts, the hypothesis seems to stand: normalmindedness is, or at least behaves like, a unit character; is dominant and is transmitted in accordance with the Mendelian law of inheritance."[46]

Goddard's work also confirmed another important assertion concerning the reproductive characteristics of the mentally retarded. A. F. Tredgold, a leading British mental retardation worker, maintained that "the average number of children in a mentally defective family was 7.3, or considerably more than half as many again as the general average for the whole population."[47] In New Jersey, the 287 mothers of the Vineland research sample had a total of 1,781 children, or an average of 6.2 per female.[48] These statistics made all the more meaningful Goddard's earlier warning that "there are Kallikak families all about us. They are multiplying at twice the rate of the general population . . . ." This apparent situation alarmed observers who feared race suicide. They especially condemned a marriage which threatened to produce inferior offspring. Some eugenicists frankly urged a woman to divorce a "drunkard or criminal husband," charging that to bear a child with such a man constituted "a crime against the race."[49]

The study of defective families lured other researchers—many trained at the Eugenics Record Office—to undertake investigations similar to Goddard studies.[50] Generally, the depopulated rural areas of the states proved the ancestral homes and breeding grounds for such groups as the Hill Folk, the Nam Family, the Dacks, the Jukes (restudied in 1915), the Family of Sam Sixty, or the "C" Family.[51] Fernald explained that in many backwoods counties the vigorous and enterprising moved, "while the inefficient and the feeble are apt to be left at home . . . with the result that if something is not done, we are to have intensified breeding of the less desirable elements in our native stock," in these isolated areas "where the entire population is below par—shiftless, immoral, drunken, with illegitimate children, nests of criminals."[52] These studies confirmed the worst fears of professionals. America's most important institutions of social control—the family and the community—failed to check mental retardation. Indeed, because of the laws of inheritance, they actually served to perpetuate mental defect and deviant behavior.

Prominent eugenicists such as Davenport and Laughlin demanded that society take positive action to prevent the country from being overwhelmed by a stream of bad germ plasm and degeneracy. Laughlin insisted:

It now behooves society in consonance with both humanitarianism and race efficiency to provide more humane means for cutting off defectives. Society must look upon germ plasm as belonging to society and not solely to the individual who carries it. Humanitarianism demands that every individual born be given every opportunity for decent and effective life that our civilization can offer. Racial instinct demands that defectives shall not continue their unworthy traits to menace society.[53]

Laughlin listed ten classes of cacogenic elements in society, including the feeble-minded, the pauper class, the criminal class, the deformed class, and the caaesthenic class (loss of an organ). He also suggested ten possible remedies ranging from segregation, sterilization, and restrictive marriage laws to polygamy, euthanasia, and laissez-faire.[54] The most widely accepted appeal of the eugenicists was "to the right of the child to be well-born," which received the support of social workers, physicians, and administrators.[55]

"In this day of *conservation*," Davenport declared, "protoplasm is our most valuable national resource,"[56] a point that justified denial of rights to the defective. Many contentions of the eugenicists had been aired as early as 1909, when Reverend Karl Schwartz of Syracuse addressed an AASF convention and inveighed against misguided philanthropy which, in his view, kept alive defectives that nature would reject. "We are directing our philanthropies," he declared, "toward a perpetuation of the unfit and the multiplication of their numbers." Suggesting "it is the disease that proves fatal that becomes the greatest agency in the maintenance and the progression of the race," Schwartz brushed aside any ethical reservations because "ethics are rightly applied only when the social interest is made paramount."[57] In any case, ethics applied only in dealing with similar beings and, as Davenport pointed out, the differences between the mentally handicapped and the average man "are not incidental, due to some accident of environment—they are *fundamental*, they are the marks of a different species, for these differences are inheritable, and may be traced through the generations."[58] The mentally defective were to be denied rights of liberty and of reproduction on the basis of the superior rights of the nation, of the race, and of the future. "Eugenics is supremely the business of the state, for a government must consider not only the present good of its citizens but the future welfare of the race."[59]

Superintendents were definitely aware of these attitudes toward their inmates and in many cases shared them. J. M. Murdock, Superintendent, State Institution for the Feeble-minded of Western Pennsylvania (Polk), summarized: "We talk less of pathology and therapeutics and physical training and industrial occupations for the feeble-minded and more of eugenics, segregation and sterilization; not so much of the individual, but more of the larger problem, the group; of prevention—and in our zeal to push forward to the goal, sometimes of extinction."[60]

To most superintendents, the basic inability of the feeble-minded to act like other people was at the heart of the problem. "They are not only deficient in mind, but they are weak and unstable in will, lacking in self-control and motivated by unconventional standards of behavior."[61] Even when their abilities enabled them to act in pursuit of some goal, they did not follow conventional forms of behavior. Thus the retarded could never compete equally in the community. E. J. Emerick, Doren's successor at Ohio, phrased it cogently: "The feeble-minded individual is a menace to society because he is incapable of social development . . . . We must understand that the feeble-minded person cannot be made into a normal citizen. He lacks the judgement, will power, and comprehension of situations necessary to enable him to react to his surroundings alright."[62] Social performance was therefore the basic criterion for feeble-mindedness. If any individual exhibited indications of incompetency, he or she was likely to be considered feeble-minded, regardless of the specific nature of the antisocial action. Mental retardation seemed to be the basic cause of almost all deviant behavior.[63]

This concern for the menace of the feeble-minded reached a peak in the years 1912–1917. Committees mushroomed to alert the public. In 1910 Johnstone organized the friends and families of children awaiting entrance to Vineland into a Committee on Provision for the Feeble-minded. Through an extensive letter–writing campaign, pressure was brought on the New Jersey legislature to pass bills providing for mental and physical examinations in the schools (1909); creation of special classes and a sterilization law (1911); establishment of farm colonies (1913); and a Commission on the Care of Defectives (1914). Realizing the value of such campaigns for other states, Johnstone utilized the resources of the Committee in 1912 to create the Vineland Extension Department, a lecture and propaganda bureau. His brother-in-law, Alexander Johnson, became director and in 1914 enlarged the department into a National Committee on Provision for the Feeble-minded, headquartered in Philadelphia with Joseph P. Byrers as executive secretary. Johnson remained as a field secretary and made a number of extensive lecture trips across the country, notably in the South, proclaiming the need to provide adequate facilities for the mentally defective.[64]

R. Bayard Cutting organized the New York Committee on Feeble-mindedness in 1916 for a similar purpose. It distributed literature which recounted the "hurt of feeble-mindedness to society," calling attention to the large number of retarded (33,000) estimated in the state of New York and the relatively small number (5,399) in institutions. A special objective of the committee was pressuring the state legislature into granting sufficient funds for the completion of Letchworth Village, a facility capable of accommodating 3,000 persons.[65] The Philadelphia Department of Public Health and Charity engaged in extensive pamphleteering campaigns; some of the documents bore disturbing titles—*The Degenerate Children of Feeble-minded Women* or *The Feeble-minded World*—and were prone to exaggerated statements. "Practically all poor feeble-minded women at large," declared one, "become mothers of illegitimate children soon after reaching the age of puberty."[66] Many additional forums helped

transmit the message. A symposium on "The Right to Be Well-
Born" comprised an entire issue of the *Survey* and included articles by Davenport, Goddard, Kite, and others. A whole issue
of the *State Charities Aid Association News* consisted of a single
article by a charity worker, Homer Folks, "State Knows How
to Deal With The Feeble-minded But Doesn't Do It." [67] Along
with the National Conference of Charities and Corrections, state
conferences such as the Indiana Conference on Mental Deficiency and Child Welfare and the Wisconsin State Conference
of Charities and Correction were instrumental in informing local administrators and officials. [68]

Reactions to this agitation varied from state to state. In a few
places, commissions were formed to survey the needs of the
retarded and to report recommendations. New York's commission was typical in both its organization and its final suggestions. It had five major recommendations and some were
adopted in New York and elsewhere. The Commission proposed: (1) statewide standardization of the principles for determining retardation with the responsibility for such diagnosis in
the hands of competent state authorities; (2) adequate and separate state provision for the custodial care of defective and dependent delinquents; (3) character building and vocational
training in state training schools with special upgraded classes
for the education of defectives returned to the community; (4)
further research into the etiological and social causes of feeble-
mindedness; and (5) establishment of a system of friendly supervision for high-grade defectives who should also be trained
to maintain themselves in the community. [69] As a result of these
findings, a Hospital Development Commission was established
to study further the issues. It urged the creation of a permanent State Commission for Mental Defectives which began operations in 1918. [70]

Sterilization laws continued to be enacted and many states
increased institutional provisions for the retarded. At least sixteen states and the District of Columbia established new facilities for the feeble-minded and the number of inmates in all institutions increased from 20,731 in 1910 to 51,731 in 1923. [71] By
1917 fifteen states had enacted some variety of eugenical sterilization law: Indiana (1907); California, Connecticut, and Wash-

ington (1909); Iowa, Nevada, and New Jersey (1911); New York (1912); Kansas, Michigan, North Dakota, Oregon, and Wisconsin (1913); Nebraska (1915); and South Dakota (1917).[72] These laws varied greatly in content, scope, and purpose, but generally they required that, before sterilization, an individual be certified as hereditarily feeble-minded (or insane, epileptic, or criminal) by a consulting board of examiners.[73] Although many laws were never or rarely used and some ruled unconstitutional as class legislation or denial of due process, 3,233 sterilizations were performed on all classes by 1921.[74]

Eugenicists figured strongly among the supporters of sterilization, but opinions of institutional officials were mixed. Eugenicists also endorsed marriage restriction laws in principle, but questioned their practicality. "Laws against the marriage of the feeble–minded are futile in any case. It would be as sensible to hope to control by legislation, the mating of rabbits."[75] Many superintendents agreed with Goddard's position that sterilization should be used in conjunction with segregation and not as a substitute for it.[76] Sterilization appeared to have the greatest utility in dealing with borderline cases. "It may be that we shall be willing to sterilize all of the borderline cases," Goddard maintained, "and then there will be no longer any objection to their marrying."[77]

Walter E. Fernald was the most prominent superintendent opposing sterilization. He contended that the "normal carriers" of defect would not be affected. The presence of these sterile people in the community, with unimpaired sexual desire and capacity, would be a direct encouragement of vice and a prolific source of venereal disease."[78] Favoring sterilization, Alexander Johnson pointed to the difficulties of providing custodial facilities for approximately one person in 250. He believed simply that sterilization was "a real necessity" because of "the impossibility of segregating all the morons."[79]

The degree of support for a sterilization law varied across the country. A. Wilmarth, for example, Superintendent, Wisconsin Home for the Feeble-minded, strongly advocated such a measure and was credited with aiding the passage of the law in 1913.[80] In New York, however, Homer Folks reported that the state sterilization law "was neither proposed nor urged , . . .

by those who have been prominently connected with social work in this state . . . . Neither was it opposed."[81] In other states there generally was a measure of custodial support for sterilization laws sufficient for their adoption.[82] Folks noted that any lack of support in the legislature was balanced by the absence of opposition. For years state legislatures had been deluged with both expert and popular assertions that retardation was responsible deviant behavior. Sterilization appeared to be an economical, effective, scientific, and permanent measure to safeguard the public welfare.

Penologists were among the first officials to express misgivings about the utility and justification of sterilization. Thirteen of the fifteen state laws had authorized the operation for criminals deemed habitual, incorrigible, hereditary, or perpetrators of heinous crimes.[83] A few individuals raised damaging questions about the punitive and therapeutic value of sterilization, but most reserved criticism for its supposedly eugenic benefits. One observer concluded that "the critics of such legislation are right in asserting that criminal inheritance remains yet to be proved."[84] Three committees appointed by the American Institute of Criminal Law and Criminology studied the issue and reported that sterilization might conceivably have some eugenic value for the general population, but no substantial proof justified reliance on sterilization to diminish crime.[85]

The uncritical use of Binet intelligence tests to diagnose mental retardation also came under examination. In 1913, Fernald contended that "the Binet tests corroborate where we do not need corroboration, and are not decisive where the differential diagnosis of the higher grade defective from the normal is in question."[86] He suggested a combination of factors—physical condition, family history, record of school progress, personal and developmental history, practical knowledge, and economic efficiency—be evaluated along with testing to determine mental defect.[87] Edgar A. Doll, a psychologist, educator, and researcher at Vineland, agreed that the intelligence test "is not in itself a complete diagnostic method," and cautioned colleagues "that a little ground gained permanently is better than yards of territory that later must be given up."[88]

J. E. Wallace Wallin, a maverick clinical psychologist, challenged the credibility of the tests when his examination of a group of successful Iowa farmers revealed all to be morons. These findings, if correct, contradicted the social definition of a higher grade defective. It was evident that these prosperous individuals were managing their affairs with ordinary prudence and that the tests must be in error. Wallin concluded that levels of education were highly significant in intelligence testing and established that there was an inverse proportion between degree of education and success on the tests.[89]

Further qualifications of the applicability and accuracy of intelligence testing did not deter the psychologists who administered the Army's program of testing in World War I. The tests revealed that 47.3 percent of the white draft and 89 percent of the black draft had mental ages of twelve or lower. Instead of questioning these results, the report on the tests concluded that "feeble-mindedness . . . is of much greater frequency of occurrence than had been originally supposed."[90] Some persons did not doubt the findings because they coincided with their own preconceived ideas. Goddard envisioned a future time when 211 persons would be mentally tested and assigned an appropriate job depending on whether they were A, B, C, D, or E individuals.[91]

While officials may have believed that mental deficiency was widespread in the general population, there was a feeling that "many feeble-minded persons can live their lives without the restraint of an institution and yet without injury to society."[92] Proof of this assertion came from Fernald's study of the careers of 646 inmates who had left his Massachusetts school. Finding more than half of the ex-inmates free of legal difficulties and public relief, he concluded that "the survey shows that there are bad defectives and good defectives."[93] The work of Charles Bernstein, Superintendent, Rome State Custodial Asylum, furnished additional evidence of the ability of the retarded to succeed in a nonrestrictive setting. In 1906, Bernstein placed inmates on small farm colonies with a minimum of supervision. The colonies proved largely troublefree and in 1911 he established a parole system which was equally successful.[94]

The results of these surveys and institutional experiments prompted some custodians to reconsider their beliefs. Fernald tentatively suggested: "There has been too great a tendency to regard feeble-mindedness as a definite entity, and to assume that all defectives are equally dangerous as to the possibility of dependency, immorality, or criminality, or as to the possibility of the transmission of their defect to their progeny."[95]

An editorial in *Mental Hygiene*, the organ of the National Committee for Mental Hygiene, echoed Fernald's remarks and questioned the validity of the policy of segregation. This 1917 commentary pointed out that "once we admit the existence of a section of the feeble-minded population which is so harmless, we must consider modifying any plan which contemplates wholesale and indiscriminate segregation."[96]

Heredity studies and Goddard's work in particular came under criticism for the manipulation of data and the use of haphazard research techniques.[97] Edward Lindsay, a Pennsylvania lawyer, provided a sophisticated critique of the eugenics movement. He asserted:

There seems to be a turning to the purely biological study of human development to find the explanation of social phenomena and as in biological thought there seems now current a return to the old preformist doctrines which are virtually a denial of development. We see their influences on the views now advanced as to conduct and social relations in a metaphysical predetermination as rigid as the old theological predeterminism.[98]

This determinism had been welcomed by those seeking an answer to persistent recidivism or continued reliance on public charity. Belief in biological inevitability condoned the abandonment of reform efforts and substituted a pervasive concern for control, domination, and mastery.

6

A Return to the Community

In the 1920's, the need for the care and supervision of the mentally retarded in the community gained acceptance.[1] While the institution remained the central agency of care, it was no longer viewed solely as a place of segregation, a permanent residence removed and hidden from the wider society and designed for all mentally deficient persons. It acquired extra-institutional responsibilities, notably to reintegrate the mentally retarded back into the community.

Pressure for change came from several sources. Every institution had a waiting list of several hundred children. Although facilities were overcrowded, parents and relatives of potential clients grew impatient with delays and pressured authorities to make more living space available. In short, an alternative was needed to relieve the congestion in existing institutions. A precedent for community care was the colony which achieved a major success under the direction of Charles Bernstein of Rome who insisted that morons and borderline cases could become happy and useful workers. The Rome training program focused on providing two kinds of labor: farm help for boys and domestic service for girls. In 1919, Bernstein administered eleven farm colonies, each with twenty inmates and a farmer and his wife, and, seven city colonies, each supervised by a matron and a social worker, having a total inmate population of 172 girls.[2]

New assumptions and facts on the number of mentally deficient individuals in the general population contributed to changing institutional priorities. For example, a report of the Surgeon General of the Army, *Defects Found in Drafted Men*, published in 1920, confirmed the growing belief that feeblemindedness was much more prevalent than had been realized. It had been assumed that four persons per one thousand in the total population were feeble-minded. The Surgeon General's report specified twelve per one thousand, and in the 1920's, numerous surveys, conducted by local school authorities throughout the country, produced findings ranging from twenty to twenty-five per one thousand. For some observers, the figures stirred alarm, generating opinion that mental retardation was increasing. Yet, there was an obvious conclusion: some kind of community supervision was needed because it was simply not possible to institutionalize all mentally deficient people. More important, the evidence suggested that many mentally retarded persons did not require or need incarceration; they lived, largely undetected, in society, performing useful, menial tasks.[3] Here was encouragement for administrators to experiment with programs which would release some of their residents in the community.

In the decade after World War I, a major effort of institutions consisted of preparing the "high-grade" or moron resident for community living. As has been noted, substantial professional opinion emphasized that many of the retarded could become valuable members of society.[4] This opinion was verified in numerous reports which analyzed institutional parole programs.

When O. J. Cobb, Superintendent, Syracuse School for Mental Defectives, for example, demonstrated that the trained moron was capable of self-support, the important elements in his program included learning how to select friends, utilize leisure time, and manage personal finances. Over a period of four years, Cobb paroled 190 boys and girls to live and work in homes and on farms and he counted only six failures.[5]

The Massachusetts School for the Feeble-minded at Waverly also developed an effective parole system. Parolees worked in offices, factories, and on farms. They carried messages, ran errands, loaded trucks, swept floors, and cleaned kitchens. At school, they were taught the importance of punctuality and responsibility on the job, and cleanliness and thrift in daily living. Mabel A. Matthews, head social worker at Waverly, identified the successful parolee as a trained person with a positive, nondemanding attitude toward work. Often humiliated and scorned for his or her slowness at school and play, the parolee found a feeling of satisfaction and accomplishment, a sense of respectability, in a job. The monotonous work was not boring; he or she rarely complained and willingly accepted directions without question. Above all the parolee needed approbation; in fact, success was dependent upon the strong support and approval of co-workers, friends, and relatives. Matthews stressed that placing the boys and girls in the community brought happiness to them and their families, saved money for the state, and made room for new students at the school.[6]

Wrentham State School, Massachusetts, justified its parole system with the argument: each successful parolee created a vacancy for another child. The program operated on a careful screening process, especially for girls. A girl was never sent to a hotel or a boardinghouse but to a private home, ideally to a place with young children and located in a small town. A family requesting a retarded child wrote directly to the school superintendent. With his recommendation, a social worker visited the home, talked with the family, and left instructions on the care of deficient children. If information about the family was favorable, a girl was chosen who would fit well into the household.[7] Other reports claimed positive results: a study of 278 parolees from Letchworth Village, Thiells, New York, consisting of 80 percent morons, maintained that two-thirds of the group achieved successful adjustment in the community. A survey of 636 parolees of Rome State School, New York, specified that the majority were laborers and members of the armed forces.[8]

The outpatient clinic of a state school represented another type of community care for the mentally deficient. The Massachusetts School for the Feeble-minded at Waverly operated a model clinic which offered free information, advice, and counsel. At the request of local authorities, a team consisting of a psychia-

trist, a social worker, a teacher, and a psychologist conducted
school clinics throughout the state, providing extensive examination and diagnostic services. The clinic's most important
function was providing help to parents and guardians. A diagnosis of mental deficiency, clinic administrators noted, had
little value unless it included suggestions on how to improve
the child's condition. One important general recommendation
was stressed: parents should scale down or modify their expectations and demands of the child. They must learn to accept
the child's own level of comfort and happiness. Additional advice related to the level of retardation: for the idiot, suggestions
dealt with the importance of habit training, the types of exercises, and the aids in walking; for the imbecile, it was important for the child to learn household chores; and the moron
needed special class or institutional occupational training. Administrators pointed to a striking conclusion: of the thousands
of children diagnosed as mentally deficient at this facility, the
majority had remained at home, visiting the clinic for examination and guidance once or twice a year.[9]

The success of this outpatient clinic owed much to Waverly's
superintendent, Walter E. Fernald, still one of the most influential leaders of the profession. He served as president of the
AASF in 1893 and again in 1923, and over this thirty-year period underwent a major attitudinal change. His transformation
reflected the new forces and pressures which were altering care
in the opening decades of the century. Sensitive to these influences, he presented, in his 1923 presidential address, a thirty-
year perspective on institutional policy. In the 1890's, he noted,
superintendents believed that the retarded formed an undesirable community element requiring permanent incarceration. This
view became "the legend of the feeble-minded," which was
based on "very depressing information," the "study of the only
known large groups of defectives . . . who had got into trouble and were in institutions, who were largely of the hereditary
class and had behaved badly and were shiftless and lazy as a
group." It seemed logical to conclude that "all defectives had
similar history and tendencies."[10]

A new perspective emerged around World War I, Fernald
observed, when it became clear that a large number of the re-

tarded lived largely unnoticed in the community. Numerous studies, conducted at schools and clinics, he claimed, showed that the majority of the deficient exhibited good behavior and a very small percentage engaged in troublesome or antisocial activities. This new information deflated "the legend of the feeble-minded," and necessitated new priorities. Fernald urged the profession to concentrate on assisting clients to adjust to home and community life and, more important, on finding employment for the larger class of morons. He commented: "The idle defective has no money, feels inferior, and does his worst. The defective who works all day at good wages seldom makes trouble." Looking to the future with optimism, Fernald saw the special class as an important job–training agency for the moron.[11]

From crucial early beginnings, the special class in the public school became a major third component in the typical American social program. Along with the parole system and the outpatient clinic, it represented a nationwide agency for the training and care of the deficient in the community. At first, special classes developed slowly and were located chiefly in eastern and midwestern cities; by 1930, there was an estimated national enrollment of over fifty thousand students.

While serving as a place for pupils who continually failed and repeated grades, the special class aimed at resolving a major difficulty: normal and deficient children did not mix well either academically or socially. A 1927 report, for example, dealing with the problems of the retarded in Cincinnati schools noted that vocational training offered to a heterogeneous group in the same classes frustrated the slower students who found the experience too difficult and frequently ruined materials. Other studies pointed out that the deficient in the regular classroom complicated the instructor's work, to the disadvantage of normal children. The retarded had frequent behavioral problems and could not grasp the subject matter, difficulties which consumed too much of the teacher's time and energy. This situation was complicated by the negative and hostile attitudes of normals toward the deficient. Taunted as a "boob" or a "dummy" and unable to compete scholastically with normal peers, the retarded pupil developed a sense of inferiority and became trap-

ped on a treadmill of failure and humiliation. The child often
floundered and eventually sought relief in truancy, petty crime,
and random acts of hostility. In effect, traditional education, well-
suited in aims, methods, and subject matter to the average student, injured the deficient pupil by emphasizing his or her
weaknesses and failures. The special class, on the other hand,
provided a haven which enabled the student to discover and
develop his or her strengths. The pace of school life was re-
laxed, the demands of regular classwork were modified, and a
structured learning environment obviated feelings of inferiority
by training the retarded in practical pursuits related to their own
experiences and to their occupational future in the unskilled labor market.[12]

This program shared the goal of traditional education, namely,
to develop the potential of each individual to fullest capacity,
and it held the common objective of citizenship training which
many administrators accepted as its major justification. Indeed,
in the years between the World Wars, they saw the special class
as a safety valve, a place for the child to learn how to get along
with others and become a good citizen. Without this opportunity, they argued, many of the deficient dropped out of regular
school, fell in with a bad crowd, and became juvenile delinquents. Eleanor Rowlett, instructor at the Jeb Stewart School,
Richmond, Virginia, commented that the special class helped
to prevent "future gangsters from developing" by channeling
the retarded into productive outlets. It also had the advantage
of being inexpensive. Institutions could not train all of the
mentally retarded; if more of them lived at home and attended
special classes in the public schools, she noted, their care would
be handled in a practical and reasonable way for the tax-
payer.[13]

As was true from the late experimental school era, the most
important function of education was to prepare the student for
the work world. Recognizing that a limited mental endowment
narrowed employment opportunities, educators called for
strengthening those qualities of the deficient which would enable them to compete with normal persons for unskilled jobs,
the only realistic employment outlet for the retarded. Charles
Scott Barry, a professor of educational psychology, University

of Michigan, argued that the mentally deficient had the characteristics necessary for success in the unskilled labor market, namely, good health, a strong body, and physical endurance. These qualities should be enhanced in the activities and instruction of the special class. Above all, the content of the curriculum must be drawn from the experiences and needs of the child. Training in reading, for example, should emphasize street names, traffic signs, household articles, food and family words, newspaper headlines, and want ads; in writing, the importance of legibility was stressed along with the ability to spell common words; and being able to make change was deemed sufficient mastery of math. Habit training, a concept and method of teaching applicable to all levels of mental retardation, was also important to the special class. Retarded children, educators noted, enjoyed doing the same things together, imitating each other. In the special class, the pupils acquired habits of obedience, punctuality, attentiveness, and cooperation; each one was important to their future job success.[14]

Most of the students enrolled in public school special classes were identified as borderline cases or morons and were placed in an ungraded setting. St. Louis, Missouri, and Dayton, Ohio, provided another type of school for children below the moron classification who had the potential for completing the third grade. Minneapolis had the more typical arrangement: a program for students with IQ's ranging from 50 to 80 and placed into groups labeled, pre-primary, primary, intermediate, advanced I, advanced II, and junior high. Mental ability, chronological age, scholastic achievement, and social adjustment determined the student's group placement. Through habit and manual training aimed at making each student employable, the pupil advanced until reaching his or her highest level."[15]

Before World War II, the special class had a limited impact. There was a shortage of personnel capable of training the deficient and through indifference or lack of funds and public support, many parts of the country remained unaffected. Still, the special class marked an advance in the care of the retarded in the community. It enhanced the image of the deficient by showing that they could complete a school program and find a productive place in society. Through the special class the public school became involved in rehabilitation and it was led into a new and closer relationship with the state school for the deficient, a development which recalled S. Gridley Howe's depiction of the ideal institution as "a link in the chain of common schools."

In preparing students for life in the community, both institutional and public school authorities believed that the retardate was receptive to positive moral influences, a perspective sharply different from the late nineteenth-century view of the feeble-minded individual as an innately vicious person. The moral career of the retarded, they argued, should be guided by church, civic, and welfare groups as well as school authorities. And the ideal setting for moral training was a supportive and supervised environment which sheltered the deficient from "evil companions" and other "destructive influences"; it also provided the atmosphere in which the retarded could develop such personal attributes as cheerfulness, perseverance, and honesty.[16] A clear implication of this training was the recognition of the importance of environmental factors in molding behavior.

In the 1930's, a chorus of investigators claimed that the environment was the most important element in shaping the conduct of the retarded.[17] The research conducted by Harold M. Skeels and his associates at the Iowa Child Welfare Research Station and the University of Iowa lent support to an environmental etiology by challenging the notion that intelligence was constant and unaffected by social influences. His work showed that a person's IQ could be manipulated in either a positive or a negative way. One study, for example, involved placing an experimental group of thirteen mentally retarded infants on a ward with brighter, older girls. A contrasting group of twelve normal and dull normal infants was kept in a more deprived setting having few opportunities for play and development. At the end of two years, the mean intelligence of the experimental group increased while that of the contrast group decreased. In effect, children provided with stimulating contacts with adults developed higher IQ's than children denied positive interaction with older people.[18] Skeels concluded:

A change from mental retardation to normal intelligence in children of preschool age is possible in the absence of organic disease or physiological deficiency by providing a more adequate psychological prescription. Conversely, children of normal intelligence may become mentally retarded to such a degree as to be classifiable as feeble-minded under the continued adverse influence of a relatively unstimulating environment.[19]

Skeels presented his findings at the 1939 annual convention of the American Association on Mental Deficiency and created a major professional debate, a controversy that has persisted to the present day.[20]

The defective delinquent, a double handicapped person, also received the attention of researchers who frequently reported that a wretched, limited home milieu fostered criminal behavior; on the other hand, a mentally deficient child brought up in a positive family atmosphere did not become a delinquent. This perspective received support from the studies of William Healy, a progressive psychiatrist, and Augusta F. Bronner, a prominent psychologist. Early in the twentieth century, Healy and Bronner dominated the fields of social psychiatry and psychology, and their work showed that delinquency was a complex social problem, the result of many causes. Their studies demonstrated that mental deficiency was not a main source of crime. Indeed, they argued that in a wholesome environment coupled with "good training," the mentally deficient person was "no more susceptible to becoming delinquent" than a normal individual.[21]

Significant work and research on the problems of delinquency and retardation issued particularly from the Wayne County Training School in Michigan. It opened in 1926 and by the mid–1930's had gained a national reputation for ameliorating the disturbed behavior of select groups of high-level deficient children. The school prepared each pupil for early return to the community. Its student body consisted largely of twelve- and thirteen-year-old boys and girls with an average IQ of 67, and many were identified as "troublesome burdens" to welfare and correctional agencies. To meet this situation, rehabilitation efforts concentrated on remedial reading, trade training, achievement therapy, group and individual psychotherapy, impromptu music exercises, and extensive social programs. The school aimed at making each pupil into an independent, self-motivating person capable of functioning well with peers and adults.

The staff complemented the varied classroom and therapeutic activities with a vigorous research program covering an array of topics in education, psychology, and medicine. A sample of subjects included nocturnal enuresis in an institution for children, speech training and the mentally retarded, reading disabilities, the brain-injured mentally deficient child, the variability of intelligence quotients, the group behavior of the retarded child, and the effect of "benzedrin" on mentally deficient children.[22] This kind of research represented the vanguard in the field of mental retardation care, and it provided the evidence to support the rehabilitative perspective and activities of the Wayne County Training School.

While the higher-level retarded increasingly found accommodation in the community and in special classes, the less hopeful cases remained in the state schools, the traditional places of care where custodial concerns dominated institutional life. Harvey M. Watkins, Superintendent of the Polk State School, Pennsylvania, for example, observed that 80 percent of the children at his institution represented imbecile and idiot classifications and were best handled with work assignments. The children engaged in domestic, farm, and industrial tasks, and Watkins especially favored the training of the higher–grade children to care for the idiots. Only a small number of residents went on parole. In 1931, only eighty-eight persons, out of a school population of over twenty-seven hundred, returned to the community to live with relatives.[23]

Other professionals confirmed the observation of Watkins that the state institution was a depository for the most severe and in many instances troublesome cases of mental deficiency. For some workers, however, this was not a drawback but a challenge, and at several places they initiated important innovations and changes which brought better care to their clients.

A unique experiment in family care was administered by

Charles L. Vaux, Superintendent of the Newark State School, who placed over one hundred of the institution's residents, with an average IQ of 50, in private homes in the village of Walworth, New Jersey. Assigned to families sensitive to the needs of the retarded, the boarders learned and performed such household chores as potato peeling and setting the table; they had an active social life at a community center, and a practical nurse handled their medical needs. Vaux argued that family care satisfied the interests of each concerned party, the child, the family, the institution, and the state. It gave the child more freedom; the family had an outlet for its altruism; the institution was relieved of some custodial cases; and family care provided the state with an inexpensive way of handling the retarded, a method far cheaper than building new facilities.[24]

A successful training experience with a group of imbecile girls at Letchworth Village, Thiells, New York, represented another expression of concern for improving the quality of institutional care. The girls could not dress and undress themselves; they were always dirty and unkempt, and frequently they created noisy disturbances that irritated matrons and attendants. This experiment required that a girl be able to walk to class and use at least one hand. She was first taught how to unbutton clothing: the teacher held her hands over those of the child and pushed the button through the hole, an act repeated many times before the girl could do it without assistance. At the end of three months, the girls could dress and undress themselves as well as attend to their personal needs. With this success, the experiment evolved into a knitting and crocheting program which provided the girls with permanent work, supplying materials for the school.[25] Here was a demonstration that imbeciles could improve their habits and appearance and become producers. It elicited a concern similar to the dedication given to pupils of the antebellum experimental schools.

Recreational and music programs improved institutional morale. Administrators insisted that children needed activities to develop confidence and social skills, noting that many of the mentally deficient had been robbed of home and community play. The research of play therapists showed that an aggressive recreational program brightened a school's atmosphere. Movies, ball games, scouting, hiking, ministrel shows, and musical plays made children happier and reduced the number of discipline problems. By contrast, when institutionalized children remained idle, they constantly fought and quarreled with each other, and destroyed property.[26]

One of the most difficult and constant issues confronting state institutions was finding an effective staff to care for the residents. C. S. Little, Superintendent of Letchworth Village, reflecting in 1923 on his twenty-five-year administrative career, observed a sharp contrast between the employee of his time and the worker of yesteryear. In the past, he claimed, institutional employees were guided by a strong sense of dedication and loyalty. They developed personal friendships with residents, attended promptly to their needs, assured their neatness, kept rooms and floors clean, and slept in areas off the wards. Now, Little asserted, the typical employee was inadequate, insensitive, and mercenary. Whether employees had become more self-serving and incompetent was a moot point, but one fact remained: in many states they worked a twelve-hour day, six days a week, and received a wage below that of an unskilled worker.[27]

Long hours and low pay invariably caused a rapid turnover of personnel, a problem particularly acute in Southern institutions. The source of the problem of insufficient funding, Southern superintendents believed, rested with legislators who viewed all mentally retarded persons as custodial cases. Without understanding or appreciation for the variety and the plight of the mentally retarded, these public policy makers assumed little responsibility for the care of the deficient. One curtly argued that it was "a waste of energy and money to attempt to do anything for individuals who had no brains."[28]

Medical research lagged at institutions and for good reasons: only a few places had pathologists, and superintendents were too preoccupied with administrative matters to become involved in research projects. A dearth of medical activity may also be attributed to the segregation of the retarded from society, and to the fact that mental deficiency rarely demanded emergency treatment or heroic crisis intervention. The condition lacked drama or excitement, an ingredient often necessary to stimulate a medical imagination to search for a way to relieve distress.

Another general factor which hampered medical science was the wide publicity given to the purported connection between retardation and heredity. The popular studies of the Nam family, the Jukes, and the Kallikaks emphasized the part heredity played in causing retardation. Early twentieth-century professional opinion supplied these studies with statements and testimony attributing most cases of mental deficiency to poor heredity. This overpowering popular and professional dogma went largely unchallenged until the 1920's, and it left little need or room for medical inquiry. Indeed, medicial intervention was neither possible nor desirable when 90 percent of all cases of mental deficiency had a purported family linkage. Medical research was also discouraged by the enthusiasm for mental testing and the psychological ramifications of retardation which, inadvertently, downgraded the biological aspects of deficiency. The prevailing educational model of retardation diverted research interests away from physiology to areas related to the teaching and controlling of clients.[29]

In the 1920's and 1930's, medical findings revealed that many mentally retarded persons were biologically defective, having unusual pathology or brain damage. Research also pointed to the susceptibility of the retarded to infectious diseases, notably those affecting the respiratory system. Tuberculosis, according to some studies, occurred most frequently among individuals with a low IQ.[30] Other investigators found that life expectancy related directly to a person's intelligence. A 1931 study showed that the average normal male lived about fifty-seven years but the male idiot only twenty years, the male imbecile about thirty years, and the male moron fifty-two years.[31]

Physicians had two common complaints regarding mental retardation care. They noted that the terms—idiot, imbecile, and moron—were convenient designations which facilitated institutional routines but revealed little about etiology or pathology. Along with the unscientific classifications of feeble-mindedness, they pointed to another troublesome problem which hampered treatment—the retarded person's low level of self-

awareness and self-preservation. A mentally deficient individual might ignore or accept such general warnings of sickness
as a chill, a cough, a headache, a visual disturbance, a loss of
weight. This insensitivity to one's own physical self coupled with
a short memory and poor communication skills thwarted medical care.[32]

In a period when the prestige of psychiatry was growing, administrators of state schools increasingly brought mental health
specialists into the institutions, chiefly to resolve practical problems. In some states, for example, the mentally deficient were
sent to mental hospitals, and to facilitate the proper placement
of patients a psychiatric liaison between school and hospital was
necessary. Also the diagnosis of young problem children required professional expertise; often blurred distinctions existed
between mental illness and retardation. Mental illness could be
masked in mental deficiency, and psychiatric observation would
clarify the matter.

But psychiatry still had little constructive to offer. Treatment
options for the psychiatrically impaired persons were limited by
the prevailing assumption that retardation stunted emotional
development. In other words, mental deficiency narrowed a
person's capacity to suffer from mental illness. If a low IQ individual had fewer mental conflicts than a brighter person, then
clinicians of the interwar period concluded that there was no
need for special therapy. The traditional ways of training the
retarded in a sheltered environment would suffice.[33]

The great economic depression of the 1930's created new
hardships for the mentally deficient. Institutional budgets were
slashed; plans for expansion were dropped; and all projects were
sharply cut back. Public schools curtailed special education
programs and often dumped the retarded into large consoli-
dated classes made up of all sorts of handicapped children.
Parolees took the hardest blows; financially strained families
returned them to institutions and others came back after losing
work. Residents awaiting parole could not find employment
because a large number of jobless mentally deficient people
languished in the community.[34] As a social worker noted in 1934:
"Your feebleminded clog the wheels and we can't do anything
for them."[35] The federal government offered some relief, pro-

viding jobs in CCC camps. Federal funds supported projects for repairing and remodeling state schools and for upgrading staffs. The Rome State School, New York, for example, received a federal grant to train one hundred high school graduates and college students on the care of retarded children.[36] The Rome grant did not mark the beginning of a new federal policy of caring for the mentally deficient. It was merely part of a massive government effort at relieving unemployment, a major problem of the economically depressed 1930's.

During World War II, mental retardation care continually deteriorated and at many places grim, oppressive conditions developed. These were years of neglect when the country faced the large issues of survival and defense and could easily overlook and ignore the needs of its mentally retarded citizens. The harsh picture of life at the Rainier State School, Buckley, Washington, reflected institutional realities throughout the country. Inadequate and insufficient equipment and rooms, a shortage of key personnel, including teachers and psychologists, and limited training and educational programs created a snake-pit atmosphere. There was a frank admission that the institution was "crowded beyond the point of decency and humanitarianism for children." A special problem involved caring for the needs of children with multiple handicaps and afflictions; administrators noted that two hundred attendants were needed to handle the epileptic, crippled, and enuretic cases.[37] This dismal scene was similar to the conditions existing in many state mental hospitals and in the immediate postwar years critics demanded institutional reform and the dissolution of all large custodial establishments.[38]

A major professional concern was the impact of institutionalization upon residents. Research findings on this problem revealed largely negative effects: in one study both young and old residents declined in IQ with their length of stay; other investigators found that short-term residents scored higher on verbal tests than long-term inmates. A comparative study of institutional and noninstitutional groups showed that the institutionalized had more negative values toward self and others than those persons who remained at home. Another experiment removed children from an institution to a home-like setting where they were encouraged to talk and play with housemothers. After several months, these children scored higher on speech and sound tests than a similar group which stayed behind in the institution. Numerous sociological studies concluded that institutions characterized by a rigid conformity to rules and routines, an excessive demand for maintaining order, and an atmosphere of depersonalization adversely affected the social relations of the resident children.[39] All of this research confirmed a professional opinion that the institution, notably the large understaffed facility, created an environment detrimental to the care and development of retarded persons. These findings were consonant with other negative evaluations of institutionalization in the postwar years exemplified by Erving Goffman's well-known book *Asylums*.

The pressure and power of parents groups eventually became another important force in the movement to upgrade institutions. Parent associations evolved slowly. Organizational efforts may have been frustrated by feelings of guilt, shame, and fear as well as a reluctance to bring out into the open the problems of rearing a retarded family member. In 1932, the Council for the Retarded Children of Cuyahoga County, one of the first parent organizations, was established in Cleveland. A few other organizations emerged in the thirties, and an increasing number of local groups were established after World War II. In 1950, ninety delegates representing twenty-three parent groups in fourteen states met in Minneapolis to draft a constitution for a national organization. This was the founding convention of the National Association of Parents and Friends of Retarded Children, later known as the National Association for Retarded Children. Formally established in February 1951, it grew rapidly and became a powerful pressure group, demanding that training and rehabilitation replace custodial care in institutions.[40] This development paralleled the growth of special disease and social problem organizations which flourished in mid-twentieth-century America.[41]

A major change in the population of state schools stimulated the involvement of parental pressure groups in the delivery of mental retardation care. The new trend was an increase in the number of young, severely mentally deficient children, and it was most pronounced in Eastern, Midwestern, and Pacific Coast states. It represented a post–World War II development: before 1945, teenage morons accounted for the largest proportion of first admissions; after the war, their number decreased while that of young imbeciles and idiots increased. The data also showed an increase in clinical cases, notably microcephalics, hydrocephalics, and other cranial anomalies. All of these changes were apparent in New York institutions between 1950 and 1958 when the moron group increased by about four hundred cases and the idiots and imbeciles by almost thirty-three hundred. In the mid–1950's, seven out of ten residents in the New York system were classified in the lower mental status ranges. The age pattern followed the national trend, pointing to an increase in residents between five and fourteen years and over thirty-five years. This change reflected the nation's high birthrate during and immediately after World War II, and the advances in medicine which increased the life span of the severely and profoundly retarded. It also indicated that the mildly retarded found work and social acceptance in the community and did not need the institution to service their needs.[42]

A dependent and senescent resident population cast the institution in a custodial role where the maintenance of the inmates became the overwhelming concern. Disturbed by this state of affairs, particularly the downgrading of training and rehabilitation programs, parental groups aimed at improving and brightening the institutional atmosphere. The National Association for Retarded Children, for example, identified the ideal state school as a residential place devoted to the happiness of children. Guided by a sympathetic and affectionate staff, it would provide a multiplicity of services and facilities designed to train each child to his or her highest level. This was the ideal and the association urged parents to direct efforts toward achieving it at their children's state school.[43] It was a familiar refrain. In the new institutional population complex, however, it was a demand to apply to the less endowed residents the attention and effort previously given to the moron class, the most hopeful cases.

Beginning in the 1950's, parental pressures for upgrading state schools brought increased attention to a need for providing ser-

vices to the severely retarded in the community. Throughout
the country, a number of mental retardation workers were sensitive to this need and inaugurated programs for the lower–level
retardate. These efforts varied in scope, method, and activity
but produced evidence which refuted a popular premise that
the severely retarded person was nontrainable. The programs
ranged from speech improvement to recreation to toilet training and reached a common finding: the chief obstacle to effective learning was a child's short attention span. On the other
hand, the chances for a student's success improved with an optimistic staff, the establishment of a warm, positive relationship
between child and therapist, the continual praise of participants, and a recognition that the children will show only limited and slow improvement. For some workers, the encouraging results of these programs presented a tantalizing challenge
that perhaps retardates at all levels could be trained. They held
a conviction that with help any mentally retarded person could
live a fuller, better, and more constructive life than he or she
presently did.[44]

This hope and enthusiasm found expression in new counseling services for parents. At clinics and in schools, professional
staffs frequently encountered parents who had difficulty accepting retardation in their children. They believed that parental attitudes shaped a child's personality, and it was important
that a family not only accept the retarded child but promote his
or her adjustment within the home and the community.[45] In
response to this problem, mental retardation workers coun-
seled parents, urging them to participate in group therapy. The
group experience, it was argued, dissipated feelings of inade-
quacy and guilt and encouraged family members to share problems with sympathetic persons in an open, tolerant atmosphere. In short, it enabled participants to accept the diagnosis
of retardation and begin making long-range plans for their child's
future.[46]

Vocational training once again, in the 1950's, became a major
thrust of care, and a new community agency—the sheltered
workshop—had a rapid growth. It facilitated job adjustment and
improved the skills of the retarded clientele. Throughout the
decade, educators called for a new approach to vocational
training, arguing that the traditional efforts did not prepare the

retarded for the world of work. They did not simply need remedial courses, or a watered–down version of a program for
normal children, or instruction in learning a trade. Instead,
training must focus on each pupil's personality development, a
recommendation based on research which showed that successful and satisfactory employment rested on an individual's
social adequacy.[47]

Here was a new twist to vocational training, and the finding
was applied to the curriculum: while the acquisition of academic– or job–related skills remained an important aim, educators maintained that the most effective programs encouraged
and enabled the retardate to become a socially competent person, someone acceptable to the community. The goal of mental
retardation training was, as T. G. Hegge, an educator, commented in 1953, "the prevention of social failure," and social
competency was achieved by habilitation, a developmental
method of training. Rehabilitation implied overcoming an injury, handicap, or disease; in contrast, habilitation meant accepting an individual's limitations and by slow and gradual
means elevating that person to his or her highest possible level.
It involved identifying and removing obstacles of self-improvement and providing a shield to protect the retardate from isolation and exploitation. This protective umbrella included such
community services as a recreation center, a club for adults, or
a sheltered workshop, all of which facilitated the attainment of
the basic goal—helping the retardate to make a positive contribution to society.[48]

The concern over the personality growth and the social adjustment of the retardate was complemented by still further increase of psychiatric interest in the care of the retarded, a development emerging out of World War II studies and reports
on mentally deficient soldiers. This research showed that a large
number of retarded servicemen were incapacitated by mental
illness. Many recovered, however, when placed in a supportive and secure environment devoid of stress and rapid change.
One observer noted:

It is apparent . . . that many mentally deficient men may be effectively utilized, and when necessary, rehabilitated, if they are treated
with kindness and understanding; suitably placed in accordance with

their limitations; and not subjected to frequent changes with the necessity for making rapid adjustment to new duties even if those duties
are relatively uncomplicated . . . . Our army hospital experience in
dealing with these men when they are in all degrees of upheaval, including psychotic episodes, would demonstrate that a reasonably secure environment will produce quite rapid, positive effects.[49]

Other reports claimed that disordered personalities could be
detected by using such new projective techniques as the The-
matic Apperception Test and the Rorshach. From these and other
studies, a common etiological pattern emerged: the high–grade
mentally retarded person suffering from emotional disorder was
an ego-crippled individual, a condition caused by a life pattern
of rejection and humiliation which bred resentments and frustrations, culminating in mental illness. All of this research challenged the older view of the deficient individual as an emotionally insensitive person; psychoses were now found at all levels
of retardation and some observers asserted that the incidence
of mental illness among the mentally deficient was much higher
than in the general population.[50]

At mid-century, the therapeutics of mental health care fused
with the treatments for the retarded. A unique situation developed. This era stands as one of the most creative periods in the
history of American mental health care; milieu therapy, varied
psychotherapeutic measures, and psychopharmacology had a
special impact, altering the thrust and direction of the care of
both the mentally ill and the mentally retarded. Milieu therapy,
or the concept of the therapeutic community, involved creating
an institutional environment in which every staff member, from
the medical to the nonprofessional, interacted with patients to
facilitate recovery. The cleanliness of rooms, the arrangement
of furniture, the color of walls, and other elements in the physical setting bore directly on patient well-being. Treatment was
an ongoing process and never limited to a half hour a day or
week. Milieu therapy, in effect, required continuous work and
demanded a total institutional effort at restoring the patient's
health.[51]

Personnel of California state hospitals, for example, reported
that they applied milieu therapy to groups of mentally re-

tarded, emotionally disturbed persons. With one group of children, the IQ's ranged from 18 to 88, and a team composed of
a psychiatrist, a psychologist, a social worker, a chaplain, and
several mental health technicians supervised the project. The
staff created an atmosphere conductive to emotional growth, a
supportive noncritical environment where each child felt the
warmth of adult contacts. Frequent conferences evaluated the
progress of the patients; emphasis was placed on maintaining
spontaneous interpersonal relations with them, focusing on their
present needs and concerns.

This total approach was applied to merit or achievement wards
at state schools for the retarded. While milieu therapy created
an emotionally corrective environment for the recovery of the
mentally ill, the merit ward offered an educationally corrective
setting for the training of the mentally deficient. Oriented around
a reward-punishment system, the merit ward was a segregated
place where residents received privileges in return for assuming greater responsibilities. The staff observed the adaptability
and ability of the students and instilled in them a feeling of self-
confidence. As in the earliest experimental schools, the purpose of the merit ward was still the preparation of the clients
for life and work in the community.[52]

Psychotherapy captured a following among professional
workers who viewed the retarded person as an ego–stunted individual suffering from inferiority, shame, and withdrawal.
While this condition might be diagnosed as a personality disorder caused by living in an oppressive and bleak environment, psychotherapists argued that an inadequate ego development was a general characteristic of many retarded persons.
A psychological method of treatment offered a way of improving and salvaging the worth of this type of individual. Its ad-
vocates focused on building a positive self-image, a process
deemed best accomplished by group therapy. A group setting,
it was argued, encouraged socialization, permitted the controlled release of impulses and aggression, and reduced a person's feelings of fear and isolation. Occupational psychotherapy became an adjunct to the group experiences and aimed at
creating feelings of satisfaction and industry. It did not matter
what type or amount of work was accomplished; the important

factor was forming new behavioral patterns which bolstered the ego and fostered better relationships with others. In the early and mid–1950's, numerous studies produced encouraging results showing that retarded patients responded and benefitted from individual and group psychotherapy. A major obstacle to success, therapists lamented, was overcoming the stereotype of the retarded individual as a drooling idiot, an emotionally insensitive person incapable of relating to others.[53]

In the state schools and institutions, psychotherapy was found useful in conjunction with new drug treatments. Thorazine, a tranquilizing agent, was the most effective drug, and it and others were used with great success for combative, hyperactive, untidy, and destructive patients. Under medication, they became calm and cooperative and worked well with others. Their destructive tendencies diminished, creating a quieter atmosphere on the wards. Most important, their attention span lengthened, making them more receptive to training and instruction. By improving behavior, drug therapy not only facilitated the work of administrators of the defiant and disturbed, it also permitted difficult retarded children to live at home.[54]

In 1960, the election of John F. Kennedy to the presidency brought a favorable political opportunity for advancing mental retardation care. JFK had a special interest in mental retardation stemming from personal involvement with his retarded sister Rosemary. In the past, the health concerns of presidential families alerted the country to major medical problems: Franklin D. Roosevelt publicized polio and Dwight D. Eisenhower dramatized the danger of heart disease. The Kennedy family focused national attention on retardation. Throughout the 1950's, it funded treatment and maintained contacts with leading researchers and clinicians.

Soon after assuming office, John F. Kennedy engaged the federal government in mental retardation programs. He created the President's Panel on Mental Retardation, a special fact-finding task force which deliberated throughout the winter, spring, and summer of 1962 and issued a final report in October. Three needs were identified: research, a system of service to provide a "continuum of care," and social action to prevent mental retardation. To facilitate research, the report called for the establishment of university-centered research institutes. To create a "continuum of care," it recommended the integration of medical, educational, and social services into a central facility connected with such local agencies as schools and churches. Here an interdisciplinary team would concentrate on minimizing the disability of the retarded person.[55]

To deal with prevention, the report stressed the importance of finding ways to overcome cultural deprivation. It asserted that the stunted development of many children of the poor resulted from being subjected to such adverse factors as low income, inadequate medical care, family breakdown, poor parental education and guidance, and a social milieu of low aspirations. While its major finding, the high correlation between incidence of retardation and deprived or low socioeconomic status, posed a massive preventive dilemma involving the reconstruction of society over a long period of time, the report did recommend measures for modifying and correcting the problem. These included programs for alleviating distress and equalizing opportunity, notably expanded health and community services, vocational rehabilitation, unemployment compensation, and urban renewal projects. The report also emphasized the importance of the child care center, a place devoted to enrichment programs which instilled new and positive attitudes and skills in children. Above all, a full-scale attack on adverse environmental conditions was, the 1962 report concluded, "our greatest hope for a major victory over mental retardation."[56]

While the White House and federal agencies, notably in HEW, followed up the presidential report by preparing legislation, Kennedy, in a special message to Congress in February 1963, linked the care of the mentally ill with that of the mentally retarded and called for a "bold new approach" to resolve the twin problems of mental illness and mental retardation. These "critical health problems . . . occur more frequently, affect more people, require more prolonged treatment, cause more suffering by the families of the afflicted, waste more of our human resources, and constitute more financial drain upon both the Public Treasury and the personal finances of the individual families than any other single condition."[57]

Taking cues from the 1962 presidential report, Kennedy's

program embraced three objectives: to find the causes of illness and retardation and eradicate them, to train and expand the number of personnel who care for the retarded, and to strengthen and improve programs and facilities. On this last point, his message stressed the desirability of community-based facilities. The mentally retarded especially needed a community agency which provided "diagnostic, health, educational, training, rehabilitation, employment, welfare, and legal protection services." When such institutions were created, Kennedy envisioned, "reliance on the cold mercy of custodial isolation will be supplanted by the open warmth of community concern and capability. Emphasis on prevention, treatment, and rehabilitation will be substituted for a desultory interest in confining patients to an institution to wither away." He held out the promise of a dramatic breakthrough, noting that "we stand on the threshold of major advances in this field."[58]

The efforts of the Kennedy Administration were rewarded with the passage of the Mental Retardation Facilities and Community Mental Health Centers Construction Act of 1963. It allocated funds to train teachers of the mentally handicapped and to construct research centers as well as clinical facilities for treating retarded persons. The act marked an important advance in federal mental retardation programs. In short, with the Kennedy Administration, mental retardation became a federal health policy and a social reform issue.[59]

Reform drives and radical agitation persisted throughout the mid and late 1960's. This was a tumultuous era of protest and rising expectations and many mental retardation workers acquired a new sense of purpose and dedication which reflected much of the furor and commitment expressed in antiwar demonstrations, civil rights protests, and the war on poverty. In their vision, retardation was a social problem, a fact of life common to the lower socioeconomic levels of American society. Their view was supported by numerous studies and research projects specifying poverty as the prime cause of both mental illness and mental retardation.[60]

Optimistic about solving social problems and preventing retardation, mental retardation workers turned their hopes into demands intertwined with a complex of issues agitating na-

tional life. Appeals from the rostrums of professional organizations called for the involvement of all members in the reso-
lution of contemporary social problems.[61] Richard Koch, in his
1969 presidential address at the annual convention of the
American Association on Mental Deficiency, convening in San
Francisco, directed a sharp rhetorical question to the membership: "Why should an organization such as ours have had such
little social conscience, when day in and day out we deal with
the products of that social neglect?"[62] He attributed 75 percent
of all cases of handicapped children to poverty and called for a
major effort of the profession at ending the war in Vietnam,
correcting racism, and economic deprivation.[63] Koch and others dramatized the retarded as "environmentally damaged individuals," whose numbers would be sharply reduced only by
eliminating poverty and discrimination.[64] Clearly, the retarded
were no longer viewed as a menace requiring incarceration or
sterilization; they had become once again a problem of education and social welfare.

The drive for social change intensified the demand for community-based facilities, accelerating the movement away from
large state institutions. Deinstitutionalization became a popular
and professional cry and it was frequently accompanied with
charges of dehumanization and warehousing. Institutions were
depicted as archaic places enveloped in a lifeless, empty atmosphere of routine and monotony. The demand for decarceration or deinstitutionalization called for community-based corrections and noninstitutional treatment of the mentally ill as well
as neighborhood residences for the retarded.[65]

The concept of normalization provided a rationale for phas-
ing out large facilities for the developmentally disabled. Initiated and promoted by Bengt Nirje of the Swedish Association
for Retarded Children, and implemented throughout Scandi-
navia, normalization represented a cluster of assumptions and
ideas, and it captured a large following among American mental retardation workers. Nirje insisted that normalization applied to every retarded person regardless of age, sex, degree of
handicap, and home or institutional setting. It meant providing
and assuring a normal life by encouraging a daily routine of such
mundane tasks as getting out of bed, dressing, and eating as

well as facilitating movement from home to work to places of
leisure and recreation. Too often, Nirje noted, the retarded were
confined to a building, creating an abnormal environment which
thwarted a natural desire to explore the community. Normalization stressed the importance of treating the retarded as normal persons: they should not be sent to bed earlier than their
peers; they should utilize community agencies and facilities
rather than remain dependent on special settings; they should
enjoy the normal rhythm of the year including holidays, family
days, and vacations. Normalization fostered the development
of the retarded at each stage of life: preschool children required
direction, warmth, and security; the social and educational atmosphere of the school was as vital to the health of the retarded as it was to normal youths; achieving independent living was a normal goal, and retarded young adults should be
trained and encouraged to become as self-sufficient as possible.

Nirje's concept also meant taking input from the retarded
themselves, showing respect for their choices and desires. It
accepted the mixing of the sexes and approved of marriage
among the mildly retarded. Economic normalcy entailed giving
the retarded the basic monetary rewards and privileges available to others, including allowances and pensions, and if employed in a sheltered workshop or a private business, the retarded employee should receive a salary equal to that of an
average person completing the same work. Normalization further demanded that the same standards of hygiene, maintenance, and design for physical plants of hospitals, schools, and
other public facilities be applied to institutions for the retarded,
and in planning for the future, any new building should always relate to its neighborhood and never be isolated solely because it would house retarded persons.[66]

Normalization represented a statement of rights and benefits
of the retarded person as a citizen and a human being; it asserted that the retarded individual had the same basic rights as
other citizens. It contrasted with paternalism and the long-
standing belief of many workers that restricted routines best
developed a retardate's potential and equanimity. This normalization perspective became the professional ideology of the 1970's
and many mental retardation workers labored enthusiastically

at making it a reality.[67] At the 1974 annual convention of the American Association on Mental Deficiency, David Rosen, president of the organization, observed that the most distinguishing feature of the 1970's was "a campaign for human rights," and he called for the aid and cooperation of parents, professionals, and lawyers in securing a fundamental right for the retarded, a right "to return and reside in neighborhoods with the rest of us." He recognized that this goal was not attainable through the traditional institution, and that most communities did not have sufficient facilities for their developmentally disabled citizens. Rosen urged direct action, recommending legal moves against authorities for failing to provide adequate resources.[68]

Several legal rulings and cases had, in fact, altered the civil rights and the care of the mentally retarded. The practice of employing institutional residents without pay, often labeled involuntary servitude or institutional peonage, was challenged. A sentence of involuntary incarceration of a retarded person deemed incompetent was struck down as an unconstitutional denial of due process. The Supreme Court ruled that involuntary sterilization was an infringement of the right to procreate. Most important, in a 1972 Federal District Court decision, *Wyatt* v. *Stickney*, involving the residents of two mental hospitals and an institution for the retarded, Judge Frank M. Johnson of Alabama established "the right to treatment and habilitation," justifying confinement only if an institution met approved standards of care. As a result, programs and facilities were upgraded and many residents were sent to community habilitation places. Other rulings created institutional standards for staff-patient ratios and nutrition, and established the right to a least restrictive alternative setting. This meant that the retarded individual had the right to be free of restrictions, and in an environment where services were similar to those for regular nonhandicapped persons.[69]

Education came under legal scrutiny, notably in two landmark cases, *Pennsylvania Association for Retarded Children* v. *Commonwealth of Pennsylvania*, best known as the PARC case, and *Mills* v. *Board of Education*. In 1971, the Pennsylvania Association for Retarded Children contested a policy of excluding re-

tarded children from public schools. While declaring the practice unsound, a federal district court stated that most
developmentally disabled persons were capable of attaining self-
sufficiency through education and training, and the earlier a
program began the more thoroughly the child benefitted. The
case resulted in opening free public education to all Pennsylvania children guaranteeing the right of due process to parents
and a child before a school administration altered the child's
educational status. The same conclusions were reached in *Mills*
v. *Board of Education*, involving the public school system of the
District of Columbia where authorities failed to provide education or training to all exceptional children and used such devices as excluding, expelling, suspending, and transferring exceptional children from regular classes without due process.

The success of the PARC and Mills rulings led to the filing of
other right-to-education cases and further support for the
handicapped came from Congress with the passage of the Rehabilitation Act of 1973, the Education for All Handicapped
Children Act of 1975, and the Developmental Disabilities Assistance and Bill of Rights Act of 1975. This legislation constituted
a major step toward securing the civil rights of the handicapped and included affirmative action measures and guidelines for implementing nondiscriminatory practices. The Bill of
Rights Act authorized grant support for planning, coordinat-
ing, and delivering services, and it specified that the retarded
had the right to treatment and habilitation in a setting designed
to maximize the potential of the individual.[70]

In the late 1970's and early 1980's, the basic thrust of mental
retardation care remained in the area of human rights. Professionals expressed a guarded optimism about the future and for
good reasons. There were problems: callous and insensitive
practices and attitudes persisted; in some areas, resistance to
housing the developmentally disabled in the community became a formidable obstacle; also, a reaction set in against the
rhetoric and practices of the community movement of the early
1970's when workers, anxious to legitimize new programs and
capture political support, aroused high expectations which could
not be fulfilled. As Gerald Caplan has noted, the expansive
claims and promises of the community mental health move-

ment, a prerequisite for political backing, generated overconfidence and created unattainable goals.[71] This may be an inevitable problem in the inauguration of any new health care or human services delivery system.

Still, the court rulings and legislation of the seventies and early eighties established the legal framework for enforcing the principle of normalization, returning many retarded persons to their home communities. Waiting lists of state schools were shortened, and institutions modified their custodial image, becoming training, diagnostic, and socialization centers where back wards were eliminated and habilitative services were offered at every level of disability. New types of facilities proliferated, notably family care homes, group homes, halfway houses, placement and counseling centers, along with programs directed at fostering independent community living. Mental retardation workers expected and demanded that the developmentally disabled themselves assume more responsibilities and direction for their lives. With this positive and dynamic view of their clientele, professionals focused on mainstreaming the retarded with normal persons in the schools and the community.

7
Conclusion

This has been a remarkable story about American society and its most unfortunate and luckless persons—the mentally retarded. It has been an excursion across the border of the everyday normal world and into the realm of unique environments, notably, the experimental school, the "village of the simple," and more recently, the sheltered workshop and the supervised independent home in the community. In each setting, the residents were governed by rules different from those applied to the outside world. They lived at a slow pace and followed a structured regimen which facilitated the attainment of goals commensurate with their abilities. Enveloped in this noncompetitive atmosphere removed from the dynamics of society, their institutions represented environments of concern, not convenience, and each one offered a supportive milieu for the residents, a place which afforded them relief and protection from clashes with society.

The sheltered facility has remained the constant in the history of American mental retardation care. To the pre–Civil War administrator, the experimental school shielded students from awkward community encounters and created a special learning environment in which pupils were trained to work and live harmoniously with others. At the end of the nineteenth century, superintendents designed an independent world for their wards, a self-sufficient facility physically and psychologically remote from society. Since World War II, mental retardation workers have built environments of solace and regeneration where clients received encouragement and assistance on how to become better citizens. In every instance, the institution, whether a school, a colony, or a community agency, controlled, sheltered, and trained persons who could not survive or function independently in society.

This status, this perceived need for a special environment to cushion the blows of society—a fact dictated by the low mental, and in some cases, physical capabilities of the retarded— has made them the most exploitable of all dependent groups. They were different from the sick, the mentally ill, and the criminal, the major dependents of society. While every disability has carried a stigma, along with an accompanying loss of social status, a basic hopeful assumption underpinned these dependencies—recovery was possible. The sick would be restored to good health, a cure would be found for the mentally ill, and the criminal would be rehabilitated. Ideally, their dependent condition was limited, temporary, and finally overcome. On the other hand, the fate of the mentally retarded was not clearly determined. While shackled to a disability which could be ameliorated but not radically changed, they were left to the trust of their caretakers who often held ambivalent feelings toward the mentally handicapped. And unlike the sick and the criminal who might demand better treatments, the retarded accepted the policies and conditions imposed on them.

Over the years this vulnerability elicited paternalistic responses from administrators who assumed that the retarded were children requiring the care, discipline, and guidance of a superintendent, a substitute father. Paternalism has pervaded the history of American mental retardation care, conferring an inferior status upon the mentally deficient. Until quite recent times, they have been patronized by normal persons who did not allow them to grow up and become adults.

Their defenselessness also made them exceedingly susceptible to outside pressures and controls which fluctuated with the changing temper of the times. The reform period before the Civil

War was an altruistic age, an era dominated by humanitarian concern for the less fortunate members of society. Imbued with confidence and optimism, administrators of the experimental schools eagerly promoted their work to the public and anticipated success in rehabilitating their most promising students. In this age, the interests of society and the institution coincided; each had a positive influence on the other.

At the end of the century, the "village of the simple" reflected an era overwrought from the tensions caused by industrialization and the growing bureaucratization of society. Labor violence, war, dramatic urban growth, and widespread dissent challenged traditional values and assumptions. Xenophobic reactions were commonplace, and isolation or segregation became a means for coping with a difficult problem. This was demonstrated by the immigration restriction drives and the enactment of Jim Crow laws as well as the movement to contain the retarded in permanent facilities. In each instance, removing the issue from the mainstream of society seemed the best option. Sensitive to the societal demand for restriction, tempered by decades of experience and disappointment, and alert to purportedly scientific studies identifying the retarded as the main cause of crime, prostitution, degeneracy, and other social problems, administrators accepted custodialism and built and maintained a separate world for the retarded themselves. More than at any other time, late nineteenth-century societal pressures and controls imposed a pariah status on the retarded, identifying them as undesirable and inferior persons who required quarantine from the community. The community viewed them as a threatening menace and demanded their permanent removal to a facility physically and psychologically distant from the everyday social world.

The temper of American society in the 1960's exerted an equally powerful impact on mental retardation care. This was an age of liberation movements, civil rights agitation, and peace demonstrations. Protestors were armed with nonnegotiable demands and a fervent righteousness and they advanced their causes by engaging in confrontation tactics. A powerful sense of rising expectations permeated every area of society. In mental retardation care, interest focused on securing the civil rights

156

of clients as well as bringing them into the normal social and
economic life of the community. Integration into society rather
than isolation from it became the major thrust of care. Now sharp
distinctions between normal people and developmentally disabled citizens were blurred. Practitioners argued that handicapped persons grew, albeit at a slower rate than normals, and
had the same needs and feelings as other members of society.

Throughout our study, a central issue, preoccupying the attention and concern of both administrators and lay persons, dealt
with determining the ultimate place of the retarded in society.
Debate on this problem first focused on the question: what was
the purpose of the institution? Consistently, the answer was
simple, obvious, and direct: the institution's objective was to
ameliorate the condition of each resident. While this mission of
the facility aroused little dissent, controversy raged over the final disposition of the retarded. In other words, a more fundamental question was posed: what was the institution's purpose
in improving the life of its residents? If the institution did indeed reach its goal, if it made the clients into better functioning
human beings, or socially and morally acceptable persons, then
where did they go? Did the improved retarded person remain
institutionalized or was that individual discharged into the
community?

In the pre–Civil War era, these questions received easy and
ready answers. The experimental schools aimed at returning their
pupils to the community. The retarded held a largely benign
position in society. There was no ambiguity, no conflict of interest between institution and community, no public resistance; administrators concentrated on achieving the stated goal
of the school. By the end of the century, however, the retarded
had been relegated to the fringes of society and identified as
outright menaces to the community. The question of whether
they could or should live outside of institutions was intensely
debated. Viewed as a threat to society, the retarded then really
had no place in the community. They were outcasts, and discussion about their disposition concentrated on the best means
of confining and controlling them.

Given this early twentieth-century perspective, the changes
of America's developmentally disabled citizens over the past fifty

years have been remarkable. Many have left the institutions and moved into the community, enrolling in public schools, finding jobs, and renting apartments. This drift into the community encountered setbacks—federal and state retrenchment policies resulted in greatly reduced programs and services, and significant local resistance to neighborhood group homes flared up in many areas.

Community opposition and hostility to the retarded has rested partly on a haunting fear of the mentally deficient, a perennial theme in our story. Initially the apprehension centered on the moral imbecile, the most undesirable type of retardate, who was first identified by Samuel Gridley Howe in the antebellum era. Howe dispelled community anxiety, however, with the argument that the moral imbecile suffered from defective "moral faculties" and could be redeemed and trained to fulfill a positive role in society. He commented that the condition resulted from "dormant or underdeveloped" moral sentiments which could be invigorated.

By 1900, this altruistic idealism had dissipated. The moral imbecile became a despicable person capable of committing any crime or act of cruelty without inhibition or remorse. This kind of retardate was held responsible for causing the country's major social ills ranging from alcoholism to prostitution. In 1904, Walter E. Fernald observed that the moral imbecile was "idle, thievish, cruel," and sexually precocious. And the prevailing opinion held that there was no cure for moral imbecility. It represented a condition beyond redemption, demanding permanent care and supervision in special custodial facilities.

Later in the twentieth century, the moral imbecile was named the defective delinquent, and the etiology underpinning the concept changed. While moral imbecility rested on a hereditarian assumption, defective delinquency held to a largely environmental base and the chances of improving the condition increased. The harsh determinism of the early 1900's was softened and once again, as in antebellum America, amelioration seemed possible, notably by placing the individual in a wholesome, constructive social setting.

Still, while historically the focus of concern has been the moral imbecile or the defective delinquent, the fear of the mentally deficient, mixed with disdain, persisted. Over the years, it has generated negative attitudes, encouraged retrenchment policies, and thwarted efforts at integrating the developmentally disabled into normal society.

Since the mid-twentieth century, the most painful problems in the care of the retarded have rested with handling the severe and profound cases, a striking parallel to the grave difficulties involved in dealing with the chronic mentally ill. On this question professional opinion has wavered between the extremes. Some have argued that any person with an IQ below 35 should be institutionalized. Releasing such individuals endangers both them and the community and may indeed be cruel since many have physical as well as mental handicaps. Yet numerous professionals have demanded the closing of institutions, insisting that even the severely disabled can be placed successfully in the community. Keeping them confined, it has been argued, not only violates their individual rights and freedom but stands as a testimony to administrative insensitivity and lack of creativity.

Another issue that polarized the profession was caring for badly deformed babies. The question has been highlighted by the growth of sophisticated delivery room procedures that permitted the survival of the many partly paralyzed or brain damaged newly born. A traditional way of handling a malformed baby was parental and, at times, unofficial medical negligence, resulting in the infant's starvation. After the mid-twentieth century, this procedure was challenged and a bewildering mix of medical, legal, and theological considerations confounded individual and institutional responsibilities.

While controversy over the disposition of the severely retarded agitated the profession and the public, optimism and confidence pervaded and guided clinicians in their care of the mild and borderline cases of the developmentally disabled. Here the slow accumulation of the work of the past half century produced encouraging results. Based on experience and research, clinicians point to a basic fact: with proper training the majority of the retarded have the potential for becoming self-supporting adults. They can master job skills, and if placed in a work situation which matches their abilities, they find satisfaction and become loyal and reliable employees.

This return of the retarded to the community, a largely mid-twentieth-century development, dramatically altered the mission of the institution. Indeed, a similar circumstance, the drive to reintegrate the mentally ill into society, changed the function and nature of the mental hospital. For over a century, insane asylums and institutions for the retarded shared a dual policy of providing therapy or training as well as offering custody for their wards. These facilities existed for changing or remodeling their clients; the objective of therapy or training was to modify the identity of the residents, making them more acceptable to society. Ideally this modification involved imposing new skills and proper behavioral patterns upon the patients. While fostering change on some of their clients, the institutions also had the custodial function of maintaining a large class of persons deemed unacceptable to the wider society. This group consisted largely of the more severe cases of mental disorder or retardation, those individuals physically and mentally incapable of surviving without major institutional support.

In recent times, as more of the retarded and mentally ill were sustained in the community, custodial or welfare work became the function of the institution. Its historic role of isolating clients from the rest of society, for their own sake and for the sake of others, and providing them with therapy or training as well as custody, was declared obsolete and inhumane. A bit of irony emerged here. With the community movement, the institution, historically at the center of care and concern, was transformed into the very type of facility its critics had condemned. It became a warehouse, a place of last resort, offering custody and subsistence to the homeless and unwanted.

Notes

INTRODUCTION

1. Leo Kanner, *A History of the Care and Study of the Mentally Retarded* (Springfield, 1964); idem, "Medicine in the History of Mental Retardation: 1800–1965," *American Journal of Mental Deficiency* 72 (1967), 165–70, (hereafter cited as *AJMD*); Stanley Powell Davies, *The Mentally Retarded in Society* (New York, 1930); Eugene E. Doll, "A Historical Survey of Research and Management of Mental Retardation in the United States," in E. Philip Trapp, ed., *Readings on the Exceptional Child* (New York, 1972), pp. 49–97; idem, "Trends and Problems in the Education of the Mentally Retarded: 1800–1940," *AJMD*, 72 (1967), 175–83; idem, "A Historical View of the Private Residential Facility in the Training and Study of the Mentally Retarded in the United States," *Mental Retardation*, 8 (1970), 3–8; B. M. Luckey, "The Contribution of Psychology to the Problems of Mental Retardation with some Implications for the Future," *AJMD*, 72 (1967), 170–75; C. Haffter, "The Changeling: History and Psychodynamics of Attitudes to Handicapped Children in European Folklore," *Journal of the History of the Behavioral Sciences*, 4 (1968), 55–61; J. E. Wallin, "Training of the Severely Retarded, viewed in Historical Perspective," *Journal of General Psychology*, 74 (1966), 107–27; Albert Deutsch, *The Mentally Ill in America: A History of Their Care and Treatment from Colonial Times* (New York, 1949), chapters 16 and 17; Robert H. Haskell, "Mental Deficiency over a Hundred Years," *American Journal of Psychiatry*, 100 (1944), 107–18; R. C. Scheerenberger, *A History of Mental Retardation* (Baltimore, 1983).

CHAPTER 1

1. Harlan Lane, *The Wild Boy of Aveyron* (Cambridge, 1976), p. 7. Lane's book, a masterful blend of historical research and psychological insight, is the best account of the events surrounding the savage and his teachers. Also see Edward (Édouard) Seguin, *Idiocy and Its Treatment by the Physiological Method* (New York, 1866), pp. 16–36; Martin W. Barr, *Mental Defectives: Their History, Treatment and Training*, 1910 ed. (Philadelphia, 1904), pp. 24–35; Leo Kanner, *A History of Care and Study of the Mentally Retarded* (Springfield, 1964), pp. 10–17.

2. Robert M. Zingg, "Feral Man and Extreme Cases of Isolation," *American Journal of Psychology*, 530 (1940), 487–517; J.A.L. Singh and Robert M. Zingg, *Wolf Children and Feral Man* (New York, 1942); Lucien Mason, *Wolf Children and the Problem of Human Nature*, trans. Edmund Fawcett, Peter Ayrton, and Joan White (New York, 1972).

3. Pierre-Joseph Bonnaterre, *Notice Historique sur le sauvage de l'Aveyron* (Paris, 1799), p. 50, quoted by Seguin, *Idiocy and Its Treatment*, p. 19. Emphasis Seguin's.

4. Lane, *Wild Boy of Aveyron*, chapter 4.

5. William Boyd, *From Locke to Montessori* (New York, 1914); George Rosen, "The Philosophy of the Ideology and the Emergence of Modern Medicine in France," *Bulletin of the History of Medicine*, 20 (1940), 328–31.

6. Ruth E. Bender, *The Conquest of Deafness*, rev. ed. (Cleveland, 1970).

7. Eric T. Carlson and Norman Dain, "The Psychotherapy that was Moral Treatment," *American Journal of Psychiatry*, 117 (1960), 519–24; Walther Reise, *The Legacy of Philippe Pinel: An Inquiry into Thought on Mental Alienation* (New York, 1964); Erwin H. Ackerknecht, *Medicine at the Paris Hospital 1794–1848* (Baltimore, 1967), pp. 47–51.

8. Jean-Marc-Gaspard Itard, *The Wild Boy of Aveyron*, trans. George and Muriel Humphrey (New York, 1932), pp. 10–11. This is from Itard's first report, "On the Education of a Man of the Wild, or the First Physical and Mental Developments of the Young Sauvage d'Aveyron," written in 1801.

9. Seguin, *Idiocy and Its Treatment*, p. 22; John F. Gaynor, "The 'Failure' of J.M.G. Itard," *Journal of Special Education*, 7 (1973), 439–44.

10. Itard, *Wild Boy of Aveyron*, pp. 86, 99–101. This is from Itard's second report, "On the New Developments and Current State of the Sauvage de l'Aveyron," written in 1806.

11. Jean-Marc-Gaspard Itard, *Rapport sur le Sauvage de l'Aveyron* (Paris, 1807), p. 12, quoted by Seguin, *Idiocy and Its Treatment*, p. 26.

12. Seguin, *Idiocy and Its Treatment*, p. 28.

13. E. Esquirol, *Des Maladies mentales*, 2 vols. (Paris, 1838), 2, 284–85.

14. *Appleton's Cyclopedia of American Biography*, s.v. "Seguin, Edward"; *In Memory of Édouard Seguin, M.D.: Being Remarks Made by Some of his Friends at the Lay Funeral Service: Held October 31, 1880* (n.p., n.d.).

15. Kanner, *History of the Care*, pp. 35–38; Lane, *Wild Boy of Aveyron*, pp. 261–66.

16. Édouard Seguin, *Hygiène et éducation des idiots* (Paris, 1843); idem, *Traitement moral, hygiène et éducation des idiots et des autres enfants arriérés* (Paris, 1846); idem, *Idiocy and Its Treatment* (1866). The discussion of Seguin is drawn largely from this last major study.

17. Mabel E. Talbot, *Édouard Seguin: A Study of an Educational Approach to the Treatment of Mentally Defective Children*, TC Series in Special Education (New York, Bureau of Publications, Teachers College, Columbia University, 1964). Chapter 2 is an excellent account of Seguin's use of ideas and methods from special and regular education, medical sources, philosophy, and his own education.

18. Edward (Édouard) Seguin, *New Facts and Remarks Concerning Idiocy* (New York, 1870), p. 40.

19. Henry Holman, *Seguin and His Physiological Method of Education* (London, 1914).

20. Seguin, *Idiocy and Its Treatment*, pp. 98–126.

21. Edward (Édouard) Seguin, "Psycho-Physiological Training of an Idiotic Hand," *Proceedings of the Association of Medical Officers of American Institutions for Idiotic and Feeble-minded Persons*, Barre, Mass., June 1880 (Philadelphia, 1880), 119–23 (hereafter cited as *PAMO*); idem, "Psycho-Physiological Training of an Idiotic Eye," *PAMO* (1880), 124–34.

22. Talbot, *Édouard Seguin*, p. 90.

23. Seguin, *Idiocy and Its Treatment*, pp. 133–209.

24. Ivor Kraft, "Edward Seguin and the 19th Century Moral Treatment of Idiots," *Bulletin of the History of Medicine*, 35 (1961), 393–419.

25. Edouard Seguin, "Origin of the Treatment and Training of Idiots," *Barnard's American Journal of Education*, 2 (1856), 151.

26. Thomas S. Ball, *Itard, Seguin and Kephart: Sensory Education—A Learning Interpretation* (Columbus, 1971), pp. 49–78.

27. William W. Turner to Linus P. Brockett, March 3, 1856, appended to *Report of the Commissioners on Idiocy to the General Assembly of Connecticut* (New Haven, 1856), 62–65. Turner reported that thirty-four retardates had been admitted to the American asylum; Frank R. Levstik, "A History of the Education and Treatment of the Mentally Retarded in Ohio, 1787–1920" (Ph.D. Dissertation, The Ohio State University, 1981), pp. 5–8.

28. *Twenty-eighth Massachusetts* (1876), 26 (this type of citation will designate the annual report of an institution); Harold Schwartz, *Samuel Gridley Howe: Social Reformer, 1801–1876* (Cambridge, 1956), pp. 137–47; F. E. Williams, "Dr. Samuel G. Howe and the Beginnings of Work with the Feeble-minded in Massachusetts," *Boston Medical and Surgical Journal*, 178 (1917), 481–84; Leo Kanner, "Itard, Seguin, Howe—Three Pioneers in the Education of Retarded Children," *AJMD*, 65 (1960), 1–10.

29. Kanner, *History of the Care*, pp. 17–31, 45–62, for a good summary of European developments; Levstik, *History of the Education and Treatment of the Mentally Retarded in Ohio*, pp. 15–16; Amariah Brigham, "Schools in Lunatic Asylums," *American Journal of Insanity*, 1 (1845), 326–40 (hereafter cited as *AJI*); "Schools and Asylums for the Idiotic and Imbecile," *AJI*, 5 (1848), 19–33; Pliny Earle, "European Institutions for Idiots," *AJI*, 8 (1852), 313–32.

30. *Third Annual Report of the New York State Lunatic Asylum at Utica* (Albany, 1845), 59.

31. *First New York* (1852), 10.

32. *Idiots. Report of the Committee on the Expediency of Appointing Commissioners to Inquire into the Condition of Idiots.* House No. 72 (Boston, 1846), 1.

33. *Idiots. Report of the Committee,* 3.

34. *Idiots. Report in Part by S. G. Howe to Which is Appended a Letter on the School for Idiots in Paris by George Sumner.* House No. 152 (Boston, 1847), 17.

35. *Idiots. First Complete Report Made to the Legislature of Massachusetts upon Idiocy by S. G. Howe.* Senate No. 51 (Boston, 1848). The original draft of the *Report* as well as records of Howe's examinations are in the Library of the Walter E. Fernald State School, Waltham, Massachusetts.

36. Ibid., 32.

37. Ibid., 32–34.

38. Ibid., 2.

39. Ibid., 56–57.

40. Ibid., 59.

41. Ibid., 57.

42. Ibid., 19.

43. Ibid., 16.

44. Ibid., 19–20. The concept of moral idiocy, related to moral insanity, has a complex history mostly unrelated to developmental disability, except as noted later in the text.

45. Harold Schwartz, "Samuel Gridley Howe as Phrenologist," *American Historical Review*, 57 (1952), 644–51; John D. Davies, *Phrenol-*

ogy: *Fad and Science, A Nineteenth Century American Crusade* (New Haven, 1955).

46. Samuel G. Howe, "The Causes and Prevention of Idiocy," *Massachusetts Quarterly Review*, 1 (1848), 318.

47. Ibid., 314.

48. *Idiots. First Complete Report*, 35–53.

49. Ibid., 60.

50. Mary Swift Lamson, *Life and Education of Laura Bridgeman* (Boston, 1892).

51. Charles E. and Carroll S. Rosenberg, "Pietism and the Origins of the American Public Health Movement," *Journal of the History of Medicine*, 23 (1968), 16–35; John L. Thomas, "Romantic Reform in America, 1815–1865," *American Quarterly*, 17 (1965), 656–81.

52. *Idiots. Second Report, Being the First Annual Report of the Experimental School for Teaching and Training Idiotic Children, by S. G. Howe.* Senate No. 38 (Boston, 1850) has a full discussion of the school's earliest period.

53. *Appleton's Cyclopedia of American Biography*, s.v. "Wilbur, Hervey B."; *Dictionary of American Biography*, s.v. "Wilbur, Hervey B."

54. "Remarks by H. B. Wilbur of Syracuse, N.Y." in *In Memory of Édouard Seguin*, 38.

55. *Circular of the Institution for the Education of Idiots, Imbeciles, and Children of Retarded Development of Mind*, Barre, Mass., January 1, 1851 (Worcester, 1851), 18.

56. *First New York* (1852), 2–3; Bernard John Graney, "Hervey Backus Wilbur and the Evolution of Policies and Practices toward Mentally Retarded People" (Ph.D. Dissertation, Syracuse University, 1979).

57. There is a constant skirmishing in the early documents as to which state was really first to aid the retarded. Wilbur's first *Annual Report* (1852), 10–12, pressed New York's claim. Howe in an "Appendix" to the *Third and Final Report of the Experimental School for Teaching and Training Idiotic Children; Also, the First Report of the Trustees of the Massachusetts School for Idiotic and Feeble-minded Youth. Reprinted with Corrections by the Writer from House Document No. 57* (Cambridge, 1852), 25–29, recalled the work of Perkins as early as 1839. Wilbur replied in his own "Appendix" in the *Account of the Ceremonies at the Laying of the Corner-stone of the New York Asylum for Idiots at Syracuse, September 8, 1854* (Albany, 1854), 38–42, by mentioning the influence of Backus on Woodward. Howe responded in his *Seventh Massachusetts* (1855), 9–11, by reprinting a letter from Christopher Morgan, the ex-secretary of the New York Board of Education, who thanked Howe for his visit in 1851. These claims can be resolved easily: New York introduced the first legislation and constructed the first building, while Massachusetts

passed the first bill and established the first public and private schools. There were other claimants for the title; see "Appendix C" in *First Ohio* (1858), 28–29.

58. Alonzo Potter et al., *Education of Idiots: An Appeal to the Citizens of Philadelphia* (Philadelphia, 1853).

59. *Memorial of the Board of Directors of the Pennsylvania Training School for Idiotic and Feeble-minded Children to the Senate and the House of Representatives of the Commonwealth of Pennsylvania in General Assembly Met Together, with Their First Annual Report*. 1854, Philadelphia. Reprint (Elwyn, 1928).

60. *Constitution and the By-Laws of the Massachusetts School for Idiotic and Feeble-minded Youth* (Boston, 1851).

61. Louis Hartz, *Economic Policy and Democratic Thought: Pennsylvania, 1776–1860* (Cambridge, 1948).

62. *Anniversary Report Read at the Ninth Annual Meeting of the Directors of the Pennsylvania Training School for Feeble-minded Children Held at the Institution, May 6, 1862* (Media, 1862). Almost all of the reports of the institutions have reviews of their past histories in each decennial year.

63. *First Ohio* (1858); *Report of the Superintendent of the School for Imbeciles at Lakeville, Conn., to the General Assembly, May Session, 1861* (Hartford, 1861); "Brief History of the Institution" in *Report of the Commissioners of the Kentucky Institution for the Education and Training of Feeble-minded Children to the General Assembly of Kentucky at Adjourned January Session 1869* (Frankfort, 1869).

64. *Report of the Commissioners of Connecticut* (1856), 5. This commission, chaired by Brockett, made an investigation and report quite similar to Howe's in Massachusetts.

65. James B. Richards, "Causes and Treatment of Idiocy," *New York Journal of Medicine*, 3 (1856), 378.

66. Linus P. Brockett, "Idiots and Institutions for Their Training," *Barnard's American Journal of Education*, 1 (1856), 600.

67. *Idiots. Third and Final Report, Being the Second Annual Report on the Experimental School for Teaching and Training Idiotic Children, by S. G. Howe*. Senate No. 9 (Boston, 1851), 3.

68. Ibid., 15–16.

CHAPTER 2

1. *First New York* (1852), Report of the Superintendent, 15.

2. *Third New York* (1854), 5.

3. Ibid., 15–16; *First Ohio* (1857), 32–33; *Fifth Massachusetts* (1853), 12–14.

4. *First Report of the Trustees of Massachusetts School for Idiotic and Feeble-minded Youth.* House Doc. No. 57 (Cambridge, 1852), 35.

5. *Third New York* (1854), Report of the Superintendent, 18–19.

6. *First New York* (1852), Report of the Superintendent, 14.

7. *Ninth Massachusetts* (1857), Report of the General Superintendent, 7.

8. For a representative daily schedule, see *Second Ohio (1859), Report of the Superintendent, 16–17;* also *Seventh Pennsylvania* (1860), 15–17.

9. *Second Ohio* (1859), 16–17.

10. *Second New York* (1853), 6; *Seventeenth Ohio* (1874), 14.

11. *Idiots. First Complete Report* (1850), 33.

12. Edward (Édouard) Seguin, *Idiocy and Its Treatment by the Physiological Method* (New York, 1866), pp. 165–66.

13. *Thirteenth Massachusetts* (1869), Report of the Trustees, 4.

14. *First Ohio* (1857), 16.

15. Bernard Wishy, *The Child and the Republic: The Dawn of Modern American Child Nature* (Philadelphia, 1968).

16. *Third Pennsylvania* (1856), 4.

17. *First New York* (1852), 15.

18. *Sixth Ohio* (1863), 8–9.

19. *Third New York* (1854), 4.

20. *Report of the Commissioners of the Institution for the Education and Training of the Feeble-minded Children to the General Assembly of Kentucky for the Years 1864 and 1865* (Frankfort, 1866), 7.

21. *Eighth Massachusetts* (1856), Report of the General Superintendent, 17.

22. *Fifth Pennsylvania* (1858), Report of the Superintendent, 24.

23. *Third New York* (1854), 5.

24. *Ibid.*, 20; *Seventh New York* (1858), 25.

25. For a good summary of these attitudes see *Fifty-fourth Massachusetts* (1902), 10–23.

26. *Report of the Superintendent of the School for Imbeciles at Lakeville, Connecticut to the General Assembly, May Session, 1861* (Hartford, 1861); *Report of the Commissioners of the Kentucky Institution for the Education and Training of Feeble-minded Children to the General Assembly of Kentucky at the Adjourned January Session, 1862* (Frankfort, 1862). Report of the Superintendent, 7–9.

27. *Fifteenth New York* (1866), 5–8.

28. *Forty-first Pennsylvania* (1893), 37–54; "Isaac N. Kerlin," *Dictionary of American Biography* X, 352 (hereafter cited as *DAB*) and *National Cyclopedia of American Biography* IV, 229.

29. "Charles T. Wilbur," *Appleton's Cyclopedia of American Biography* 6, 503 and *National Cyclopedia of American Biography* 10, 451.

30. *First Report. Institution for Idiots* (1866), 3–4; *Sixth Annual Illinois* (1870), 13, 25–26.

31. *Sixth Annual Illinois* (1870), 9.

32. *Seventh Annual Illinois* (1871), 16.

33. For examples see ibid., 27–39; *Fifteenth New York* (1866), 16–25; *Thirteenth Pennsylvania* (1866), 11–13.

34. On the constant change in state legislatures see Gerald N. Grob, "The Political System and Social Policy in the Nineteenth Century: Legacy of the Revolution," *Mid-America*, 58 (1976), 5–19.

35. Oscar Craig et al. "History of the State Boards," *National Conference of Charities and Correction*, 20 (1893), 32–51 (hereafter as *NCCC*).

36. *Tenth New York* (1861), 11.

37. *Eighth Annual Illinois* (1872), 20.

38. *Seventh Annual Illinois* (1871), 59.

39. *Sixth Biennial Illinois* (1877), 54.

40. *Sixth Annual Illinois* (1870), 23.

41. Norman Dain, *Changing Concepts of Insanity in the United States, 1789–1865* (New Brunswick, 1964), p. 64.

42. *Second Ohio* (1859), 14.

43. *Tenth Ohio* (1867), 10.

44. *Eighth Pennsylvania* (1861), 9.

45. *Seventeenth Massachusetts* (1864), 8.

46. *Seventh Ohio* (1864), 18.

47. *Fourteenth Pennsylvania* (1867), 17, 19.

48. *Tenth Ohio* (1867), 14–15.

49. *Seventh Ohio* (1864), 18.

50. Massachusetts, *Idiots. First Complete Report* (1850), 59.

51. *Seventh Pennsylvania* (1860), 10.

52. *Tenth Ohio* (1867), 16.

53. Leland V. Bell, *Treating the Mentally Ill. From Colonial Times to the Present* (New York, 1980), pp. 19–22.

54. *Eighth Massachusetts* (1856), 15.

55. *Fourteenth Pennsylvania* (1867), 21; For earlier discussion of this issue see *Fourth Pennsylvania* (1857), 17–18; *Tenth Pennsylvania* (1863), 26.

56. *Sixteenth Pennsylvania* (1869) and *Eighteenth Pennsylvania* (1871).

57. *Nineteenth Pennsylvania* (1872), 6.

58. *Fourteenth New York* (1865), 10–11.

59. *Seventeenth New York* (1868), 9.

60. *Nineteenth New York* (1870), 11–14.

61. *Twentieth New York* (1871), 11.

62. *Fourteenth Ohio* (1870), 9 and *Tenth Pennsylvania* (1863), 26.

63. There was little variation in the terms employed by the various schools.

64. *Ninth New York* (1860), 18; *Fourth Ohio* (1866), 9; *Eleventh Massachusetts* (1859), 27.

65. *Ninth New York* (1860), 18; *Fifteenth Massachusetts* (1863), 4.

66. *Eleventh New York* (1862), 13.

67. *Twentieth Pennsylvania* (1873), 9; see *Twenty-second Pennsylvania* (1875), 13–15 for Kerlin's observations about the success of other schools.

68. *Twenty-seventh Massachusetts* (1875), 22.

69. *Twenty-second Pennsylvania* (1875), 18.

70. *Fourteenth Ohio* (1870), 7–8.

CHAPTER 3

1. George E. Shuttleworth, *Notes of a Visit to American Institutions for Idiots and Imbeciles* (Lancaster, England, 1877), 3. For a survey of nineteenth-century British developments see Spencer Hugh Gelband, "Mental Retardation and Institutional Treatment in Nineteenth Century England, 1845–1886" (Ph.D. Dissertation, University of Maryland, 1979). Gelband discusses the growth of "imbecile asylums," demonstrating the wide support of professional and lay groups for institutionalizing mentally retarded persons.

2. Shuttleworth, *Notes*, 4.

3. Ibid., 6.

4. Ibid., 5.

5. Ibid.

6. Ibid., 6.

7. Ibid., 7.

8. Ibid., 8–9.

9. Ibid., 7–8.

10. Ibid., 5.

11. Ibid., 9.

12. Ibid., 10.

13. Shuttleworth had visited nine schools in 1875. The oldest, South Boston, had been founded in 1848, while the most recently occupied was the New York City Idiot Asylum at Randalls Island in 1870. In the twenty years following his visit, ten state institutions and an important private school were established. This was an average of more than one every two years. The Iowa Institution for Feeble-minded Children was organized in 1876 in Glenwood in what previously had been the Soldiers' Orphans Home. (See *First Biennial Iowa* [1877]; Henry M. Hurd, *The Institutional Care of the Insane in the United States and Canada*, 4 vols.

[Baltimore, 1916], III, 426–28; and "Status of the Work: Iowa," *PAMO* [1879], 105–7.) Indiana also utilized the facilities of its Soldiers' and Sailors' Orphanage at Knightstown (later moved to Fort Wayne) to house the Indiana School for Feeble-minded Youth in 1879. (See *First Indiana* [1879]; Hurd, *Institutional Care, III, 386–88; and "Status of the Work: Indiana*," *PAMO* [1880], 168–70.) The same year Minnesota opened a School for the Feeble-minded in conjunction with the state institutions for the deaf and the blind at Faribault. (See *First Biennial Minnesota* [1880]; Hurd, *Institutional Care*, III, 813–17; and "Status of the Work: Minnesota," *PAMO* [1879], 107–8.) The old state university building at Lawrence was used in 1881 for the Kansas State School for Feeble-minded Youth that was relocated at Winfield. (See *First Biennial Kansas* [1881], Hurd, *Institutional Care*, II, 448–49; and "Status of the Work: Kansas," *PAMO* [1883], 268–69.) The year 1885 saw the state assumption of responsibility for the California Home for the Care of Feeble-minded Children (Glen Ellen) and the establishment of the New York State Custodial Asylum for Feeble-minded Women at Newark as an independent institution apart from the control of Syracuse. (See "Status of the Work: California," *PAMO* [1886], 354–55; "Report from the States: California," *NCCC*, 12 [1885], 29; and Hurd, *Institutional Care*, II, 55–58; *First Newark* [1885]; "Report from the States: New York," *NCCC*, 12 [1885], 69; "Status of the Work: New York," *PAMO* [1886], 364–66; and Hurd, *Institutional Care*, III, 150–51.) Three years later in 1888, New Jersey created the State Institution for Feeble-minded Women at Vineland, where the private New Jersey Home for the Education and Care of Feeble-minded Children had been established for a year. (See *First Vineland* [1889]; James Leiby, *Charity and Correction in New Jersey* [New Brunswick, 1967], pp. 102–4; and "Status of the Work: New Jersey," *PAMO* [1889], 77.) The Nebraska legislature authorized the building of the Nebraska Institution for Feeble-minded Youth at Beatrice in 1887 and the Maryland Asylum and Training School for the Feeble-minded at Owings Mills opened as a state-supported school the following year. (See *First Biennial Nebraska* [1886]; "Report from the States: Nebraska," *NCCC*, 14 [1887], 58; "Status of the Work: Nebraska," *PAMO* [1888], 362–64; *First Maryland* [1879]; "Report from the States: Maryland," *NCCC*, 15 [1888], 332; "Status of the Work: Maryland," *PAMO* [1887], 454–55; and Hurd, *Institutional Care*, II, 575–77.) Finally, in 1892, the state of Washington built a School for Defective Youth at Medical Lake. (See Hurd, *Institutional Care*, III, 800–801; and "Status of the Work: Washington," *PAMO* [1892], 249.)

14. Because the schools all developed in much the same way, little would be gained by a recapitulation of the individual histories.

15. *Twenty-fourth Pennsylvania* (1876), 13.

16. Edward (Édouard) Seguin, *Idiocy and Its Treatment by the Physiological Method* (New York, 1866), p. 289.

17. *PAMO* (1877), 3–6.

18. *NCCC*, 1 (1874), 3.

19. Frank J. Bruno, *Trends in Social Work as Reflected in the Proceedings of the National Conference of Social Work, 1874–1946* (New York, 1948), pp. 1–24.

20. *NCCC*, 11 (1884), 18.

21. Thomas L. Haskell, *The Emergence of Professional Social Science: The American Social Science Association and the Nineteenth Century Crisis of Authority* (Urbana, 1977) and Mary O. Furner, *Advocacy and Objectivity: A Crisis in the Professionalization of American Social Science, 1865–1905* (Lexington, 1975).

22. Gerald N. Grob, *Mental Institutions in America: Social Policy to 1875* (New York, 1973), pp. 132–73.

23. *PAMO* (1878), 8.

24. Aside from Kentucky and Maryland, no southern states created institutions for the retarded until the twentieth century. This situation deserves further study, but occasional references indicate that the wealthy sent their relatives North, while the poor were housed in the county almshouses.

25. *PAMO* (1887), 387.

26. Ibid., 388.

27. *PAMO* (1879), 41.

28. Isaac N. Kerlin, "Etiology of Idiocy," *PAMO* (1880), 150–62.

29. *Twenty-sixth Pennsylvania* (1878), 5.

30. *Fourteenth Annual Report of the Massachusetts Board of State Charities* (Boston, 1877), xiv.

31. Isaac N. Kerlin, "The Organization of Establishments for the Idiotic and Imbecile Class," *PAMO* (1878), 20.

32. First published in 1875 as an appendix to the *Thirty-first Annual Report of the New York Prison Association* (New York, 1875), 130–83, and was titled "A Record and Study of the Relations of Crime, Pauperism, and Disease." We have cited the first edition, published by G. P. Putnam's Sons, New York, in 1877.

33. Mark H. Haller, *Eugenics: Hereditarian Attitudes in American Thought* (New Brunswick, 1963), pp. 21–22 for an excellent summary of Dugdale's life and work.

34. Dugdale, *Jukes*, p. 9.

35. Haller, *Eugenics*, p. 21.

36. Dugdale, *Jukes*, p. 12.

37. Ibid., p. 14.

38. Ibid., p. 15.

39. Ibid., pp. 18, 25, 28, 36, 39, 60.

40. Ibid., p. 17.

41. Dugdale used both terms in much the same way as they are employed by sociologists today, see *Jukes*, pp. 16, 24.

42. Ibid., p. 57.

43. Ibid., pp. 49–50.

44. Ibid., p. 50.

45. Ibid., pp. 53–54.

46. Ibid., p. 55.

47. Ibid., pp. 59–62.

48. Ibid., p. 58.

49. *Fourteenth Massachusetts Charities* (1877), xv.

50. Dugdale, *Jukes*, p. 28.

51. For an interesting biographical portrait of Mrs. Lowell, see the memorial number of *Charities and the Commons* 15 (December 2, 1905), 309–35.

52. *Twenty-eighth New York* (1878), 14; *First Newark* (1885), 6; *PAMO* (1878), 100; James C. Carson, "A History and Plea for State Provision for the Feeble-minded," *Proceedings of the Twenty-first Annual Convention of the New York State County Superintendents of the Poor* (Albany, 1891), 45.

53. *Thirty-first New York* (1883), 14.

54. *Second Newark* (1887), 7; Peter L. Tyor, "Denied the Power to Choose the Good: Sexuality and Mental Defect in American Medical Practice, 1850–1920," *Journal of Social History*, 10 (1977), 472–89.

55. *Fourth Newark* (1889), 6.

56. Kerlin in particular was upset about what he termed the lack of "sexual separateness" in county poorhouses; he angrily declared, "The laws of heredity are undeviating here, and too well known to allow any trifling or neglect." *Twenty-sixth Pennsylvania* (1878), 11.

57. *Thirtieth Massachusetts* (1877), 14; *Twenty-seventh Pennsylvania* (1879); *Eighth Biennial Illinois* (1880), 8, 16; *Twenty-second Connecticut* (1880), 6; *Twenty-fifth Ohio* (1881); *Thirtieth New York* (1880), 17.

58. *Twenty-ninth Massachusetts* (1878), 23–26; *Thirtieth Massachusetts* (1879), 16.

59. *Thirty-sixth Massachusetts* (1884).

60. Ibid., 22.

61. *Thirty-seventh Massachusetts* (1885), 20–21.

62. *Eighth Biennial Illinois* (1880), 16. Wilbur had called for an asylum in 1868, see *Fourth Annual Illinois* (1869), 31.

63. *Thirtieth New York* (1882), 14–15.

64. *Thirty-second New York* (1884), 3–4, 11.

65. *Twenty-ninth Pennsylvania* (1882), 8–10.

66. *Twenty-sixth Ohio* (1883), 12.

67. *Thirty-second New York* (1884), 6.

68. *Thirtieth Pennsylvania* (1882), 16.

69. Forty-fifth Massachusetts (1893), 18–19.

70. Isaac N. Kerlin, "Provisions for Idiotic and Feeble-minded Children," *NCCC*, 11 (1884), 246.

71. Ibid., 247.

72. Hervey B. Wilbur, "The Classification of Idiocy," *PAMO* (1877), 29–35, and idem, "Some of the Abnormalities of Idiocy and the Methods Adopted in Obviating Them," *PAMO* (1881), 190–201.

73. This was the subject of the second paper prepared by Kerlin's committee; see H. M. Greene, "The Obligations of Civilized Society to Idiotic and Feeble-minded Children," *NCCC*, 11 (1884), 264–77.

74. Kerlin, "Provisions," 253.

75. Ibid., 254.

76. Ibid., 255.

77. A. W. Wilmarth, "Notes on the Anatomy of the Idiotic Brain," *PAMO* (1884).

78. Kerlin, "Provisions," 256.

79. Ibid., 256–58.

80. Ibid., 257.

81. Ibid., 258–62.

82. Ibid., 262–63.

83. Ibid., 262.

84. Isaac N. Kerlin, "Report of the Standing Committee: Provision for Idiots," *NCCC*, 12 (1885), 174.

CHAPTER 4

1. For a parallel development in mental hospitals see Gerald N. Grob, *Mental Institutions in America: Social Policy to 1875* (New York, 1973) and Leland V. Bell, *Treating the Mentally Ill: From Colonial Times to the Present* (New York, 1980).

2. *Thirty-ninth New York* (1890), 26; *Forty-sixth Massachusetts* (1894), 13.

3. *Tenth Pennsylvania* (1863), 9; *Sixth Ohio* (1863), 10–11.

4. *Fortieth Pennsylvania* (1892), 12–13.

5. *Fifteenth Biennial Illinois* (1894), 15.

6. *Forty-fifth Massachusetts* (1893), 21.

7. *Thirteenth Biennial Iowa* (1901), 16.

8. Ibid.

9. *Plans and Specifications for the Erection of Asylum Buildings of the Pennsylvania Training School for Feeble-minded Children* (Philadelphia, 1891).

10. Samuel G. Howe, *Idiots. First Complete Report Made to the Legislature of Massachusetts upon Idiocy* (Boston, 1848), 19–20; Anon. (S. G. Howe), "The Causes and Prevention of Idiocy," *Massachusetts Quarterly Review*, 3 (1848), 9–10.

11. *Thirty-second Pennsylvania* (1884), 10.

12. Isaac N. Kerlin, "The Moral Imbecile," *NCCC*, 17 (1890), 244.

13. Ibid., 244–45.

14. *Thirty-fourth Pennsylvania* (1886), 8–10.

15. Moral insanity was thought to be a distinct disease entity, responsible for "certain types of compulsive and asocial behavior" without overt psychosis; see Charles E. Rosenberg, *The Trial of the Assassin Guiteau: Psychiatry and Law in the Guilded Age* (Chicago, 1968), p. 68. Rosenberg presents a good discussion of the issue. Also see Eric T. Carlson and Norman Dain, "The Meaning of Moral Insanity," *Bulletin of the History of Medicine*, 36 (1962), 130–40; Arthur E. Fink, *Causes of Crime: Biological Theories in the United States, 1800–1915* (Philadelphia, 1938), pp. 48–75; and Isaac N. Kerlin, "Moral Imbecility," *PAMO* (1898), 30.

16. Kerlin, "Moral Imbecile," 245.

17. This definition was adopted by the Royal Commission on the Care and Control of the Feeble-minded (1908) and was cited in Alfred F. Tredgold, *Mental Deficiency (Amentia)* (London, 1908), p. 79.

18. Kerlin, "Moral Imbecile," 246 and see 246–48.

19. Mark H. Haller, *Eugenics: Hereditarian Attitudes in American Thought* (New Brunswick, 1963), pp. 14–17, 40–44, provides an inclusive summary of this thought; Fink, *Causes of Crime*, pp. 99–150, comprehensively reviews the criminal anthropologists and their theories; see also Stephen Jay Gould, *The Mismeasure of Man* (New York, 1981).

20. Kerlin, "Moral Imbecility," 37.

21. Ibid., 35.

22. *Sixth Biennial Iowa* (1887), 20; the same words are used by F. M. Powell, the superintendent at Iowa, in his paper, "The Care and Training of Feeble-minded Children," *NCCC*, 14 (1887), 255. This sort of repetition was common.

23. *Thirty-fifth Connecticut* (1893), 6.

24. Kerlin, "Moral Imbecile," 249.

25. Ibid., 250.

26. Ibid.

27. Isaac N. Kerlin, "Report of the Committee on the Care and Training of the Feeble-minded," *NCCC*, 15 (1888), 99.

28. Kerlin, "Care and Training," 99.

29. Ibid., 100.

30. Ibid.

31. Ibid.

32. William P. Letchworth, "Provision for Epileptics," *NCCC*, 21 (1894), 193–200.

33. "Oscar C. McCulloch," *DAB* 12, 8; "Tributes to Oscar C. McCulloch," *NCCC*, 14 (1888), 230–50.

34. Oscar C. McCulloch, "The Tribe of Ishmael: A Study in Social Degradation," *NCCC*, 14 (1888), 154.

35. Ibid., 155–57.

36. Ibid., 158.

37. Ibid.

38. Ibid., 158–59.

39. William N. Ashman, "A Medico-Legal Study of Idiocy," *PAMO* (1887), 28.

40. F. M. Powell, "Presidential Address," *PAMO* (1886), 390–91.

41. *Thirty-eighth Massachusetts* (1886), 26.

42. *Thirty-sixth Massachusetts* (1884), 10.

43. *Fortieth Massachusetts* (1888), 35–38.

44. Ibid.

45. George M. Kline, ed., *Bulletin of the Massachusetts Department of Mental Diseases*, 14 (1930), Fernald Memorial Number.

46. *Fifty-second Massachusetts* (1900), 8.

47. Walter E. Fernald, "The Massachusetts Farm Colony for the Feeble-minded," *NCCC*, 29 (1902), 487–96 and "The Templeton Farm Colony for the Feeble-minded," *The Survey*, 27 (March 2, 1912), 1873–1877. Colonies were known in Indiana, Ohio, California, and New York; see Stanley P. Davis, *Social Control of the Feeble-minded* (New York, 1923), pp. 108–70.

48. Fernald, "Massachusetts Farm Colony," 490.

49. Ibid., 489.

50. Ibid., 490.

51. *PAMO* (1890), 29.

52. Albert M. Salisbury, "The Education of the Feeble-minded," *PAMO* (1891), 220; Mark Friedberger, "The Decision to Institutionalize Families with Exceptional Children in 1900," *Journal of Family History*, 6 (1981), 396–409.

53. Walter E. Fernald, "The History of the Treatment of the Feeble-minded," *NCCC*, 20 (1893), 211. The entire 1893 proceedings of the NCCC were devoted to a historical review of the many facets of the conference's work. Fernald's paper is an excellent source for superintendent beliefs concerning the progress and problems of the profession. See also Dennis I. Wool and Thomas M. Stephens, "Twenty-five

Years of Caring for and Treating Feeble-minded Persons in the United States: A Review of the Literature from 1874 to 1900," *The Journal of Special Education*, 12 (1978), 219–29.

54. Fernald, "History of the Care," 212; C. W. Winspear, "The Protection and Training of Feeble-minded Women," *NCCC*, 22 (1895), 160–63; Madeline C. Bragar, "The Feeble-minded Female: An Historical Analysis of Mental Retardation as a Social Definition, 1890–1920" (Ph.D. Dissertation, Syracuse University, 1977).

55. For representative statements see *Forty-fifth Massachusetts* (1892), 12; *Forty-second Pennsylvania* (1894), 11; *Fifty-third Biennial Maryland* (1899), 18; *First Michigan* (1896), 22; *Forty-second Ohio* (1900), 11.

56. Salisbury, "Education of the Feeble-minded," 229.

57. Department of the Interior, Census Office, John S. Billings, *Report on the Insane, Feeble-minded, Deaf and Dumb, and Blind in the United States at the Eleventh Census: 1890* (Washington, 1895), p. 65; and Department of Commerce and Labor, Bureau of the Census, Special Reports, *Insane and Feeble-minded in Hospitals and Institutions: 1904* (Washington, 1906), p. 206.

58. Alexander Johnson, "Permanent Custodial Care," *NCCC*, 23 (1896), 214, for an illustration of this technique.

59. *First Michigan* (1896); *Fourth Biennial Report of the Wisconsin State Board of Control* (Madison, 1899); *First Biennial Missouri* (1901); *First Biennial New Hampshire* (1902); *First Biennial Oregon* (1909); Henry H. Hurd, *The Institutional Care of the Insane in the United States and Canada* (Baltimore, 1916), 4 vols., II, 759; III, 850; II, 888; III, 45, 294, 371–72, 380; Walter E. Fernald, "Care of the Feeble-minded," *NCCC*, 31 (1904), 38.

60. *First Rome New York* (1896); *First Western Pennsylvania* (1898); *First Wrentham Massachusetts* (1908).

61. See the discussion following Isabel Barrow, "What's Next—An Editor's Suggestions," *PAMO* (1895).

62. Martin W. Barr, "Presidential Address," *Journal of Psycho-Asthenics*, 1 (1896), 23–33 (hereafter cited as *JPA*).

63. J. E. Wallace Wallin, *The Mental Health of the School Child* (New Haven, 1914), p. 389 and Tables II–IV, pp. 405–20.

64. Lydia Gardiner Chase, "Public School Classes for Mentally Deficient Children," *NCCC*, 31 (1904), 394. Miss Chase, a Providence resident, drew upon the *Report of the School Committee*, Providence, 1899–1900 (n.p., n.d.), pp. 212, 222, which she cites.

65. Lawrence A. Cremin, *The Transformation of the School: Progressivism in American Education, 1876–1957* (New York, 1964), pp. 127–28.

66. J. E. Wallace Wallin, *Problems of Subnormality (Yonkers-on-Hudson, 1917), pp. 59–109; The Education of Handicapped Children* (Cam-

bridge, 1924). Wallin was considered a leading contemporary authority.

67. Wallin, *Mental Health*, pp. 397–99; the first such clinic was established at the University of Pennsylvania in 1896.

68. James H. Van Sickle, Lightner Witner, and Leonard Ayers, *Provision for Exceptional Children in Public Schools*, United States Bureau of Education Bulletin, 1911, No. 14 (Washington, 1911), p. 33, reported 99 cities as having special classes for the mentally defective and 220 cities with ungraded classes for "backward" children.

69. National Educational Association, *Journal of the Proceedings and Address of the Thirty-sixth Annual Meeting, 1898* (Chicago, 1897), 36–37 (hereafter cited as *NEA*).

70. NEA (1902), 826.

71. Fernald appears to have been the first; see Walter E. Fernald, *Feeble-minded Children* (Boston, 1897), a paper read before the New England Association of School Superintendents.

72. *Eighteenth New Jersey* (1905).

73. Walter E. Fernald, "Mentally Defective Children in the Public Schools," *JPA*, 8 (1903), 33–35; Fernald makes the point that while feeble-minded children might be tolerated in the community, adults would not be tolerated.

74. Chase, "Public School Classes," 397.

75. Antrim E. Osborne, "Presidential Address," *PAMO* (1894), 395.

76. F. M. Powell, "Report of the Standing Committee," *NCCC*, 28 (1900), 71.

77. Albert O. Wright, "The Defective Class," *Proceedings of the Fourth Minnesota State Conference of Charities and Corrections* (St. Paul, 1895), 17 (hereafter cited as *Minn. CCC*). Wright, a president of the NCCC, used the term "troublesome tumors of the body politic," to describe the defective class (ibid., 14).

78. James C. Carson, "Prevention of the Feeble-minded from a Moral and Legal Standpoint," *NCCC*, 25 (1898), 296 (emphasis ours).

79. *Sixteenth New Jersey* (1903), 22–23.

80. Wright, "Defective Class," 17.

81. Charles R. Henderson, *Introduction to the Study of Dependent, Defective, and Delinquent Classes and Their Social Treatment* (Boston, 1901, 2nd ed.).

82. Martin W. Barr, "The How, the Why, and the Wherefore of the Training of Feeble-minded Children," NEA (1898), 1048–49.

83. *Fifty-sixth Massachusetts* (1903), 13–14.

84. *Forty-second Pennsylvania* (1894), 11.

85. *Forty-fifth Massachusetts* (1892), 12; *Seventh Newark, New York* (1892), 7.

86. Haller, *Eugenics*, pp. 58–75; and William E. Castle, "The Beginnings of Mendelism in America," *Genetics in the 20th Century*, ed. L. C. Dunn (New York, 1951).

87. Martin W. Barr, "The Influence of Heredity on Idiocy," *Journal of Nervous and Mental Disease*, 20 (1895), 344–53; "Some Studies in Heredity," *JPA*, 1 (1896), 1–7; "Feeble-mindedness and Viciousness in Children: An Inheritance," *Proceedings of the Association of Directors of the Poor and Corrections of the State of Pennsylvania*, 8 (Philadelphia, 1897), 131–37; Ernest Bicknell, "Feeble-mindedness as Inheritance," *NCCC*, 23 (1897), 219–26.

88. *Fifty-fifth New York* (1905).

89. Martin W. Barr, *Mental Defectives: Their History, Treatment, and Training* (Philadelphia, 1904), p. 122.

90. Ibid., 123.

91. "Editorial," *JPA*, 11 (September 1906), 31–32.

92. See the discussion focusing on M. H. Brewer's rejection of Weismann, *PAMO* (1895), 607. Brewer was given a vote of thanks by the Association.

93. Arthur C. Rogers, "The Future of the Feeble-minded and Epileptic," *Third Minn. CCC* (1895), 102.

94. *Sixteenth New Jersey* (1903), 22.

95. Barr, "Some Studies in Heredity," 2.

96. Robert M. Phelps, "The Prevention of Defectiveness," *Fourth Minn. CCC* (1895), 38.

97. Haller, *Eugenics*, pp. 3, 8–14, 17–20. We have benefitted from this study and are indebted to it for our treatment of eugenics.

98. E. Carleton MacDowell, "Charles Benedict Davenport, 1866–1944: A Study of Conflicting Influences," *Bios*, 17 (March 1946), 3–50.

99. Carnegie Institution of Washington, *Yearbook No. 1, 1902* (Washington, 1903).

100. The American Breeders Association was organized in 1903 by stockmen and biologists; its Committee on Eugenics, established in 1906, "was the first group in the United States to advocate eugenics under the name eugenics," Haller, *Eugenics*, pp. 62–63.

101. Carnegie Institution of Washington, *Yearbook No. 5, 1906* (Washington, 1907), 93.

102. Charles E. Rosenberg, "Charles B. Davenport and the Beginning of Human Eugenics," *Bulletin of the History of Medicine*, 35 (1961), 266–76.

103. A. W. Wilmarth, "Presidential Address," *PAMO* (1895), 518; *Tenth Biennial Iowa* (1895), 32; *Thirty-ninth Connecticut* (1897); *Third Biennial Wisconsin* (1902), 355.

104. Stevenson Smith, et al. *A Summary of the Laws of the Several States*

Governing I.—Marriage and Divorce of the Feeble-minded, the Epileptic, and the Insane . . . , Bulletin of the University of Washington, No. 82 (Seattle, 1914); Jessie S. Smith, "Marriage, Sterilization and Commitment Laws Aimed at Decreasing Mental Deficiency," *Journal of Criminal Law and Criminology,* 5 (1914), 364–69.

105. Kate G. Wells, "State Regulation of Marriage," *NCCC,* 24 (1897), 301.

106. Carson, "Prevention of Feeble-mindedness," 303; George H. Knight, "Prevention from a Legal and Moral Standpoint," *NCCC,* 25 (1898), 364–68; Arthur C. Rogers, "Recent Attempts at Restrictive Marriage Legislation," *NCCC,* 28 (1901), 200–203; L. G. Kline, "Prevention of the Propagation and Increase of Defectives, Delinquents, and Criminals," *Tenth Minn. CCC* (1901), 68; A. W. Wilmarth, "Report on the Committee on Feeble-minded and Epileptic," *NCCC,* 39 (1902), 152–61; Edward R. Johnstone, "Defectives: Report on the Committee," *NCCC,* 32 (1906), 240–41.

107. *Forty-eighth Pennsylvania* (1900), 9–10.

108. *Fifty-first* (1903) and *Fifty-second Pennsylvania* (1904).

109. Walter E. Fernald, "The Care of the Feeble-minded," *NCCC,* 31 (1904), 382.

110. Ibid., 383.

111. Ibid., 384.

112. Ibid., 385.

113. Ibid.; *Fifty-fifth* (1902), 17 and *Fifty-eighth Massachusetts* (1905), 18.

114. Fernald, "Care of the Feeble-minded," 385–86.

115. Ibid., 387.

116. Ibid., 387–88.

117. Wilmarth, "Report on Committee," 157–58; *Fifty-second Pennsylvania* (1904), 15.

118. Wilmarth, "Report on Committee," 157.

119. *Sixth Biennial Maryland* (1899), 18; Smith, *Laws of the Several States,* pp. 79–81, for a summary of the institutional commitment and discharge laws. Michigan was the first state, in 1905, to vest the power of detention solely in the superintendent.

120. Knight, "Prevention from a Legal and Moral Standpoint," 306.

121. Martin W. Barr, "The Imbecile and Epileptic *versus* the Tax-Payer and the Community," *NCCC,* 29 (1902), 163.

122. Ibid.

123. Alexander Johnson, "Concerning a Form of Degeneracy: I," *American Journal of Sociology,* 4 (July 1898–May 1899), 469. Johnson was very active in charity organizations; he was secretary of the Indiana State Board of Charities, became superintendent without a medical

degree, and was general secretary for the NCCC. See his autobiography, Alexander Johnson, *Adventures in Social Welfare* (Fort Wayne, 1923).

124. *Forty-sixth Massachusetts (1893)*, 13; Fernald noted that Waltham had forty-six inmates over twenty years old, out of a total inmate population of 420, while the number of feeble-minded in Massachusetts was estimated to be at least three thousand. Also see *Forty-seventh Pennsylvania* (1899), 13, for Barr's comments on the need to balance the training school population with that of the custodial department, and Arthur C. Rogers, "The Relation of the Institutions for Defectives to the Public School System," *NCCC*, 34 (1907), 469–77; Edward R. Johnstone, "The Institution as a Laboratory for the Public School," *NCCC*, 34 (1907), 477–86.

125. Orpheus Everts, "Asexualization as a Penalty for Crime and the Reformation of Criminals," *Cincinnati Lancet-Clinic*, 20 (March 1888), 377–80; cited in Fink, *Causes of Crime*, p. 189. Fink provides an excellent narrative of this debate, as well as a comprehensive bibliography, especially of medical journals; see Fink, *Causes of Crime*, pp. 188–210.

126. Kerlin, "Presidential Address," 278; for other early statements favoring asexualization see Martin W. Barr, "Moral Paranoia," *PAMO* (1895), 531; and *Fourth Biennial Maryland* (1895), 21.

127. *Ninth Biennial Report of the Kansas Board of Charities and Corrections* (Topeka, 1896); *Eleventh Biennial Report of the Kansas Board of Charities and Corrections* (Topeka, 1900); F. C. Cave, "Report of Sterilization in the Kansas State Home for the Feeble-minded," *JPA*, 15 (1911), 123–25; Barr, *Mental Defectives*, pp. 195–96.

128. Martin W. Barr, "Presidential Address," *JPA*, 2 (1897), 6; and "Results of Asexualization," *JPA*, 9 (1905), 129.

129. A. J. Ochsner, "Surgical Treatment of Habitual Criminals," *Journal of the Americal Medical Association*, 32 (1899), 867–68, first discussed the utilization of vasectomy as a eugenic measure (hereafter cited as *JAMA*); Daniel R. Brower, "Medical Aspects of Crime," *Boston Medical and Surgical Journal*, 140 (1899), 570–74.

130. Harry C. Sharp, "Rendering Sterile of Confirmed Criminals and Mental Defectives," *Proceedings of the Annual Congress of the National Prison Association* (1907), 178; "The Severing of the Vas Deferentia and its Relation to the Neuropathic Constitution," *New York Medical Journal*, 75 (1902), 411–14; "Vasectomy as a Means of Preventing Procreation in Defectives," *JAMA*, 53 (1909), 1897–1902; *The Sterilization of Degenerates* (n.p., n.d. [1910?]).

131. Sharp, "Rendering Sterile," 180.

132. G. H. Makuen, "Some Measures for the Prevention of Crime, Pauperism, and Mental Deficiency," *Bulletin of the American Academy of Medicine*, 5 (1900), 1–15; "Asexualization of Criminals and Degenerates," *Michigan Law Journal*, 6 (1897), 284–316; Barr, *Mental Defectives*, pp. 193–95.

133. Barr, *Mental Defectives*, p. 192.

134. Ibid., p. 195.

135. Samuel D. Risley, "Is Asexualization ever Justified in the Case of Imbecile Children," *JPA*, 9 (1905), 92–98.

136. The preamble of the bill read: "Whereas: Heredity plays a most important part in the transmission of idiocy and imbecility"; Barr, *Mental Defectives*, p. 195.

137. Harry H. Laughlin, *Eugenical Sterilization in the United States* (Chicago, 1922), 35–36.

138. For example, see the discussion, pro and con, following Harry C. Sharp, "The Indiana Plan," *Proceedings of the Annual Congress of the American Prison Association* (1901), 40–48.

139. Sharp, "Rendering Sterile," 179, and the *Eighteenth Report of the Board of State Charities made to the Legislature of Indiana for One Year, 1907* (Indianapolis, 1908), 9, 11.

140. Laughlin, *Eugenical Sterilization*, p. 15.

141. Alexander Johnson, "Report of Committee on Colonies for Segregation of Defectives," *NCCC*, 30 (1903), 248–49; there were other occasional hints of euthanasia; see Mauken, "Some Means for Prevention," 5, and C. C. Vanderbeck, *Résumé of the History, Classification, Causation, Diagnosis, and Treatment of the Feeble-minded Defective* (n.p., 1899), p. 27; George Mogridge, "State Care of the Feeble-minded," *Bulletin of Iowa Institutions*, 9 (1907), 166.

142. Mary E. Perry, "Minority Report," *NCCC*, 30 (1903), 253–54.

143. Martin W. Barr, "State Care of the Feeble-minded," *N.Y. Med. Jour.*, 77 (1903), 1159.

144. "Editorial," *JPA*, 3 (1899), 144.

145. Amos W. Butler, "The Burden of Feeble-mindedness," *NCCC*, 34 (1907), 8 (emphasis ours).

CHAPTER 5

1. For the significance of intelligence testing, see Haller, *Eugenics: Hereditarian Attitudes in American Thought*, pp. 95–110; Deutsch, *The Mentally Ill in America*, pp. 354–62; Davies, *Social Control of the Feeble-minded*, pp. 43–55; Kanner, *A History of the Care*, pp. 117–37; Margaret Adams, *Mental Retardation and its Social Dimensions* (New York, 1971), pp. 30–36; Fink, *Causes of Crime*, pp. 214–34.

2. Isabel Barrows, "What's Next—An Editor's Suggestions," *PAMO* (1895), 542.

3. *Forty-eighth Pennsylvania* (1900); for the early history of intelligence testing, see Joseph Peterson, *Early Conceptions and Tests of Intelligence* (Yonkers-on-Hudson, 1925), pp. 72–96.

4. For Johnstone, see the *Eighteenth New Jersey* (1905), and Alexander Johnson, *Adventures in Social Welfare*, pp. 180–87; for Vineland and Goddard, see Joseph Byers, *The Village of Happiness: The Story of the Training School* (Vineland, 1934); Edgar Doll, ed., *Twenty-fifth Anniversary: Vineland Laboratory, 1906–1931* (Vineland, 1932); and James Leiby, *Charity and Corrections in New Jersey*, pp. 104–9.

5. *Eighteenth New Jersey* (1905), 27; research departments were seen as great aids in the struggle for prevention of mental defect; by 1912, Illinois, Iowa, and Minnesota had research laboratories.

6. Henry H. Goddard, "The Research Work," in Supplement to *Training School Bulletin*, 1 (1907), 1–13; "A Side Light on the Development of the Number Concept," ibid., 20–25; "A Group of Feeble-minded Children with Special Regard to Their Number Concepts," in Supplement to *Training School Bulletin*, 2 (1908), 1–16; Goddard was a prolific author: Doll, *Twenty-fifth Anniversary*, pp. 112–19, lists thirty-six "Research Articles," sixty-one "General Articles," and six books produced by Goddard from 1907 to 1918; many were published in the *Training School Bulletin* which gave full reports of institutional development, research in progress, and current events.

7. Henry H. Goddard, "Two Months Among European Institutions for the Mentally Defective," *Training School Bulletin*, 5 (1908), 11–16; Goddard learned of their work in Brussels and published a short account of their 1905 series of tests: "The Binet-Simon Tests of Intellectual Capacity," *Training School Bulletin*, 5 (1908), 3–9.

8. Goddard collected their work from L'Année Psychologique and had it published as Alfred Binet and Thomas Simon, *The Development of Intelligence in Children*, trans. Elizabeth S. Kite, Publication of the Training School at Vineland, New Jersey, Department of Research, No. 11, May 1916 (Baltimore, 1916); the three versions are also available in Peterson, *Early Conceptions and Tests*, pp. 172–75, 193–95, 234–35. Binet and Simon were not dogmatic about their tests; they believed that they could be improved further, and that they should be used in conjunction with other testing methods.

9. Binet and Simon, *Development of Intelligence*, Introduction by Henry H. Goddard, p. 5; Goddard published this version in 1910, "A Measuring Scale of Intelligence," *Training School Bulletin* 6 (1910), 146–55.

10. Henry H. Goddard, "Suggestions for a Prognostical Classification of Mental Defectives," *JPA*, 14 (1910), 49.

11. Henry H. Goddard, "Four Hundred Children Classified by the Binet Method," *JPA*, 15 (1910), 17–30.

12. See the *Twenty-fourth Biennial Illinois* (1912) for the work of Edmund B. Huey, the head of Illinois' research department; Edmund B. Huey, "Retardation and the Mental Examination of Retarded Chil-

dren," *JPA*, 15 (1910), 31–43; and idem, *Backward and Feeble-minded Children* (Baltimore, 1912), p. 19, where he stresses the importance of the twelve-year division. The 1909 Binet scale called for the subject to pass five tests: repeat seven digits, find in one minute three rhymes for a given word, repeat a sentence of twenty-six syllables, answer problem questions, and give interpretations of pictures—at this time, all Binet tests were given by personal interview, and were variously interpreted by different examiners; the 1911 revision made these tests serve for the measurement of normal fifteen-year mentality.

13. "Report of the Committee of Classification of the Feeble-minded," *JPA*, 14 (1910), 61–67.

14. Quoted by Alfred E. Tredgold, *Mental Deficiency (Amentia)* (London, 1908), pp. 75–76; Tredgold was a medical expert to the Royal Commission on the Feeble-minded and his work was well known in America. In 1904 the Commission began the investigations and by 1908 it had examined 248 witnesses, conducted sixteen detailed surveys of urban and rural districts in Great Britain, and finally issued its findings as *Report of the Royal Commission on the Care and Control of the Feeble-minded*, 5 vols. (London, 1908).

15. A.R.T. Wylie, "President's Annual Address," *JPA*, 16 (1911), 4; Frank L. Christian, "The Defective Delinquent," *Albany Medical Annals*, 34 (1913), 281.

16. Fred Kuhlmann, "The Binet-Simon Tests of Intelligence in Grading Feeble-minded Children," *JPA*, 16 (1912), 173–94; Kuhlmann was research director at Faribault.

17. Henry H. Goddard, "Two Thousand Children Tested by the Binet Measuring Scale for Intelligence," *NEA*, 39 (1911), 870–77; as a result of this large–scale testing Goddard was able to revise the Binet tests to suit American conditions. He published this work as, "A Revision of the Binet Scale," *Training School Bulletin*, 8 (1911), 56–62.

18. Henry H. Goddard, "Ungraded Classes," *Report on Educational Aspects of the Public School System of the City of New York, Part II, Sub-Division I, Section E, 1911–1912* (New York, 1912); also see the *Thirteenth Annual Report of the City Superintendent of Schools, 1910–1911*, "Reports on Defective Children" (n.p., 1911). Goddard expanded his views in *School Training of Defective Children* (Yonkers, 1914); and see also City of New York, Board of Education, "Ungraded Classes" (Document No. 2, n.p., 1914). At the time of Goddard's initial investigation there was another of equal significance and publicity, Anne Moore, *The Feeble-minded in New York: A Report Prepared for the Public Education Association of New York*, Special Committee on Provision for the Feeble-minded of the State Charity Aid Association (New York, 1911). To facilitate further research the New York State Board of Charities, De-

partment of State and Alien Poor, organized a Bureau of Analysis and Investigation which published a series of *Eugenics and Social Welfare Bulletins* from 1912 to 1917; these were taken over by the newly organized State Division of Mental Defect and Delinquency in 1917; see *Fifty-first Annual Report of the New York State Board of Charities* (Albany, 1917).

19. J. E. Wallace Wallin, *The Problem of Subnormality* (Yonkers-on-Hudson, 1917), pp. 123–88, reviews forty-three of the most prominent investigations undertaken in prisons, courts, reformatories, homes for the wayward, industrial schools, juvenile courts, detention homes, hospitals for the insane, and public school systems. As Binet testing was popularized, there were literally thousands of these examinations.

20. *Report of the Commission for the Investigation of the White Slave Traffic, So-Called* (Boston, 1914), 30.

21. Henry H. Goddard, *Feeble-mindedness: Its Causes and Consequences* (New York, 1914), p. 8; among criminals, Goddard cites percentages of retardation varying from 28 to 89 percent (p. 9).

22. Victor V. Anderson, "Mental Disease and Delinquency: A Report of a Special Committee of the New York State Commission of Prisons," *Mental Hygiene*, 3 (1914), 177–98; Anderson presents in tabular form the results of twenty-one investigations which revealed that between 11 and 50 percent of prison, reformatory, penitentiary, workhouse, and industrial training school inmates were feeble-minded; another table indicates that an average of 30 percent of drug users, immoral women, shoplifters, drunken women, and vagrants were retarded. Fink, *Causes of Crime*, pp. 217–34, has extensive bibliographic citations to studies of the mentality of criminals, delinquents, and other offenders.

23. *Report of the Commission to Investigate the Question of the Increase of Criminals, Mental Defectives, Epileptics and Degenerates* (Boston, 1911); Fernald may have directed this commission.

24. *Commission to Investigate*, 27.

25. *Fifty-fifth Massachusetts* (1902), 11–17; *Fifty-eighth Massachusetts* (1905), 18–19.

26. *Sixty-third Massachusetts* (1910), 18.

27. The act was not operational until 1922 as the legislature did not appropriate funds for the institutions for eleven years. Fernald's role in drafting the bill is revealed by his correspondence that is contained in a collection of contemporary newspaper stories, speeches, and other memorabilia that was compiled by Fernald, and is kept with the librarian at the Walter E. Fernald State School, Waverly, Massachusetts. This material, bound in loose–leaf scrapbooks, was most helpful in determining the state of public reaction to the mentally retarded.

28. Massachusetts, *Commission to Investigate*, 32; Walter E. Fernald, "The Imbecile with Criminal Instincts," *American Journal of Insanity*, 65 (1909), 731–49; a more precise terminology was suggested by Victor V. Anderson, "A Classification of Borderline Mental Cases Among Offenders," *Jour. Crim. Law, Criminol.*, 6 (1916), 689–96.

29. Walter E. Fernald, "The Diagnosis of the Higher Grades of Mental Defect," *JPA*, 18 (1913), 73.

30. *Sixty-fourth Massachusetts* (1911), 10. For further comment on the link between retardation and crime see Henry H. Goddard, "Mental Defectives Who Are Also Delinquent," *NCCC*, 38 (1911), 64–65; Frank Moore, "Mentally Defective Delinquents," ibid., 65–68; Ernest K. Coulter, "Mentally Defective Delinquents and the Law," ibid., 68–70; O. F. Lewis, "The Feeble-minded Delinquent," *Twelfth Annual New York State Conference of Charities and Corrections* (Albany, 1911), 190–204; Henry H. Goddard and Helen F. Hill, "Feeble-mindedness and Criminality," *Training School Bulletin*, 8 (1911), 3–6; Henry H. Goddard, "Feeble-mindedness and Crime," *Proceedings of the Annual Congress of the American Prison Association* (1912), 353–57; Olga Bridgman, "Mental Deficiency and Delinquency," *JAMA*, 61 (1914), 471–72; Mary Storer, "The Defective Delinquent Girls," *JPA*, 19 (1914), 23–30; Nicolas F. Hahn, "The Defective Delinquent Movement: A History of the Born Criminal in New York State" (Ph.D. Dissertation, State University of New York, Albany, 1978). The work of William Healy and Augusta Bronner in the 1910's challenged the view that there was a direct connection between mental deficiency and criminal behavior. See below chapter 6.

31. For the possibilities of brutal and senseless crimes see Henry H. Goddard, *The Criminal Imbecile: An Analysis of Three Remarkable Murder Cases* (New York, 1915); for studies of juveniles and lesser offenders, see William G. Eynon, "The Mental Measurement of Four Hundred Juvenile Delinquents by the Binet-Simon System," *N.Y. Med. Jour.*, 98 (1913), 175–78; Clinton P. McCord, "One Hundred Female Offenders: A Study of the Mentality of Prostitutes and 'Wayward Girls,' " *Jour. Crim. Law, Criminol.*, 6(1915), 385–407; Victor V. Anderson, "An Analysis of One Hundred Cases Studied in Connection with the Municipal Court of Boston," *Bos. Med. Surg. Jour.*, 171 (1914), 341–46.

32. Goddard, *Feeble-mindedness*, p. 514.

33. Victor V. Anderson, *The Relationship of Mental Defect and Disorder to Delinquency*, Massachusetts Commission on Probation (Boston, 1918), 3; on the role of mental defect and recidivism, see Paul E. Bowers, "The Recidivist," *Jour. Crim. Law, Criminol.*, 5 (1914), 404–19; Victor V. Anderson, "Feeble-mindedness as Seen in Court," *Mental Hygiene*, 2 (1917), 260–65. A conclusion was reached that the parole system was successful with normal criminals, but not with the mentally defective.

34. Hasting H. Hart, *The Extinction of the Defective Delinquent*, Russell Sage Foundation, Department of Child Helping, Publication No. 10 (New York, 1912), 6. Hart was director of the Department and delivered this paper before the American Prison Association in 1912. For more extensive plans concerning the defective delinquent, see New York Committee on Feeble-mindedness and Mental Health Committee, State Charities Aid Association, *Defective Delinquents: Facts about Defective Delinquents, Their Nature, Prevalence, Institutional and Legislative Needs in the State of New York*, Memorandum submitted to the Hospital Development Commission, November 1917; LeRoy Bauman, *A Program of State Provision for the Feeble-minded*, New York Committee on Feeble-mindedness (New York, 1917); George H. Hastings, *What Shall Be Done with Defective Delinquents*, New York Committee on Feeble-mindedness (New York, 1918).

35. Henry H. Goddard, "Heredity of Feeble-mindedness," Eugenics Record Office, Bulletin No. 1 (Cold Springs Harbor, 1911), reprinted from *American Breeders Magazine*, 1 (1910), 165–78.

36. Haller, *Eugenics*, pp. 64–66; Carnegie Institution of Washington, *Yearbook No. 8, 1909* (Washington, 1910).

37. Carnegie Institution of Washington, *Yearbook No. 17, 1918* (Washington, 1919); Harry H. Laughlin, Eugenics Record Office, Report No. 1 (Cold Springs Harbor, 1913). Davenport was director of the Office while Laughlin was superintendent; by 1920, *Eugenical News*, begun in 1916 as the Eugenics Research Association's house organ, had a circulation of one thousand, and 205 field workers had been trained.

38. Charles B. Davenport, "Some Social Applications of Modern Principles of Heredity," *Transactions of the Fifteenth Annual International Congress on Hygiene and Demography* (Washington, 1912), 2; and "Eugenics and Charity," NCCC, 39 (1912), 281. These statements were made to audiences of believers in some measure of environmentalism. An earlier statement on charity had brought Davenport the singular distinction of having the editor of the NCCC add: "This is probably the furthest from an accurate statement of the position of organized charity, that has ever appeared in the Proceedings of the National Conference."

39. Harry H. Laughlin, "The Legal, Legislative and Administrative Aspects of Sterilization," Eugenics Record Office Bulletin No. 10B, *Report of the Committee to Study and to Report on the Best Practical Means of Cutting Off the Defective Germ-Plasm in the American Population* (Cold Springs Harbor, 1914), 59; Davenport used the phrase in a lecture delivered at the "Golden Jubilee Celebration of the Battle Creek Sanitarium," (n.p., n.d.).

40. Carnegie Institution of Washington, *Yearbook No. 13, 1914*

(Washington, 1915), 125; Charles E. Rosenberg, "Charles Benedict Davenport," 271–72.

41. Charles B. Davenport, *Heredity in Relation to Eugenics* (New York, 1911), pp. 66–67; and for Davenport's more precise biological explanation see Charles B. Davenport, "Feeble Inhibitionless," *JPA*, 17 (1914), 147–49.

42. Henry H. Goddard, *The Kallikak Family: A Study in the Heredity of Feeble-mindedness* (New York, 1912), pp. 17–19, 29–30; on the significance of the infant mortality rate see Henry H. Goddard, "Infant Mortality in Relation to Hereditary Effects of Mental Deficiency," An Address Delivered Before the American Association for the Study and Prevention of Infant Mortality, Cleveland, October 3, 1912 (n.p., n.d.).

43. Goddard, *Kallikak*, p. 50. Goddard faulted such earlier studies as A. E. Winship, *The Jukes-Edwards: A Study in Education and Heredity* (Harrisburg, 1900) because of the divergence in environments of the two families; as for the *Jukes*, the lack of a control group made it difficult to say if the work proved the hereditary nature of crime, although feeble-mindedness was the best material for making criminal careers (Goddard, *Kallikak*, p. 54).

44. Goddard, *Kallikak*, p. 111. Goddard attempted to impress the reader with his objectivity: "We have preferred to err on the other side and have not marked people feeble-minded unless the case was such that we could substantiate it beyond a reasonable doubt" (ix); yet he admitted (unwittingly) the basic unsoundness of his research methods "in determining the mental condition of people in the earlier generations . . . , one proceeds in the same way as one does to determine the *character* of a Washington or a Lincoln or any other man of the past" (p. 14, emphasis ours). As other critics were to note, there is a considerable difference between the determination of *character* and that of *mental defect*.

45. Goddard, *Feeble-mindedness*, pp. 438–65.

46. Ibid., p. 556.

47. A. F. Tredgold, "The Feeble-minded," *Contemporary Review*, 97 (1910), 720; for an excellent contemporary opinion of the importance of birthrates see Edward A. Ross, "The Causes of Race Superiority," *Annals*, 18 (1910), 67–89. Ross helped popularize the term "race suicide."

48. Goddard, *Feeble-mindedness*, pp. 472–73.

49. Goddard, *Kallikak*, p. 72; and Henry H. Goddard, "Heredity as a Factor in the Problem of the Feeble-minded Child," *Troisième Congress International D'Hygiène Scolaire* (Paris, 1910); "Mental Deficiency from the Standpoint of Heredity," Massachusetts Society for Mental Hygiene, Publication No. 15 (Boston, 1915).

50. Charles B. Davenport et al., "The Study of Human Heredity,"
Eugenics Record Office, Bulletin No. 2 (Cold Springs Harbor, 1911);
idem, "The Trait Book," Eugenics Record Office, Bulletin No. 6 (Cold
Springs Harbor, 1912); the Trait Book listed virtually every conceivable
human characteristic with handy symbols.

51. Florence H. Danielson and Charles B. Davenport, "The Hill Folk:
Report on a Rural Community of Hereditary Defectives," Eugenics
Record Office, Memoir No. 1 (Cold Springs Harbor, 1912); Arthur H.
Esterbrook and Charles B. Davenport, "The Nam Family: A Study in
Cacogenics," Eugenics Record Office, Memoir No. 2 (Cold Springs
Harbor, 1912); Anna Finlaynon, "The Dark Family: A Study in Hered-
itary Lack of Emotional Control," Eugenics Record Office, Bulletin No.
15 (Cold Springs Harbor, 1916); Arthur H. Esterbrook, *The Jukes in 1915*
(Washington, 1916); Mary S. Kostir, "The Family of Sam Sixty," Ohio
Board of Administration, Publication No. 8 (Columbus, 1916); Amos
W. Butler, "The 'C' Family," *Proceedings of the Indiana Academy of Science* (Indianapolis, 1915); Nina Sessions, "The Feeble-minded in a Rural County of Ohio," Ohio Board of Administration, Publication No.
12 (Columbus, 1918).

52. Walter E. Fernald, "Menace of the Feeble-minded," *Report of the
Fifteenth Annual Meeting of the New Hampshire Conference of Charities and
Corrections* (Concord, 1915), 1; see Guy G. Fernald, *Report of the Maine
Commissioner for the Feeble-minded and of the Survey by the National Com-
mittee for Mental Hygiene* (Augusta, 1918), 16–18, for other references
to this condition, especially in New England.

53. Laughlin, "Aspects of Sterilization," 16.

54. Ibid., 18–57.

55. Franklin B. Kirbride, "The Right to be Well Born," *Survey*, 27
(1912), 1838–40; Edward B. Pollard, *The Rights of the Unborn Race*,
American Baptist Publication Society (Philadelphia, 1914); Michael F.
Guyer, *Being Well Born: An Introduction to Eugenics* (Indianapolis, 1916);
E. J. Emerick, "Segregation of the Mentally Defective," *Ohio Bulletin of
Charities and Corrections*, 19 (1913), 10–20.

56. Charles B. Davenport, "Influence of Heredity on Human Society," *Annals*, 24 (1909), 20.

57. Karl Schwartz, "Nature's Corrective Principle in Social Evolution," *JPA*, 13 (1909), 83, 76, 88.

58. Charles B. Davenport, "Medico-Legal Aspects of Eugenics,"
Medical Times, 92 (1914), 300.

59. *Forty-sixth Annual Report of the New York State Board of Charities*
(Albany, 1912), 167.

60. J. M. Murdock, "State Care for the Feeble-minded," *JPA*, 18
(1913), 34; idem, "Quarantine Mental Defectives," *NCCC*, 36 (1909),
64–67.

61. *Report of the Commission on the Segregation, Care and Treatment of Feeble-minded and Epileptic Persons in the Commonwealth of Pennsylvania* (n.p., 1913), 43.

62. E. J. Emerick, "Problem of the Feeble-minded," Ohio Board of Administration, Publication No. 5 (Columbus, 1915), 3–4; Emerick was partly responsible for the establishment of the Bureau of Juvenile Research in 1914 under the Board of Administration. The Bureau's goal was "to find the defectives and psychopaths while they are yet young . . . to devise ways and means to control their lives" (11).

63. Walter E. Fernald, "Some Phases of Feeble-mindedness," *Proceedings of the Third Annual New York City Conference of Charities and Corrections* (New York, 1912), 157; Fernald makes the same point in "The Burden of Feeble-mindedness," Massachusetts Society for Mental Hygiene, Publication No. 4 (Boston, 1912), 5; for the issue of common causation, Charles H. Cooley, *Human Nature and Social Order* (New York, 1902), p. 375.

64. Leiby, *Charity and Correction*, pp. 108–9; Byers, *Village of Happiness*, pp. 76–80; Johnson, *Adventures*, pp. 391–417; Edward R. Johnstone, "Stimulating Public Interest in the Feeble-minded," NCCC, 43 (1916), 205–15; Joseph P. Byers, "State Plan for the Care of the Feeble-minded," NCCC, 43 (1916), 223–29; *Report of the New Jersey Commission on the Care of Mental Defectives* (Trenton, 1914).

65. New York Committee on Feeble-mindedness, "Facts About the Feeble-minded; The Need for Additional Accommodations for the Feeble-minded in the State of New York" (New York, 1917); *First Annual Report of the New York Committee on Feeble-mindedness* (New York, 1917).

66. Philadelphia, Department of Public Health and Charities, "The Degenerate Children of Feeble-minded Women" (Philadelphia, 1910).

67. *The Survey*, 27 (1912); *State Charities Aid Association News*, 2 (1914).

68. "Indiana Conference on Mental Deficiency and Child Welfare," State Board of Charities of Indiana, *The Indiana Bulletin*, 107 (1916), 378–450; three sessions—"Mental Defect as a Home and School Problem," "Mental Defect as a Medical Problem," and "Mental Defect as a Legal Problem," *Proceedings of the Wisconsin Conference of Charities and Corrections, Sheboygan, October 17 to October 19, 1916* (Madison, 1917).

69. *Report of the State Commission to Investigate Provision for the Mentally Defective* (Albany, 1915), 113; the commissions of New Jersey, Massachusetts, and Pennsylvania have been cited; in addition see *Mental Defectives in Indiana: Report of the Committee on Mental Defectives Appointed by Governor Samuel M. Roston* (Indianapolis, 1916); Lillian C. Streeter, "Existing Conditions Relating to Defectives and Feeble-mindedness in New Hampshire," *Report of New Hampshire Children's Commission to the Governor and the Legislature* (n.p., 1915); Fernald sug-

gested a program similar to that of New York's, Walter E. Fernald, "What's Practicable in the Way of Preventing Mental Defect," *NCCC*, 42 (1915), 189–98. The National Committee for Mental Hygiene, working with a grant from the Rockefeller Foundation, carried out thirty-five surveys of this nature; see Clifford W. Beers, *A Mind That Found Itself*, Twenty-fifth Anniversary Edition Issued March 1935, with Additions (New York, 1908), pp. 330–32.

70. *Report of the Hospital Development Commission* (Albany, 1918), and *First Annual Report of the State Commission for Mental Defectives, July 1, 1918 to June 30, 1919* (Albany, 1920).

71. Department of Commerce, Bureau of the Census, *Feeble-minded and Epileptic in Institutions* (Washington, 1923), 17–19, 25.

72. Harry H. Laughlin, *Eugenical Sterilization in the United States* (Chicago, 1922), pp. 1–14; Ezra S. Gosney and Paul Popenoe, *Sterilization for Human Betterment* (New York, 1929); *Collected Papers on Eugenical Sterilization in California* (Pasadena, 1930); J. H. Landsman, *Human Sterilization: A History of the Sexual Sterilization Movement* (New York, 1932); Leon F. Whitney, *The Case for Sterilization* (New York, 1934); Abraham Myerson, et al., *Eugenical Sterilization: A Re-Orientation of the Problem* (New York, 1936); Kenneth Ludmerer, *Genetics and American Society: A Historical Appraisal* (Baltimore, 1972), pp. 91–92 for the eugencists, role in the campaign to pass sterilization laws; D. K. Pickens, "The Sterilization Movement: The Search for Purity in Mind and State," *Phylon*, 28 (1967), 78–94.

73. See Laughlin, *Eugenical Sterilization*, pp. 52–92, 99–140, for a detailed examination of the laws, methods of sterilization, groups eligible, executive agencies, court procedures, and family studies.

74. Laughlin, *Eugenical Sterilization*, pp. 96, 142–289.

75. Charles B. Davenport, "Marriage Laws and Customs," First International Congress of Eugenics, *Problems in Eugenics* (London, 1912), p. 154; for representative pro-sterilization arguments see M. E. Von Meter, "Stamping Out Hereditary Diseases by Sterilizing the Sexes," *American Journal of Surgery*, 21 (1907), 18–22. J. Ewring Mears, *The Problem of Race Betterment* (Philadelphia, 1910); Theodore Diller, "Some Practical Problems Relating to the Feeble-minded," *JPA*, 16 (1911), 20–26; R. H. Grube, "Sterilization of Defectives for the Betterment of the Human Race," Ohio State Board of Health, Monthly Bulletin (August 1911); Hasting H. Hart, *Sterilization as a Practical Measure*, Russell Sage Foundation, Department of Child Helping (New York, 1913); Bleecker van Wagenen, "Surgical Sterilization as a Eugenics Measure," *JPA*, 18 (1914), 185–97; J. T. Haynes, *Vasectomy*, Ohio Board of Administration, Publication No. 13 (Columbus, 1919); Charles H. Clark, *The Prevention of Racial Deterioration and Degeneracy*, Ohio Board of Administration, Publication No. 15 (Columbus, 1920).

76. Henry H. Goddard, *Sterilization and Segregation*, Russell Sage Foundation, Department of Child Helping (New York, 1913).

77. Goddard, *Feeble-mindedness*, pp. 588–89; for the question of what to do with borderline cases see Samuel C. Kohs, "The Borderline of Mental Deficiency," *NCCC*, 43 (1916), 279–91.

78. Fernald, "Burden of Feeble-mindedness," 8.

79. "Discussion," *Twenty-fifth Minn. CCC* (1916), 49; for Johnson's earlier views, Alexander Johnson, "Race Improvement by Control of Defectives," *Annals*, 34 (1909), 22–29; Johnson said: "I must consider it [sterilization] a most serious and dangerous attack on public morals" (25). Estimates of retardation in the general population varied from 1 in 136 to 1 in 294, Davies, *Social Control*, pp. 43–45.

80. Rudolph J. Vecoli, "Sterilization: A Progressive Measure?" *Wisconsin Magazine of History*, 43 (1960), 190–202; *Twelfth Biennial Report of the State Board of Control of Wisconsin—Reformatory, Charitable and Penal Institutions* (Madison, 1914).

81. Homer Folks, "Report of the Committee on the Mentally Defective in Their Relation to the State," *Proceedings of the Thirteenth Annual New York State Conference of Charities and Corrections* (Albany, 1912), 176; Folks, "State Knows," 7.

82. *Seventh Annual Report of the Department of Charities and Corrections, 1911, State of New Jersey* (Trenton, 1912), 17; Harry A. Lindsay, "Sterilization of Degenerates," *Bulletin of Iowa State Institutions*, 14 (1912), 52–60; Edwin A. Down, "Sterilization of Degenerates—Connecticut's New Law," *Proceedings of the First Annual Connecticut State Conference of Charities and Corrections* (Hartford, 1911), 160–62.

83. Laughlin, *Eugenical Sterilization*, pp. 117–24.

84. Arthur J. Todd, "Sterilization and Criminal Heredity: An Editorial," *Jour. Crim. Law, Crimin.*, 5 (1914), 5; Charles A. Boston, "Protest Against Laws Authorizing the Sterilization of Criminals and Imbeciles," *Jour. Crim. Law, Crimin.*, 4 (1913), 804–15; American Medical Association, "Sterilization of Criminals," prepared by the Medico-Legal Bureau of the AMA (Chicago, 1915).

85. Joel D. Hunter, "The Sterilization of Criminals," Report of Committee H of the Institute, *Jour. Crim. Law, Crimin.*, 4 (1914), 514–40; William A. White, "Sterilization of Criminals," Report of Committee F of the Institute, *Jour. Crim. Law, Crimin.*, 8 (1917), 499–502. For the questions of heredity, intelligence, and crime see Edith R. Spaulding and William Healy, "Inheritance as a Factor in Criminality," *Jour. Crim. Law, Crimin.*, 6 (1914), 837–59; J. Harold Williams, "Intelligence and Delinquency: A Study of 215 Cases," *Jour. Crim. Law, Crimin.*, 6 (1916), 697–705.

86. Fernald, "Diagnosis of Higher Grades," 80.

87. *Sixty-ninth Massachusetts* (1916).

88. Edgar A. Doll, "On the Use of Term 'Feeble-minded,' " *Jour. Crim. Law, Crimin.*, 8 (1917), 216, 221. Doll succeeded Goddard at Vineland.

89. J. E. Wallace Wallin, "Who is Feeble-minded?" *Jour. Crim. Law, Crimin.*, 6 (1916), 706–17; Wallin entered into an extended literary argument with Samuel C. Kohs, see *Jour. Crim. Law, Crimin.*, March to July 1916; for Wallin's summation see Wallin, *Problems of Subnormality*, pp. 110–277.

90. Robert M. Yerkes, ed., *Psychological Examining in the United States Army*, National Academy of Science, Memoirs, 15 (Washington, 1921), p. 789. Nicholas Pastore, "The Army Intelligence Tests and Walter Lippmann," *Journal of the History of the Behavioral Sciences*, 14 (1978), 316–27. Two excellent historical critiques are Hamilton Cravens, *The Triumph of Evolution, American Scientists and the Heredity-Environment Controversy, 1900–1941* (Philadelphia, 1978), pp. 224–65, and John M. Reisman, *The Development of Clinical Psychology* (New York, 1966), pp. 94–135.

91. Henry H. Goddard, *Human Efficiency and Levels of Intelligence* (Princeton, 1920).

92. *Report of the Special Commission Relative to the Control, Custody, and Treatment of Defectives, Criminals and Misdemeanants* (House Document No. 1403, Boston, 1919), 33. Fernald chaired the commission.

93. Walter E. Fernald, "After-Care Study of the Patients Discharged from Waverly for a Period of Twenty-five Years," Massachusetts Society for Mental Hygiene, Publication No. 39 (Boston, 1919), 8.

94. *Seventeenth Rome* (1912) and Davies, *Social Control*, pp. 108–70.

95. *Sixty-ninth Massachusetts* (1916), 22.

96. "Supervision of the Feeble-minded," *Mental Hygiene*, 1 (1917), 168.

97. Thomas Moore, "Types and Causes of Feeble-mindedness," in *The Problem of Feeble-mindedness*, ed. Thomas Moore (New York, 1917); H. C. Stevens, "Eugenics and Feeble-mindedness," *Jour. Crim. Law, Crimin.*, 6 (1915), 190–97.

98. Edward Lindsay, "Heredity and Responsibility: An Editorial," *Jour. Crim. Law, Crimin.*, 4 (1913), 3. Also see the editorial in *Survey*, 36 (1916), 266, which praised a paper by Adolf Meyer as "a welcome antidote to . . . semi-scientific literature . . . . "

CHAPTER 6

1. Z. Pauline Hoakley, "Extra-institutional Care for the Feeble-minded," American Association for the Study of the Feebleminded, *Proceedings*, 1922 Annual Meeting, 117–37 (hereafter cited as *Proceedings*); Thomas Haines, "Community Service of State Institutions for the

Mentally Defective," *Proceedings* (1923), 38–50; Katharine G. Ecob, "New York State's Accomplishments and Immediate Aims in Extra-institutional Care of Mental Defectives," *Proceedings* (1924), 19–29; Frankwood E. Williams, "Essential Elements in any plan for Community Supervision of Trained Mentally Defective Persons," ibid., 51–55; William C. Sandy, "Community Responsibility and Mental Deficiency," *Proceedings* (1926), 189–94.

2. Inez F. Stebbins, "The Institution in Relation to Community Supervision," *Proceedings* (1925), 174–90; Charles Bernstein, "Rehabilitation of the Mentally Defective," *Proceedings* (1919), 126–55; Charles Bernstein, "Colony Care for Isolating Defective and Dependent Cases," *Proceedings* (1921), 43–54.

3. Edgar A. Doll, "Community Control of the Feeble-minded," *Proceedings* (1929), 161–74.

4. C. T. Jones, "The Problem of the Feeble-minded in New Jersey," *Proceedings* (1928), 204–10; Harry C. Storris, "A Report on an Investigation Made of Cases Discharged from Letchworth Village," *Proceedings* (1929), 220–32.

5. O. J. Cobb, "Parole of Mental Defectives," *Proceedings* (1923), 145–48.

6. Mabel A. Matthews, "One Hundred Institutionally Trained Male Defectives in the Community Under Supervision," *Proceedings* (1921), 60–70.

7. Johanna D. Lillyman, "The Parole System at the Wrentham State School," *Proceedings* (1921), 103–7.

8. H. W. Potter, "A Resume of Parole Work at Letchworth Village," *Proceedings* (1926), 165–86; Roy W. Foley, "A Study of the Patients Discharged from Rome State School for the Twenty Year Period ending December 31, 1924," *Proceedings* (1929), 180–204.

9. Walter E. Fernald, "An Out-Patient Clinic in Connection with a State Institution for the Feeble-minded," *Proceedings* (1920), 81–89; Edith E. Woodhill, "Public School Clinics in Connection with a State School for the Feeble-minded," ibid., 94–103; Walter E. Fernald, "The Inauguration of a State-wide Public School Mental Clinic in Massachusetts," *Proceedings* (1922), 200–15.

10. Walter E. Fernald, "Thirty Years Progress in the Care of the Feeble-minded," *Proceedings* (1924), 211–12.

11. Ibid., 217–19.

12. Mary M. Wolfe, "The Relation of Feeble-mindedness to Education, Citizenship, and Culture," *Proceedings* (1925), 124–33; Mabel R. Fernald, "Some Problems Related to the Education of Mentally Defective Children," *Proceedings* (1927), 137–47; Edgar A. Doll, "Mental Hygiene Aspects of Special Education," *Proceedings* (1930), 73–79; Edgar

A. Doll, "A Special Class Catechism," *The Journal of Educational Research* 12 (1925), 186–203; idem, "The Next Ten Years in Special Education," *The Training School Bulletin* (1928), 145–53.

13. V. V. Anderson, "Education of Mental Defectives in State and Private Institutions and in Special Classes in Public Schools in the United States," *Mental Hygiene*, 5 (1921), 85–122; Thomas H. Haines, "Special Training Facilities for Mentally Handicapped Children in the Public Day Schools of the United States, 1922–1923," *Mental Hygiene*, 8 (1924), 893–911; Ada M. Fitts, "The Value of Special Classes for the Mentally Defective Pupils in the Public Schools," *Proceedings* (1920), 115–23; George E. McPherson, "Special Classes for Retarded Children," American Association on Mental Deficiency (organizational name change in 1933 from AASF to AAMD) *Proceedings* (1933), 202–9; Eleanor Rowlett, "Special Classes in Richmond," *Proceedings* (Part 2 1938), 82–5; Jesse H. Binford, "The Function of the Subnormal Class in City School Systems," ibid., 78–81.

14. Charles Scott Berry, "The Aims and Methods of Education as Applied to Mental Defectives," *Proceedings* (1930), 68–72; Elise H. Martens, "A Conference on Curriculum for Mentally Retarded Children," *Proceedings* (1935), 35–43.

15. Grace A. Taylor, "Education and Training of the Feeble-minded," *Proceedings* (1921), 24–31; Frank L. Wiley, "The Organization and Administration of the Education of Sub-Normal Children in the Public Schools," *Proceedings* (1922), 231–39; Stanley P. Davies, "The Institution in Relation to the School System," *JPA*, 30 (1925), 210–26; Roy F. Street and Minnie Fuller, "Community Responsibility for the Care of the Mentally Deficient Child," *Proceedings* (1935), 190–93; May E. Bryne, "Program of Education for Mentally Retarded Children in a Public School System," *Proceedings* (Part 2 1938), 116–22.

16. Sanger Brown II, "Recommendations for Training the High Grade Mental Defective in Institutions for Community Life," *Proceedings* (1931), 39–44; Abby N. Little and Betsey S. Johnson, "A Study of the Social and Economic Adjustments of 113 Discharged Parolees from Laconia State School," *Proceedings* (1932), 233–48.

17. Milton Harrington, "The Problem of the Defective Delinquent," *Proceedings* (1934), 166–75; Eleanor T. Glueck, "Mental Retardation and Juvenile Delinquency," *Proceedings* (1935), 267–85; Edgar A. Doll and Kathryn A. Fitch, "Social Competence of Delinquent Boys," *Proceedings* (1938), 137–41.

18. Harold M. Skeels and Harold B. Dye, "A Study of the Effects of Differential Stimulation on Mentally Retarded Children," *Proceedings* (1939), 114–36.

19. Ibid., 135–36.

20. M. S. Crissey, "Harold Manville Skeels," *AJMD*, 75 (1970), 1–3; Beth C. Wellman, "IQ Changes of Preschool and Non-preschool Groups During the Preschool Years: A Summary of the Literature," *Journal of Psychology*, 20 (1945), 247–68.

21. William Healy and Augusta F. Bronner, *Delinquents and Criminals* (New York, 1926), pp. 150–51; idem, *New Light on Delinquency and Its Treatment* (New Haven, 1936), p. 162.

22. Walter M. Thayer, "Institutional Training of the Defective Delinquent," *Proceedings* (1925), 38–44; Thorleiff G. Hegge, "Reading Cases in an Institution for Mentally Retarded Problem Children," *Proceedings* (1932), 149–212; Robert H. Haskell, "An Organization for the Training of Higher Grade Mental Defectives," ibid., 252–69; Thorleiff G. Hegge, "Special Reading Disability with Particular Reference to the Mentally Deficient," *Proceedings* (1934), 297–340; Samuel A. Kirk, "Attitudes Toward Behavior Problems in an Institution for High Grade Mentally Deficient Problem Children," *Proceedings* (1935), 368–84; Mabel Bowers, "Impromptu Music in Young Mental Defectives," *Proceedings* (Part 2, 1938), 62–71; Arthur H. Steele, "A Study of Nocturnal Enuresis in an Institution for Children," ibid., 127–34; Newell C. Kephart and M. H. Ainsworth, "A Preliminary Report of Community Adjustment of Parolees of the Wayne County Training School," ibid., 161–66; Robert H. Haskill, "The Development of a Research Program in Mental Deficiency over a Fifteen-Year Period," *American Journal of Psychiatry*, 101 (1944), 73–81; Thorleiff G. Hegge, "Some Aspects of the Wayne County Training School: An Institution for High Grade and Borderline Mentally Retarded Children," *AJMD*, 61 (1956), 58–93; "Children with Mental and Emotional Disabilities. A Symposium Held in Celebration of the 25th Anniversary of the Wayne County Training School, Northville, Michigan," *AJMD*, 56 (1952), 665–700.

23. Harvey M. Watkins, "Administration in Institutions of over Two Thousand," *Proceedings* (1928), 235–54; Leroy M. A. Maeder, "The Problem of Mental Deficiency in Pennsylvania," *Proceedings* (1932), 33–51.

24. Charles L. Vaux, "Family Care of Mental Defectives," *Proceedings* (1935), 168–88; Edgar A. Doll and S. Geraldine Longwell, "Social Competence of Feeble-minded in Family Care," *Proceedings* (1938), 211–16.

25. George J. Veith, "Training the Idiot and Imbecile," *Proceedings* (1927), 148–68.

26. Arthur E. Westwell, "Recreation in a State Institution," *Proceedings* (1928), 149–65; Philip S. Waters, "The Value of Play as a Means of Social Education for the Feeble-minded," *Proceedings* (1932), 357–76; William Van De Wall, "A Music Program for the Institutions for the

Mentally Deficient," ibid., 70–97; Bertha E. Schlotter, "Recreation in a State Institution for Mental Defectives," *Proceedings* (1935), 505–13; Hildegarde E. Graeve, "The Music Program in an Institution," ibid., 228–33.

27. C. S. Little, "Random Remarks on State Institutions," *Proceedings* (1923), 59–65; Sanger Brown II, "The Year's Progress in New York State in the Care of Mental Defectives," ibid., 198–203.

28. Joseph Zubin, "Regional Differences in the Care of the Mental Defect and Epilepsy," *Proceedings* (Part 2, 1938), 167–78; W. H. Dixon, "Institutional Administration," *Proceedings* (1929), 62–68; G. M. Stafford, "Some of the Problems Encountered in an Institution," *Proceedings* (1928), 229–31.

29. C. Stanley Raymond, "The Need for Research in the Field of Mental Deficiency," *Proceedings* (1933), 71–80; George S. Stevenson, "The Need for a Biological Approach to an Understanding of the Feeble-minded," *Proceedings* (1927), 23–30.

30. E. A. Whitney, "A Review of Ten Years Surgical Work in an Institution for the Feeble-minded," *Proceedings* (1935), 386–92; Ransom A. Greene, "A Survey of Tuberculosis in a School for the Feeble-minded," *Proceedings* (1931), 213–24.

31. Neil A. Dayton, "Mortality in Mental Deficiency over a Fourteen Year Period: Analysis of 8976 Cases and 878 Deaths in Massachusetts," *Proceedings* (1931), 127–205.

32. Abraham Meyerson, "Researches in Feeble-mindedness," *Proceedings* (1926), 203–9; George Van Ness Dearborn, "Amentia in Medical Diagnosis," *Proceedings* (1934), 54–65.

33. Edward J. Humphreys, "The Field of Psychiatry in Relation to the Work of the State School," *Proceedings* (1938), 80–89; Mary Vanuxem, "The Prevalence of Mental Disease Among Mental Defectives," *Proceedings* (1935), 242–49; Florentine Hackbusch, "270 Patients on the Waiting List," ibid., 319–35; Ransom A. Greene, "Conflicts in Diagnosis Between Mental Deficiency and Certain Psychoses," *Proceedings* (1933), 127–43; Kanner, *A History of the Care*, pp. 142–43; Frank J. Menolascino, "Psychoses of Childhood: Experiences of a Mental Retardation Pilot Project," *AJMD*, 70 (1965), 83–92; Lawson G. Lowrey, "The Relationship of Feeble-mindedness to Behavior Disorders," *Proceedings* (1928), 96–100.

34. Mabel Ann Matthews, "Some Effects of the Depression on Social Work with the Feeble-minded," *Proceedings* (1934), 46–50; Lloyd N. Yepsen, "Newer Trends in the Rehabilitation of the Mentally Deficient," ibid., 101–6; Meta L. Anderson, "The New Deal and Special Education, ibid., 385–88.

35. Matthews, "Some Effects of the Depression," 50.

36. Frank W. Ghent, "An Experiment in Vocational Training for High School Graduates in the Care of Defective Children," *Proceedings* (1935), 136–46.

37. H. Robert Otness, "A Population Inventory," *AJMD*, 55 (1950–51), 19–22.

38. Dean T. Collins, "Children of Sorrow. A History of the Mentally Retarded in Kansas," *Bulletin of the History of Medicine*, 39 (1965), 68–70; Samuel Levine, "Educational Problems in State Institutions for the Mentally Retarded," *AJMD*, 58 (1954), 403–7; Karl F. Heiser, "Mental Deficiency in the Urban Community," *American Journal of Orthopsychiatry*, 27 (1957), 484–89; Rudolf Kaldeck, "Psychiatric Approach to Mental Deficiency," *AJMD*, 64 (1959), 50–56; Leland V. Bell, *Treating the Mentally Ill*, pp. 153–55.

39. Mary E. Downey, "The Disturbed Wards," *AJMD*, 55 (1950–51), 334–40; Margaret W. O'Brien, "A Vocational Study of a Group of Institutionalized Persons," *AJMD*, 57 (1952), 56–62; M. I. Badt, "Level of Abstraction in Vocabulary Definitions of Mentally Retarded School Children," *AJMD*, 63 (1958), 241–46; M. R. Denny, "Research in Learning and Performance," in H. A. Stevens and R. Heber, eds., *Mental Retardation: A Review of Research* (Chicago: 1964); R. A. Dentler and B. Mackler, "The Socialization of Retarded Children in an Institution," *Journal of Health and Human Behavior*, 2 (1961), 243–52; P. Morris, *Put Away: A Sociological Study of Institutions for the Mentally Retarded* (New York, 1969); Nicholas Hobbs, ed., *Issues in the Classification of Children* (San Francisco, 1976); George M. Guthrie, Alfred Butler, and Leon Gorlow, "Personality Differences Between Institutionalized and Noninstitutionalized Retardates," *AJMD*, 67 (1963), 543–47.

40. M. A. Wirtz, "The Development of Current Thinking About Facilities for the Severely Retarded," *AJMD*, 60 (1956), 497–500; Joseph T. Weingold, "Parent Groups and the Problem of Mental Retardation," *AJMD*, 56 (1952), 484–92; Godfrey D. Stevens and Bernice Seltz, "Assisting Parent Groups in Working Together," *AJMD*, 60 (1955), 1–6; Joseph H. Levy, *Parent Groups and Social Agencies* (Chicago, 1951); Norma L. Bostock, "How Can Parents and Professionals Coordinate for the Betterment of all Retarded Children," *AJMD*, 60 (1956), 428–32; M. Willie Blance, "The Role of the Social Worker," *AJMD*, 66 (1961), 464–71.

41. Richard Carter, *The Gentle Legions* (New York, 1961).

42. Benjamin Malzberg, "Some Statistical Aspects of First Admissions to the New York State Schools for Mental Defectives," *AJMD*, 57 (1952), 27–37; Herbert Goldstein, "Population Trends in US Public Institutions for the Mentally Deficient," *AJMD*, 63 (1959), 599–604; Robert E. Patton and Abbott S. Weinstein, "Changing Characteristics of

the Population in the New York State Schools for Mental Defectives,"
AJMD, 64 (1960), 625–35; George Tarjan, Richard K. Eyman, and Harvey
F. Dingham, "Changes in the Patient Population of a Hospital for the
Mentally Retarded," *AJMD*, 70 (1966), 529–41; R. A. Kurtz, "Sex and
Age Trends in Admission to an Institution for the Mentally Retarded,
1910–1959," *Nebraska State Medical Journal*, 52 (1967), 134–43; George
Tarjan, H. F. Dingman, C. R. Miller, "Statistical Expectations of Se-
lected Handicaps in the Mentally Retarded," *AJMD*, 65 (1960), 335–41;
S. W. Wright, M. Valente, and George Tarjan, "Medical Problems on
a Ward of a Hospital for the Mentally Retarded," *American Journal of
Diseases of Children*, 104 (1962), 64–70 (hereafter cited *AJDis Child*); George
Tarjan, S. W. Wright, M. Kramer, P. H. Person, Jr., and R. Morgan,
"The Natural History of Mental Deficiency in a State Hospital. Part I:
Probabilities of Release and Death by Age, Intelligence Quotient, and
Diagnosis," *AJDis Child*, 96 (1958), 64–70; George Tarjan, S. W. Wright,
H. F. Dingman, and S. Sabagh, "The Natural History of Mental Defi-
ciency in a State Hospital. Part II: Mentally Deficient Children Admit-
ted to a State Hospital Prior to Their Sixth Birthday," *AJDis Child*, 98
(1959), 370–78; George Tarjan, S. W. Wright, H. F. Dingman, and R.
K. Eyman, "The Natural History of Mental Deficiency in a State Hos-
pital. Part III: Selected Characteristics of First Admissions and Their
Environment," *AJDis Child*, 101 (1961), 195–205; Harold A. Decker,
Edward N. Herberg, Mary S. Haythornwaite, Lois K. Rupke, and
Donald C. Smith, "Provisions of Health Care for Institutionalized Retarded Children," *AJMD*, 73 (1968), 283–93.

    43. Margaretta D. Robbins, "What Parents Expect the Institutions to
Do for Their Children," *AJMD*, 61 (1957), 672–74; E. Paul Benoit, "More
Funds for Institutionalized Retarded Children," *AJMD*, 58 (1953), 93–
107.

    44. Dorothy Dewing, "Use of Occupational Therapy in the Sociali-
zation of Severely Retarded Children," *AJMD*, 57 (1952), 43–49; Daniel
Liberman, "The Education of the Severely Retarded Child," *AJMD*, 58
(1954), 397–402; Frances A. Caine, "Public Education and the Severely
Retarded Child," *AJMD*, 59 (1954), 37–38; Al Tudyman, "A Realistic
Total Program for the Severely Mentally Retarded," *AJMD*, 60 (1955),
574–82; Charles P. Jubenville, "A State Program for Day Care Centers
for the Severely Retarded," *AJMD*, 66 (1962), 829–37; N. R. Ellis, "Toilet Training the Severely Defective Patient: An S-R Reinforcement
Analysis," *AJMD*, 68 (1963), 98–103; Philip Roos, "Changing Roles of
the Residential Institution," *Mental Retardation*, 4 (1966), 4–6.

    45. Harriet Rheingold, "Interpreting Mental Retardation to Par-
ents," *Journal of Consulting Psychology*, 9 (1945), 142–48; Gale H. Walker,
"Social and Emotional Problems of the Mentally Retarded Child,"

AJMD, 55 (1950–51), 132–38; A. E. Grebler, "Parental Attitudes Toward Mentally Retarded Children," *AJMD*, 56 (1952), 475–83; Margaret Richards, "The Retarded Child in a State School and the Problems He Presents from a Parent's Viewpoint," *AJMD*, 58 (1953), 56–59; Anne C. French, M. Levbarg, and H. Michal–Smith, "Parent Counseling as a Means of Improving the Performance of a Mentally Retarded Boy: A Case Study Presentation," ibid., 13–20; Cleo E. Popp, Vivien Ingram, Paul H. Jordan, "Helping Parents Understand Their Mentally Handicapped Child," *AJMD*, 58 (1954), 530–39; Elise F. Morris, "Casework Training Needs for Counseling Parents of the Retarded," *AJMD*, 59 (1955), 510–16; Edmund W. Gordon and Montague Ullman, "Reactions of Parents to Problems of Mental Retardation in Children," *AJMD*, 61 (1956), 158–63; Arthur Mandelbaum and Mary E. Wheeler, "The Meaning of a Defective Child to Parents," *Social Casework*, 41 (1960), 799–802; Stella Stillson Slaughter, *The Mentally Retarded Child and His Parent* (New York, 1960).

46. Joseph Rankin, "Group Therapy Experiment with Mothers of Mentally Deficient Children," *AJMD*, 62 (1957), 49–55; Glenn V. Ramsey, "Review of Group Methods with Parents of the Mentally Retarded," *AJMD*, 71 (1967), 857–63; A. Blatt, "Group Therapy with Parents of Severely Retarded Children: A Preliminary Report," *Group Psychotherapy*, 10 (1957), 133–40; J. T. Weingold and R. P. Hormuth, "Group Guidance of Parents of Mentally Retarded Children," *Journal of Clinical Psychology*, 9 (1953), 118–24; M. L. Yates and R. Lederer, "Short-term Group Meetings with Parents of Children with Mongolism," *AJMD*, 65 (1961), 467–72.

47. H. Michal-Smith, "A Study of the Personal Characteristics Desirable for the Vocational Success of the Mentally Retarded," *AJMD*, 55 (1950–51), 139–43; Elizabeth W. Buck, "Developing the Community's Responsibility for the Adjustment of the Mentally Retarded," ibid., 407–13; Naomi S. Richards, "Vocational Training in Sheltered Workshops," *AJMD*, 56 (1951), 344–48; Ann Lehman, "Dealing with the Employer in Job Finding and Placement," ibid., 445–47; Ralf A. Peckham, "Problems in Job Adjustment of the Mentally Retarded," ibid., 448–53; Janet I. Pinner, "The Public Employment Service and Effective Relationships with Other Agencies," ibid., 454–56; "Emotional, Social, and Cognitive Re-education of the Mentally Handicapped. A Symposium," *AJMD*, 62 (1958), 521–72; Shirley Mae Wolk, "A Survey of the Literature on Curriculum Practices for the Mentally Retarded," ibid., 826–39; Louis E. Rosenzweig, "The Rehabilitation of the Mentally Retarded," *AJMD*, 59 (1954), 26–34; Gordon R. Shachoy, "Training the Mentally Deficient for Community Adjustment," ibid., 226–30; Albert J. Shafter, "The Vocational Placement of Institutionalized Mental De-

fectives in the United States," ibid., 279–307; Sol L. Warren, "Problems in the Placement and Follow-up of the Mentally Retarded," ibid., 408–12; Margaret Hudson, "The Severely Retarded Child: Educable vs Trainable," ibid., 583–86; E. Arthur Whitney, "Current Trends in Institutions for the Mentally Retarded," *AJMD*, 60 (1955), 10–20; Edward C. Harold, "Employment of Patients Discharged from the St. Louis State Training School," ibid., 397–402.

48. I. Ignacy Goldberg, "New Look in the Concept of the Rehabilitation of the Mentally Retarded in a State Institution," ibid., 467–69; Isaac N. Wolfson, "Follow-up Studies of 92 Male and 131 Female Patients who were Discharged from the Newark State School in 1946," *AJMD*, 61 (1956), 224–38; "The Role of Varied Therapies in the Rehabilitation of the Retarded Child," ibid., 508–15; Salvatore G. DiMichael, "Vocational Diagnosis and Counseling of the Retarded in Sheltered Workshops," *AJMD*, 64 (1960), 652–57; S. A. Kirk and G. O. Johnson, *Educating the Retarded Child* (New York, 1951); Chris J. De Prospo and Richard H. Hungerfold, "A Complete Social Program for the Mentally Retarded," *Occupational Education*, 3 (1946), 95–107; Max Dubrow, "Sheltered Workshops for the Mentally Retarded as an Educational and Vocational Experience," *Personnel and Guidance Journal*, 38 (1960), 392–95; William A. Fraenkel, "Planning the Vocational Future of the Mentally Retarded; Current Trends in Community Programing," *Rehabilitation Literature*, 22 (1961), 4, 98–104; I. Ignacy Goldberg, "Current Status of Education and Training in the United States for Trainable Mentally Retarded Children," *Exceptional Children*, 24 (1957), 146–54; L. N. Yepsen, "Subnormal Minds are Abler Than You Think," *Journal of Rehabilitation*, 15 (1949), 8–12; Salvatore G. DiMichael, "Employment of the Mentally Retarded," ibid., 3–7; Salvatore DiMichael, ed., *Vocational Rehabilitation of the Mentally Retarded* (Washington, 1950).

49. William H. Dunn, "The Readjustment of the Mentally Deficient Soldier in the Community," *AJMD*, 51 (1946), 50.

50. Sara Neham, "Psychotherapy in Relation to Mental Deficiency," *AJMD*, 55 (1951), 557–72; Edward J. Humphreys, "Widening Psychiatric Horizons in the Field of Mental Retardation," *AJMD*, 61 (1956), 390–98; Leonard J. Duhl, "Mental Retardation. A Review of Mental Health Implications," *AJMD*, 62 (1957), 5–13; Rudolf Kaldeck, "Psychiatric Approach to Mental Deficiency," *AJMD*, 64 (1959), 50–56; Frank J. Menolascino, "Emotional Disturbance and Mental Retardation," *AJMD*, 70 (1965), 248–56; Leon Eisenberg, "Review of Psychiatric Progress: Mental Deficiency," *American Journal of Psychiatry*, 117 (1960), 606–7.

51. George S. Stevenson, "Community Organization for a General

Mental Health Program," *AJMD*, 55 (1950–51), 479–84; Warren T. Vaughan, Jr., "A Community Mental Health Approach to Mental Retardation," *AJMD*, 65 (1961), 577–81; idem, "Certain Real Problems in the Development of Community Programs for the Medical Care, Education, and Training of the Mentally Retarded," *American Journal of Public Health*, 47 (1957), 706–12; A.C.K. Hallock and W. T. Vaughan, Jr., "Community Organization—A Dynamic Component of Community Mental Health Practice," *American Journal of Orthopsychiatry*, 26 (1956), 691–706; D. Vail, "Mental Deficiency: Response to Milieu Therapy," *American Journal of Psychiatry*, 113 (1956), 170–73; Maxwell Jones, *The Therapeutic Community* (New York, 1953); Louis Rowitz, "Socioepidemiological Analysis of Admissions to a State Operated Outpatient Clinic for Retarded Children," *AJMD*, 78 (1973), 300–307; Bell, *Treating the Mentally Ill*, pp. 156–63.

52. J. M. Stubblebine and R. D. Roadruck, "Treatment Program for Mentally Deficient Adolescents," *AJMD*, 60 (1956), 552–56; Albert J. Shafter, "A Philosophy of Institutional Administration," *AJMD*, 65 (1960), 313–17; Albert J. Shafter and Charles S. Chandler, "Merit Wards—Settings for Social and Vocational Training," *AJMD*, 64 (1960), 1029–33; Ann M. Clarke and A.D.B. Clarke, eds., *Mental Deficiency— The Changing Outlook* (Glencoe, 1958).

53. C. L. Stacey and M. F. DeMartino, ed., *Counseling and Psychotherapy with the Mentally Retarded* (Glencoe, 1956); M. Cotzin, "Group Psychotherapy with Mentally Defective Problem Boys," *AJMD*, 53 (1948), 268–82; Sara Neham, "Psychotherapy in Relation to Mental Deficiency," *AJMD*, 55 (1951), 557–72; Seymour B. Sarason, *Psychological Problems in Mental Deficiency* (New York, 1949); idem, "Individual Psychotherapy with Mentally Defective Individuals," *AJMD*, 56 (1952), 803–5; Mariella Z. Menzel, "Psychotherapeutic Techniques Among the Mentally Deficient," ibid., 796–802; Louise A. Fisher and Isaac N. Wolfson, "Group Therapy of Mental Defectives," *AJMD*, 58 (1954), 486–89; Glenn Wiest, "Psychotherapy with the Mentally Retarded," *AJMD*, 59 (1955), 640–44; Myrtle Astrachan, "Group Psychotherapy with Mentally Retarded Female Adolescents and Adults," *AJMD*, 60 (1955), 152–56; Malcolm J. Farrell and Eli Forsley, "Enhancing Patients Adjustment by Means of Group Sessions with Attendants," ibid., 603–7; N. DeMaplma, "Group Psychotherapy with High Grade Imbeciles and Low Grade Morons," *Delaware State Medical Journal*, 28 (1956), 200–3.

54. Simon Horenstein, "Reserpine and Chlorpromazine in Hyperactive Mental Defectives," *AJMD*, 61 (1957), 525–29; R. L. Gatski, *JAMA*, 157 (1955), 1298; Alfred H. Johnston and Charles H. Martin, "The Clinical Use of Reserpine and Chlorpromazine in the Care of the Mentally Deficient," *AJMD*, 62 (1957), 292–94; L. H. Rudy, H. E. Himwich,

Franco Rinaldi, "A Clinical Evaluation of Psychopharmacological Agents in the Management of Disturbed Mentally Defective Patients," ibid., 855–60; H. Schiller, "Reserpine, Chlorpromazine, and the Mentally Retarded, A Report of 139 Cases," *Psychiatric Quarterly*, 33 (1959), 683–99.

55. Edward D. Berkowitz, "The Politics of Mental Retardation During the Kennedy Administration," *Social Science Quarterly*, 61 (1980), 128–32.

56. Ibid., 132–37; *President's Panel on Mental Retardation. A Proposed Program for National Action to Combat Mental Retardation* (Washington, October 1962).

57. "Message from the President of the United States Relative to Mental Illness and Mental Retardation," *American Journal of Psychiatry*, 120 (1964), 729.

58. Ibid., 730.

59. "Congress Enacts New Mental Health Programs," *Congressional Quarterly Almanac*, 88th Congress, 1st Session, 1963, XIX, 222–23; "Services and Facilities for the Mentally Retarded and Persons with Other Developmental Disabilities and Mental Health Centers," *United States Code Annotated*. Title 42 The Public Health and Welfare (St. Paul, 1964), 341–71; Berkowitz, "The Politics of Mental Retardation During the Kennedy Administration," Social Science Quarterly, 137–43.

60. Edward Zigler, "Twenty Years of Mental Retardation Research," *Mental Retardation*, 15 (1977), 51–53.

61. Martin Rosen, Gerald R. Clark, and Marvin S. Kivitz, eds., *The History of Mental Retardation Collected Papers*, Vol. 2 (Baltimore, 1976), p. 305; William Sloan and Harvey A. Stevens, *A Century of Concern. A History of the American Association on Mental Deficiency, 1876–1976* (Washington, 1976), pp. 261–304; Gunnar Dybward, "The Importance of Prevention in Mental Retardation," *Mental Retardation*, 7 (1969), 3–6; Tzuen-Jen Lei, Edgar W. Butler, Louis Rowitz, and Ronald J. McAllister, "Agency-Labeled Mentally Retarded Persons in a Metropolitan Area: An Ecological Study," *AJMD*, 79 (1974), 22–31.

62. Richard Koch, "President's Address," *AJMD*, 74 (1969–70), 2–4.

63. Ibid., 4; Wesley D. White, "President's Address: The Role of AAMD in the 1970's," *Mental Retardation*, 8 (1969–70), 2–3.

64. Wesley D. White and Wolf Wolfensberger, "The Evolution of Dehumanization in Our Institutions," *Mental Retardation*, 7 (1969), 5–9; Irving Philips, "Children, Mental Retardation, and Planning," *American Journal of Orthopsychiatry*, 35 (1965), 899–902; R. C. Scheerenberger, *Deinstitutionalization and Institutional Reform* (Springfield, Ill., 1976); Wolf Wolfensberger, "Models of Mental Retardation," *New Society*, 8 (1970), 51–53.

65. Andrew T. Scull, *Decarceration* (Englewood Cliffs, 1977).

66. Bengt Nirje, "The Normalization Principle and Its Human Management Implications," in Robert B. Kugel and Wolf Wolfensberger, eds., *Changing Patterns of Residential Services for the Mentally Retarded* (Washington, January 10, 1969), 181–95; Wolf Wolfensberger, *The Principle of Normalization in Human Services* (Toronto, 1972).

67. Michael J. Begab, "The Major Dilemma of Mental Retardation," *AJMD*, 78 (1974), 519–29.

68. David Rosen, "President's Address: Observations of an Era of Transition," *Mental Retardation*, 12 (1974), 61–63.

69. Rosen, Clark, Kivitz, *The History of Mental Retardation*, Vol. 2, pp. 305–9; *Summary of Existing Legislation Relating to the Handicapped* (Washington, August 1980).

70. E. W. Martin, "Breakthrough for the Handicapped: Legislative Breakthrough," *Exceptional Children*, 34 (1963), 493–503; idem, "A National Commitment to the Rights of the Individual—1776–1976," *Exceptional Children*, 43 (1976), 132–35; J. W. Melcher, "Law, Litigation, and Handicapped Children," ibid., 126–30; Reed Martin, *Educating Handicapped Children. The Legal Mandate* (Champaign, Ill., 1979).

71. Ruth B. Caplan, *Psychiatry and the Community in Nineteenth Century America* (New York, 1969), pp. 334–44.

Bibliographical Essay

This is a commentary on sources we found most useful and informative. It is not a comprehensive bibliography of all works consulted and does not purport to be a compilation of all materials in the field. The notes for each chapter will guide the reader to the appropriate sources.

The most useful and readily available primary sources are the reports of the superintendents and trustees of the American institutions for the mentally retarded. The majority of these reports are annual, the remainder are biennial. For the thirty years of the schools' existence, the *Annual Reports* provide invaluable insights into institutional operations as well as the medical and educational theories of the superintendents; especially useful are the early reports of Samuel G. Howe, Hervey B. Wilbur, Gustavius A. Doren, James B. Richards, Isaac N. Kerlin, and Charles T. Wilbur.

As the custodial role of the schools became more pronounced, the reports assumed a more "institutional" character; greater space and detail were devoted to agricultural and industrial matters and the physical aspects of the facilities. There were fewer discussions of individuals or of case histories, and the reports of trustees grew more perfunctory. Around 1900, superintendents used their reports in propaganda efforts intended to spur legislative and public interest in the menace of the feeble-minded. The work of Henry H. Goddard, Walter E. Fernald, Martin W. Barr, A. W. Wilmarth, Alexander Johnson, and Edward R. Johnstone are the most significant in this regard.

After 1865, the *Annual Reports* can be supplemented by the yearly statements of the various state boards of charities, which served as supervisory agencies for charitable and correctional institutions. The value of these documents varies considerably as does their titles. The state boards of charities and corrections were generally renamed as the state departments of public welfare after 1900. Many of the departments issued detailed quarterly bulletins of institutional operation, supplying good information about state policy, administrative opinion, and daily institutional life.

Other important state documents include the reports of the various commissions to investigate mental retardation. The first and one of the most significant was the *Report of the Massachusetts Commission on the Condition of Idiots in the Commonwealth* (Senate Document No. 51, Boston, 1848). Also noteworthy is the *Report of the New York State Commission to Investigate Provisions for the Mentally Deficient* (Albany, 1915) because of its size (628 pages), scope, contents, and excellent bibliography. Two additional sources of pre–1920 bibliographic references are: "Feeble-mindedness: A Selective Bibliography," *Bulletin of the Russell Sage Foundation Library* No. 15 (New York, 1916), and Leland C. Whitney, "Bibliography of Feeble-mindedness in its Social Aspects," *Journal of Psycho-Asthenics* Monograph Supplements, 1 (No. 3, March 1917).

There are only a limited number of relevant federal publications prior to World War I; most of the interest in retardation remained at the state and local level until after 1920. Beginning with the Census of 1850 and continuing through the Census of 1890 there were attempts to enumerate all the retarded. After 1890 the Census Bureau was instructed to survey institutional populations only. Prior to 1890 the census data must be used with caution as it is more suggestive than authoritative. After 1910 the publications of the Children's Bureau of the Department of Labor, notably the work of Emma O. Lundberg in the "Dependent, Defective and Delinquent Classes" series, are worthwhile; helpful also are the *United States Public Health Reports* and the *Bulletins* of the Bureau of Education.

The records, proceedings, and journals of several national, state, and local organizations are important sources. The *Proceedings of the National Conference of Corrections and Charities* are significant for their scope and national focus, and at least fourteen states and New York City had their own conferences modeled after the national organization. The *Proceedings of the Association of Medical Officers of American Institutions for Idiotic and Feeble-minded Persons* which became in 1906 *Proceedings of the American Association for the Study of the Feebleminded,* and in 1933 *Proceedings of the American Association on Mental Deficiency,* are essential for any understanding of the superintendents, their institutions, and their profession. The records and publications from the National Committee on Mental Hygiene, the Eugenics Record Office, and the Committee on Provision for the Feeble-minded are also important.

There is a great deal of periodical literature, much of it in medical journals. The best guides to these sources are the *Index Catalogue of the Library of the Surgeon-General's Office* and the *Index Medicus*. The *Journal of Psycho-Asthenics, The American Journal of Mental Deficiency, Mental Retardation, Training School Bulletin, Eugenical News*, and the *Boston Medical and Surgical Journal* have important articles in virtually every volume.

The early treatment of the mentally retarded is discussed with firsthand knowledge by Edward Seguin in "Origin of the Treatment and Training of Idiots," *American Journal of Education*, 2 (August 1856), 145–52; *Idiocy and Its Treatment by the Physiological Method* (New York, 1870); and *New Facts and Remarks Concerning Idiocy* (New York, 1870). Harlan L. Lane, *The Wild Boy of Aveyron* (Cambridge, 1976) is the best historical work but there are serviceable secondary accounts in Martin W. Barr, *Mental Defectives: Their History, Treatment, and Training* (Philadelphia, 1904); Stanley P. Davies, *Social Control of the Mentally Deficient* (New York, 1930); and Albert Deutsch, *The Mentally Ill in America: A History of Their Care and Treatment from Colonial Times* (New York, 1949).

There are few adequate studies of the men who worked with the retarded. The exception is the treatment given to Seguin in William Boyd, *From Locke to Montessori* (London, 1914); Ivor Kraft, "Edward Seguin and the Nineteenth–Century Moral Treatment of Idiots," *Bulletin of the History of Medicine*, 35 (September-October 1961), 393–419; and Mabel E. Talbot, *Edward Seguin: A Study of an Educational Approach to the Treatment of Mentally Defective Children* (New York, 1964).

The most recent historical overview of the treatment of the retarded is R. C. Scheerenberger, *A History of Mental Retardation* (Baltimore, 1983). Leo Kanner, *A History of the Care and Study of the Mentally Retarded* (Springfield, Ill., 1964) remains a good source. Marvin Rosen, Gerald R. Clark, and Marvin S. Kivitz, eds., *The History of Mental Retardation: Collected Papers* (Baltimore, 1976), 2 vols., provides many important documents and some commentary. Margaret Adams, *Mental Retardation and Its Social Dimensions* (New York, 1971) is a useful item. The following are more present-minded but offer some historical insights: Leopold D. Lippman, *Attitudes Toward the Handicapped: A Comparison Between Europe and the United States* (Springfield, Ill., 1972); Wolf Wolfensberger, *The Origin and Nature of Our Institutional Models* (Syracuse, 1975); R. C. Scheerenberger, *Deinstitutionalization and Institutional Reform* (Springfield, Ill., 1976); and Seymour B. Sarason and John Doris, *Educational Handicap, Public Policy, and Social History* (New York, 1979).

The work of Gerald N. Grob and David J. Rothman in their studies of institutions and public policy must be acknowledged although neither directly addresses mental retardation: Gerald N. Grob, *Mental Institutions in America. Social Policy to 1875* (New York, 1975) and *Mental Illness and American Society* (New York, 1983) should be compared to David J. Rothman, *The Discovery of the Asylum: Social Order and Disorder in the New Republic* (Boston, 1971) and *Conscience and Convenience: The Asylum and Its Alternatives in Progressive America* (Boston, 1980).

Recent studies have focused largely on deinstitutionalization and the ways of providing care for the retarded in the community. Some of the important works include: Burton Blatt, *Exodus from Pandemonium: Human Abuse and Reformation of Public Policy* (Boston, 1970) and *Souls in Extremis: An Anthology on Victims and Victimizers* (Boston, 1973); Robert B. Edgerton, *The Cloak of Competence: Stigma in the Lives of the Mentally Retarded* (Berkeley, 1967) and *Mental Retardation* (Cambridge, 1979); Norman R. Bernstein, ed., *Diminished People: Problems and Care of the Mentally Retarded* (Boston, 1970); David L. Braddock, *Opening Closed Doors: The Deinstitutionalization of Disabled Individuals* (Reston, Va., 1977); Bruce L. Baker, Gary B. Seltzer, and Marsha M. Seltzer, *As Close as Possible: Community Residences for Retarded Adults* (Boston, 1977); Joseph Halpern et al., *The Myths of Deinstitutionalization: Policies for the Mentally Disabled* (Boulder, 1980); Patricia T. Cegelka, ed., *Mental Retardation. From Categories to People* (Columbus, 1982); and Andrew Garoogian, *Deinstitutionalization and the Care of the Developmentally Disabled: A Select Bibliography* (Monticello, Ill., 1982).

Index

American Association for the Study of the Feeble-minded (AASF), 89, 107. *See also* Association of Medical Officers of American Institutions for Idiotic and Feeble-minded Persons; American Association on Mental Deficiency

American Association on Mental Deficiency, 147

American Asylum for the Deaf and Dumb (Hartford, Conn.), 10

American Breeders Association, 95, 111-12

American Health Association, 51

American Institute of Criminal Law and Criminology, 120

Amoros, Francisco, 9

Annual Reports: early role of, xi, 25, 27, 31-32; changing institutional roles, 71-72

asexualization, professional debate over, 100-104. *See* Barr, Martin W.

Association of Medical Officers of American Institutions for Idiotic and Feeble-minded Persons (AMO): founding of, 50-53; reorganization of, 89-90

Association of Medical Superintendents of American Institutions for the Insane, 11, 52

Asylums, 138

Aveyron, "savage" or "wild boy of" (Victor), 3-6

Awl, William, 11

Backus, Frederick J., 11-12

Barr, Martin W., 89, 92, 93, 96, 99, 102-4, 106; *Mental Defectives*, 94

Barre, Mass., first American school at, 16

Barrows, Isabel, 105

Barry, Charles Scott, 128

Beach, Fletcher, 45-49

Beers, Clifford, ix

Benedikt, Moriz, 68

Bernstein, Charles, 121, 123-24

Binet, Alfred, intelligence tests and, 106
boards of charities, 31-32
Bonnaterre, Pierre-Joseph, 4
Boyington, Horatio, 12
Bridgeman, Laura, 15
Brigham, Amariah, 11
British Royal Commission on the Care and Control of the Feeble-minded, 107-8
Brockett, Linus P., 19
Bronner, Augusta F., 131
Brown, George, 50, 72
Brown, George A., 72
Butler, Amos W., 104
Byrers, Joseph P. 117

"C" Family, 114
California: School for the Feeble-minded, 91; milieu therapy, 142
Caplan, Gerald, 150
Carson, James C., 73, 91
castration, 101
census: underenumeration, 29; Census of 1880, 67, 88; Census of 1890, 88
charity societies, 51
child stereotyping, 108
civil rights of the retarded, 99-100, 145-51
classification of the retarded: 1850's, 26-27; 1870's, 40-41; intelligence tests and, 107; 1930's, problems with, 135
Cobb, O. J., 124
Commercial Hospital and Lunatic Asylum (Cincinnati), 10
community care, xii, 123-51; Rome State Asylum and, 123-24; 1950's and, 140
Connecticut: American Asylum for the Deaf and Dumb, 10;

Commission on Idiocy, 18; School for Imbeciles (Lakeville), 29
counseling parents of retarded children, 140
Council for the Retarded Children of Cuyahoa County (Cleveland), 138
criminal anthropology, 81
custodialism, institutional, x-xi; lack of, 21-29; 1860's, 36-43; 1890's, 71-72; 1920's and 1930's, 132-34
Cutting, R. Bayard, 117

Dacks Family, 114
Davenport, Charles B., 95, 112, 115-16, 118
deaf, education of, 5
de Condillac, Etienne Bonnet, 4
defective class, 92
defective delinquent, 110-11, 131
defective families, xiii, 114-15. See also Jukes, The; Kallikak Family, The
Defects Found in Drafted Men, 124
degeneration, 6-7, 14, 26
deinstitutionalization, 147
Developmental Disabilities Assistance and Bill of Rights Act of 1975, 150
Dix, Dorothea, ix, 17
Doll, Edgar A., 120
Doren, Gustavus, 33-34, 50, 63
drug treatment, 144
Dugdale, Robert L., 54-58, 68. See also heredity; Jukes, The

economic depression of the 1930's, and retardation care, 136-37
educational model, caring for the retarded, xiv-xv

Education for All Handicapped
    Children Act of 1975, 150
Elwyn, Alfred, 17
Elwyn (Pennsylvania Training
    School for Feeble-minded Chil-
    dren), early history of, 17-18
Emerick, E. J., 116
environmental etiology of retar-
    dation, 34-36, 130-31
Epée, Charles-Michel, 5, 8
Esquirol, Jean-Etienne-Domi-
    nique, 7, 8
eugenics, 111-13, 115-16
Eugenics Record Office, 114
Everts, Orpheus, 101
experimental schools for the re-
    tarded, x, 16-19

Family of Sam Sixty, 114
farm colony, 86-87
feeble-minded, 6, 12. See also re-
    tardates; retardation
"Feeble-minded Club" (Vine-
    land, N.J.), 106
Fernald, Walter E., 86; farm col-
    ony, 86-87; moral imbecile, 97-
    98, 157; immigration and retar-
    dation, 92-93; segregation of
    the retarded, 98; retardation
    and prostitution, 109; defective
    delinquent, 110; opposition to
    sterilization, 119-20; critical
    view of IQ tests, 120; after-care
    study, 121; reassesses menace
    of the retarded, 121-22; out-
    patient clinic, 126; a thirty-year
    perspective on care, 126-27;
    legend of the feeble-minded,
    127
Folks, Homer, 118; attitudes to-
    ward sterilization law, 119-20
French Academy, 1806 report of,
    6

Galton, Francis, 95
Goddard, Henry H., 106-12; 114,
    118; Feeblemindedness: Its Causes
    and Consequences, 113; Kallikak
    Family, The, 113
Goffman, Erving, 138
Guggenbuhl, Johann J., 11

habilitation services, 140-41
Hall, G. Stanley, 106
Harriman, Mrs. E. H., 112
Healy, William, 131
Hegge, T. G., 141
heredity, 14; retardation, preven-
    tion of, 34-35, 54-58, 84-85;
    transmission of retardation, 95-
    96, 114-16; critical view of, 121-
    22
Hill Folk, 114
Howe, Samuel G., ix, 10, 12-15,
    16, 19, 22, 24, 36, 42, 62, 72;
    degrees of retardation, 14;
    moral idiocy, 14, 157; benefits
    of providing care, 15; moral
    imbecile, 80, 130, 157
human rights and the retarded,
    99-100, 149-51

idiot, 6, 26
Illinois: Asylum for Feeble-
    minded Children (Lincoln), 30-
    31, 63
imbecile, 6-7, 26
Indiana: School for the Feeble-
    minded (Fort Wayne), 100;
    sterilization law, 103; Confer-
    ence on Mental Deficiency and
    Child Welfare, 118
inmate labor, 74-78
institutions, x-xiii, 18-21; over-
    crowding, 20, 137; and nine-
    teenth-century reform, 21;
    early optimism, 21; noncusto-

dial first two decades, 22-29;
1850's, improvement not cure,
27; effect of Civil War, 29;
1890's, change in goals, 71-72;
three stages of growth, 78-79;
1890's, establishment of new,
89; impact of immigration, 92-
93; 1930's, staffing and research difficulties, 134; 1950's,
increasing proportion of severe
cases, 138-39; World War II,
negative effects of, 137-38
intelligence tests, 106-7
Iowa: Institution for Feeble-
minded Children (Glenwood),
78; Child Welfare Research
Station, 130; University of, 130
Itard, Jean-Marc-Gaspard, 4-6,
8

Johnson, Alexander, 103
Johnson, Judge Frank M., 149
Johnstone, Edward R., 106, 117
Journal of Psycho-Asthenics, 89, 94
Jukes, The, 54-58, 68, 84-85, 114

Kallikak Family, The, 113
Kansas State Home for the Feeble-minded (Winfield), 101
Kennedy, John F., 144-46; special
message to Congress, 145
Kentucky Institution for the Education and Training of Feeble-
minded Children (Frankfort),
18
Kerlin, Isaac N., 30, 34, 42, 53,
72, 89; study of dispositions,
37-38; founding of AMO, 50-
51; on heredity, 54, 63, 65, 74-
76; NCCC 1884 *Report*, 67;
ideal institution, 69-70; moral
imbecility, 79-84; custodial
care, 83

Kimball, Gilman, 12
Kite, Elizabeth S., 113, 118
Knight, George H., 72, 99
Knight, Henry M., 29, 50, 72
Koch, Richard, 147

Laughlin, Harry M., 112, 115
legal rulings and the retarded,
149-51
"legend of the feeble-minded,"
127
Letchworth Village (Thiells,
N.Y.), 125, 133-34
Lindsay, Edward, 122
Little, C. S., 134
Lowell, Josephine Shaw, 59

McCulloch, Oscar C., 84-85
marriage restriction laws, 96, 119
Massachusetts: Worcester State
Lunatic Hospital, 11; *Report
Made to the Legislature of Massachusetts Upon Idiocy*, 13; Experimental School for Teaching
and Training Idiotic Children
(South Boston and Waltham),
16, 86-87, 110; farm colony
(Templeton), 86-87; Wrentham
State School, 89, 125; *Report of
the Commission for the Investigation of the White Slave Traffic,
So-called*, 109-10; custodial facility for defective delinquents,
110; School for the Feeble-
minded (Waverly), 124-26
Matthews, Mable A. 125
medicine and retardation care,
research findings of the 1920's
and 1930's, 134-36. *See also* pediatrics and retardation; psychiatry and the retarded
"menace of the feeble-minded,"
xiii

Mendel, Gregor, 93
mental age, 108
mental health care and mental retardation care, xiii-xv
Mental Hygiene, 122
Mental Retardation Facilities and Community Mental Health Centers Construction Act of 1963, 146
merit ward, 143
Metropolitan District Asylum for Imbecile Children (England), 45
Michigan: Wayne County Training School, 131-32
milieu therapy, 142
Miller, Ambrose, 76
Mills v. *Board of Education,* 149-50
moral imbecile, fear of, 71; concept of, 79-84; changing views of, 98
moral insanity, 81
moral treatment, xiii-xiv, 9
moron, 107, 124
Murdock, J. M., 116

Nam Family, 114
National Association for Retarded Children, 138-39
National Committee for Mental Hygiene, 122
National Committee on Provision for the Feeble-minded, 117
National Conference of Corrections and Charities (NCCC), 50-51; moral imbecility and, 82; marriage restriction and, 96
National Education Association, 90
National Prison Association, 51
Newark State School, 133
New Jersey: Training School for Feeble-minded Children (Vine-

land), 91; Commission on the Care of Defectives, 117; legislation, 117; Newark State School, 133
New York: Census of 1845, 11; Asylum for Idiots (Syracuse), 17; Custodial Asylum for Feeble-minded Women (Newark), 59; State Board of Charities, 59; Rome State Custodial Asylum, 89, 121, 137; mental testing, 109; Committee on Feeble-mindedness, 117; Commission for Mental Defectives, 118; Letchworth Village (Thiells), 125, 133-34
Nirje, Bengt, 147
normalization, 147-48

Ohio: Commercial Hospital and Lunatic Asylum, 10; Deaf and Dumb Asylum, 10; Institution for Feeble-minded Youth, 64; Council for the Retarded Children of Cuyahoa County, 138
Osborne, A. E., 91
outpatient clinic for the retarded, 125-26

PARC case. See *Pennsylvania Association for Retarded Children* v. *Commonwealth of Pennsylvania*
parents: organizations of, 138; pressures of, 139; counseling services for, 140
parole of retarded, 124-25, 136
Parrish, Joseph, 17, 29, 72, 74
paternalism and the retarded, 108, 154
Patterson, R. J., 33
Pearson, Karl, 95
pediatrics and retardation, xiii

penologists, opposition to sterilization, 120

Pennsylvania: Training School for Idiotic and Feeble-minded Children (Elwyn), 17-18; Polk State School (Western Pennsylvania State Institution for the Feeble-minded), 89, 132; sterilization bill, 102-3; Philadelphia Department of Public Health and Charity, 117; Pennsylvania Association for Retarded Children, 149-50

Pennsylvania Association for Retarded Children v. *Commonwealth of Pennsylvania*, 149-50

Pereire, Jacob, 5, 8

Perkins Institution for the Blind, 10

Perry, Mary E., 103

personality development and the retarded, 141-42

Philadelphia Department of Public Health and Charity, 117

Philanthropic Index and Review, 30

physiological education (instruction), 8-9. *See also* Seguin, Edouard

Pilcher, F. Hoyt, 101

Pinel, Philippe, 4, 8

Polk State School (Pa.), 89, 132

poverty and retardation, 146-47

Powell, F. M., 52

President's Panel on Mental Retardation, 144

psychiatry and the retarded, 136, 141-44

public schools: special classes, 90-91, 127-30; mental testing, in New York, 109; ungraded classes, 129; access to, 149-50

Rainier State School (Buckley, Wash.), 137

Rehabilitation Act of 1973, 150

retardates: separation of grades, 40-41; 1870's, return to community, 43; and womanhood, 60; admission age and retention, 60-61; 1890's, apparent increase of, 91; human rights of, 99-100, 150-51; 1900's, stereotyping of, 108; 1910's, unable to act like others, 116-17; community care, 123-51; 1950's, mental illness and, 142-44; 1950's, psychotherapy, 143-44

retardation, ix, xiii-xvi; classification of, 26-27, 40-41; 1850's, etiology of retardation and mental illness, 35-36; 1870's, prevention of, 53; sexuality, 60-61; criminal pathology, 68 (*see also* moral imbecile, fear of); 1930's, psychiatry and research, 135-36; economic depression and, 136-37; environment, cultural deprivation and, 130-31, 145; 1950's, drug therapy and, 144; 1960's, 146-47; poverty and, 146-47

Richards, James B., 16, 17, 27

Rodman, James, 29

Rogers, Arthur C., 87, 90, 94

Rollin, Charles, 9

Rome State Asylum, 123-24

Rosen, David, 149

Rowlett, Eleanor, 128

Royal Albert Asylum (England), 45

Saegent, Carl M., 11

salpingectomy, 101

"savage" of Aveyron, 3-6

schools, experimental, x, 16-19

Schwartz, Rev. Karl, 115

segregation and the retarded, 100

Seguin, Édouard, 5, 7-10, 11, 16, 17, 33, 50, 51, 72; *Idiocy and Its Treatment by the Physiological Method,* 94

severely retarded: 1930's institutional care, 132-33; increasing number of, 138-39

Sharp, Harry C., 101-2

sheltered workshop, xii, 140

Shuttleworth, George E., 45-49

Sicard, Roche-Ambroise, 5, 8

Simon, Thomas, 106

Skeels, Harold M., 130-31

Smith, Asbury G., 62-63

special class, 90-91, 127-30

state boards of charities, 31-32

Station for Experimental Evolution (Cold Spring Harbor, N.Y.), 95. *See also* Davenport, Charles B.

sterilization, xiii, 101-4; penologists opposition to, 72-73; eugenics and, 101-2; laws, 102-3; numbers of, 119

Sumner, George S., 12

superintendents: and Seguin physiological approach, 10, 33; 1890's, second generation of 72-73

Surgeon General, 1920's and extent of retardation, 124

Swedish Association for Retarded Children, 147

Tarbell, George G., 62-63

teachers of public school, and classes at Vineland, N.J., 106

Tredgold, A. F., 114

"Tribe of Ishmael, The" 84-85

Tuck, Henry, 62

University of Iowa, 130

vasectomy, 101

Vaux, Charles L., 133

Victor, 3-6

"village of the simple," xi, 70

Vineland Extension Department, 131. *See also* New Jersey Training School for Boys and Girls

Wallin, J. E. Wallace, 120-21

Washington, Rainier State School (Buckley), 137

Watkins, Harvey M., 132

Wayne County Training School, 131-32

Weismann, August, 94

Western Pennsylvania State Institution for the Feebleminded, 89, 132

Wilbur, Charles T., 30-31, 33, 50, 63

Wilbur, Hervey B., 16, 29, 32, 39, 41-42, 50-51, 59, 63, 72

Wilmarth, Alfred W., 68, 98-99, 119

World War I, mental tests and, 121

World War II, studies of retarded soldiers, 141-42

Woodward, Samuel B., 11

Worcester State Lunatic Hospital of Massachusetts, 11

Wyatt v. *Stickney,* 149

About the Authors

PETER L. TYOR is Director of State Relations for Northwestern University, Evanston, Illinois.

LELAND V. BELL is Professor of History at Central State University, Wilberforce, Ohio. He is the author of *In Hitler's Shadow: The Anatomy of American Nazism* and *Treating the Mentally Ill: From Colonial Times to the Present*, as well as of articles appearing in the *Journal of Human Relations*, *Political Science Quarterly*, and *Illinois Quarterly*.